Between The Lines
A History of Haven

Between The Lines
A History of Haven

Mary O'Meara

Matador
9 Priory Busines Park
Wistow Road
Kibworth Beauchamp
Leicester LE8 0RX, UK
Tel: 0116 279 2299
Email: books@troubador.co.uk
Web: www.troubador.co.uk/matador

ISBN 978 1 78088 064 8

British Library Cataloguing in Publication Data.
A catalogue record for this book is available from the British Library.

Typeset in 9pt Courier by Troubador Publishing Ltd, Leicester, UK

Matador is an imprint of Troubador Publishing Ltd

Printed and bound in the UK by TJ International, Padstow, Cornwall

Acknowledgements

Thanks to Gary, Nat, Iwan and Jack & Tom for the music, the song, the dance, the happy trails and the magic of it all…

Thank you to Mickey Smith, Danny Donnelly, Jamie Colgan, Jim Spencer, Division of Laura Lee, Joe Moss & David Moss & Piper Ferguson.

Special thanks to my comrade in crime, Viv, for sharing a big chunk of this crazy journey with me, to Aeneas for the sublime aesthetics and to Zhohara & Julianna for being there & shining a light. Big thanks to Nick and to Steph for their encouragement and enthusiasm.

Grateful thanks to my lovely family for all their love and support.

Thanks to Haven fans everywhere, I hope you enjoy the ride.

This book is dedicated to those on the outside.

The inside has always been over-rated.

It's also dedicated to those who dare to dream, and more than that, those who dare to live their dream where there is no outside or inside, only love.

Do you remember the first time?

London town… a west-end girl, I worked in some of the caverns of bookshops that populate the Charing Cross road area. When not browsing books I was, more often than not, browsing records.

One lunch-time, during my Wednesday ritual of scanning the music press, I recall a few small column inches catching my eye. The name that leapt out of that small, black, smudgy typeface was 'Johnny Marr'. Having been a Smiths fan since my teens anything relating to them, particularly Marr, easily got my attention. What was the perpetually industrious Marr up to now?

Oh, producing a new band called Haven. Cornish. Managed by Joe Moss. This is how most people were introduced to Haven at the beginning and I was no exception. Looking back now, I find it strange that I even recall reading this small NME news item, yet I clearly do.

Strange, perhaps too, that I recall roaming around Virgin's flagship Megastore on Oxford St/Tottenham Court Road to see if there was a Haven record available so that I could hear this new band. There wasn't, at this point, but I was informed that there would be in a few weeks.

The unexplainable vivid recall continues when I remember sitting with two good friends downstairs in The George (a biker's pub or it was in those days) behind the now sadly demolished Astoria. I recollect pulling Haven's *Beautiful Thing* from the red and black polythene Virgin Megastore bag and presenting it to my friends commenting on its unusual artwork – a neat copper paint-spattered square which immediately communicated a free-flowing, bohemian aesthetic I could easily admire.

I seem to remember telling my friends these could be a special band. This was before I'd even played the record as I had only just purchased it but I somehow already knew that. I had no idea, of course, that I would end up chronicling their story but with hindsight, when I think about the unusually lucid memories I have of 'discovering' them, I wonder if I was being mysteriously appointed (subconsciously at this point) to unravel their tale and follow their journey. Each episode that got me closer to Haven seems to be a freeze-frame of fuzzy familiarity – a connection that wafted into my life so naturally that I barely noticed it on a conscious level but I embraced it all the same without questioning it.

I played *Beautiful Thing* and found it a quick passage into a world full of colour and magic, quite mesmerizing, but to be truthful, at this juncture, Haven were just another good band among many others I liked. At this point in my life I was editor of *Terrible Beauty*, a Manic Street Preacher's fanzine. I was exposed to new and exciting bands every day. The Haven record knocked gently on my door and I liked it a lot but for some reason, right then, they were a band "for future reference/consideration". I had no idea what they looked like, no idea what their names were. All I knew was the song was achingly beautiful and so was the singer's voice. The sleeve was also sublime.

19-07-2001

I saw the band live. If I remember rightly, my friend, Viv had bought me a ticket for my birthday (the day after). It was a memorable day for many personal reasons and another day I recall with that strange, seamless recollection. The gig took place in Dingwalls at Camden Lock. I stood leaning on some rails and watched Haven tear through a short but punchy set. I remember Joe Moss coming by, stopping and standing beside me and clapping very loudly. I didn't know him to speak to at this point but recognised his face from a Smiths documentary I had on an old VHS tape at home.

I remember thinking how young they looked and how boyishly cute. And the singer's voice sent shivers down my spine. I still didn't know any of their names but I was starting to get an ear for their sound and liking it more and more. I left feeling good, but not elated. That didn't happen until the second time I witnessed them perform.

17-04-2002

Again, for no apparent reason, snapshots from the day stick in my mind. Haven's debut album, *Between the Senses* had been released at this point and their popularity had taken quite a jump since Dingwalls. I'd obviously been spreading the word before this gig as I had a whole group of curious friends with me this time to check out their performance at ULU that night.

In this phase of my life I was working in University of Westminster in the shadow of Euston Tower. I remember the day unfolding, watching the traffic jamming and crawling from the window. The sky was weighed down, crammed with heavy toxic clouds.

Seven o clock, a playful mood ensued on Gower Street. I was clowning around with some friends. This continued in the ULU bar. It was a normal crowd, a normal night but then something happened that sticks in my mind even now, eight years later, that wasn't really normal at all. The band had started up and we were still giggling in the bar but the music seemed to literally summon me – not sternly, not solemnly but like a gush of gladness that said "Come on! This way!" I took my friend Jon's arm and pulled him with me and we swam upstream to the middle of the crowd. I hear the song but I don't know what it is. I swear it was about a river or rocky mountain but today, now that I know Haven's discography very well, no such song exists but that's what I heard and that's what I remember.

The crowd seemed to part in front of me like the Red Sea and the band appeared to be visions in white – this amazing song and this amazing voice. I was totally immersed in how wonderful it all was – on a complete high, not a chemical one but a musical-spiritual zenith that just happened for no reason at all other than that sometimes life really is purely magical.

In a nutshell, I felt dazzled by Haven's performance and it signalled to me that something had really fallen into place since the last time I'd seen them nine months before. Though I still knew very little about the people in the band I was beginning to be pulled towards their musical journey and I had a feeling there would be some significance to this night that I had yet to understand but it etched itself on the cosmic canvas of my memory in thick, rich shimmering brush-strokes. Many years later, here I am re-tracing the origins of this discovery, peeling back the layers to find the beginnings of their adventure. That story may or may not be over. It's currently still meandering and it's been a privilege to watch it flow over the last decade.

Beautiful things don't die, but they can transform.

Going back...

There is something intrinsically sunny about Nathan. There's also something slightly ethereal, something child-like. When I come across him against the industrial cityscapes of Manchester or even the leafy suburbs of Heaton Moor, he often seems like a fish out of water. Not necessarily unhappy or uncomfortable but not in his natural element which undoubtedly seems to be water: "I was about sixteen when I surfed for the first time – I just became completely involved in it. It's just the most amazing experience," he tells me "I can't explain to someone who's never surfed what an incredible thing it is to do. Just to be that immersed in nature. It's all cheesy stuff but it's just incredible – the longer you do it the more challenges you can find within it – you'll never master the ocean, you'll master the ride but not the ocean. It's the most – it seems to me the best thing to be doing with your time really."

This oceanic immersion, this companionship and attunement with the natural world easily manifests in Nat's music – that fluid, free-flowing quality can instantly be felt when you encounter his guitar playing, like sunlight dancing on a quivering mirror of water. It's no surprise to learn he is completely self-taught. He can't remember exactly when he first picked up a guitar:

"I can remember my brother having a guitar and he won't mind me saying he is like tone deaf and a bit shit!" Nat laughs "He had this guitar that was painted silver with animals on it and stuff but I remember him not appreciating it at all and I've got photographs of me as a very young kid playing a guitar but I don't particularly remember that – but I remember on my twelfth birthday getting a silver electric guitar and thinking it was the best thing and I remember that night being able to – I'd not been able to play the guitar before that as far as I know, but I could play *Sunshine of Your Love* that night – or my version of it that night. Only on one string, but that was it. I thought I was rocking out!

I think if you teach yourself you're relying on your ears and your love of music but if you get taught there's a kind of mental process that you go through to remember things that you're taught if people learn to read music. I've got a huge amount of respect for someone who can be given a piece of music and play it as it should sound so later on in life I tried to learn to read music and it's very difficult – it's like learning maths or something – but I think, maybe it divides you because you're using your creativity and your musical ear but you're also using a big chunk of your brain to remember all of this language. Whereas when you play just from your ear I think there's more brain space – you can just feel..."

Nat's brother, Will, who is four years older, may not have had a huge influence on him musically but he did in just about every other way:

"I kind of tended to copy him – or follow in his footsteps. Apparently, the day I was born he was trying to teach me how to ride a bike! I mean I followed in his footsteps in every respect apart from going to University – that's the one thing I didn't do that he did. I had the band, which felt very natural to me and University felt very unnatural. I didn't feel I was ready to leave home. I liked my parents – I liked the safety zone of being at home and also the comfort of having time – two or three of my best friends to play music with and it felt very safe and cosy. The idea of upping sticks and going to Plymouth or Cardiff to study Geology or something didn't sound too good!"

Will seems to have been a very positive role model for Nathan: "I was lucky enough not to make any of his mistakes – everything

he did right I did right as well." Nat's father aspired to lead a life of self-sufficiency, "At some point during the early seventies he set up a commune in Scotland," Nat reveals, "it was at the peak of sort of hippie movement and he wanted to know that he could exist and bring up a family without using money – outside the system. He literally left a note on his pillow and went on his own – stuck his thumb out and went through India and Afghanistan. I think he was looking for good dope! Along the way he came across some good music as well and it kind of filtered into him, y'know? And luckily enough I got blessed with it as a kid."

Nathan Wason was born on 12 March 1978. His father, clearly an unconventional type, also an internationally acclaimed craftsman, .was born in Liverpool "He left home when he was about eighteen or nineteen," Nat continues. "So, he created this commune with maybe sixteen other people or something and lived without money for nine years. My brother was born there and obviously they had to work very hard at that but then he finished and decided that it was kind of – that maybe he's made a point to himself or something – I don't know – and he moved down to Cornwall from Scotland and that's where I ended up. Obviously I've given my old man a hell of a lot of respect for taking something like that on board."

They settled in St Just, Cornwall. "I grew up on a farm but it wasn't a working farm. We didn't have cattle or anything. Our landlord owned the farm and the house was on it but we weren't part of it."

Nat paints an idyllic picture of his childhood – simple but joyful – and even now returning to Cornwall is a rejuvenating and welcomed experience for him:

"I still feel like a child – I still feel like I'm in my childhood," he grins. "I rush home at the drop of a hat. I get to see 'em so little. They're good people. Obviously they're my Mum and Dad but they're a good laugh and I can't shock 'em with anything I tell them. They told me that at a young age. They've been through it all – all sorts of shit so it's nice for me to know that anything that crops up in my life I can talk to them straight about it."

Nat was best friends from early childhood with Tom Lewis, the son of a local well-respected fisherman. They were and still are very close, both sharing a strong calling from the mighty sea:

"I've surfed for twenty years and feel sick if I've not been round the sea," Nat explains, "I need to get there every so often and I do – but with Tom that connection is even stronger, I think."

Nat and Tom also shared a love of music and from the age of around twelve they began playing together with the view of maybe starting a band.

It was around this time that Nat met Iwan Gronow:

"I know exactly when I met Iwan. I was in the football team at school and we went to the Isles of Scilly to play the Isles of Scilly. Iwan was in the same team as me but I'd never crossed paths with him before," Nat says, "but on the way over, me and him just happened to hit it off – senses of humour or whatever it was just playing Pac-man and stuff on the ferry and that was us – me and him we were really tight from then on."

Nat asked Iwan if he fancied joining himself and Tom in their music-making escapades.

"I remember our first rehearsal in the garage over in Zennor and Iwan had his microphone," chuckles Nat. "He turned his back on us all and set his microphone up facing the wall so he couldn't see us and we played some – I can't remember what music and Iwan belted his lungs out. Iwan's always been the enthusiast and he still is to this day. He's a good football player as well." All these years later, Nat and Iwan are still known to play football together.

Iwan was born in Sidcup, Kent on the 24 May 1978, moving from there to Cornwall when he was around three years old. "My Dad's born in Wales, he's Welsh and my Mum was born in Norwich. My Dad was actually in a band," Iwan reveals. "He lived in London for quite a while. When I was little and he was in a band called The Wolf Boys – they were really good. He was the singer and lyricist. I went through his book recently they were kind of joke/ punk lyrics but they were really good and John Peel played them loads."

Years later when Iwan's own band were featured by John Peel, he remembers his Dad summoning up the courage to ask Peel, in the kitchen, if he remembered The Wolf Boys. Not only did Peel remember them but also recalled the label they were on and other details which naturally pleased Mr. Gronow greatly.

"When I looked at his lyrics I was pretty shocked with some of them," Iwan recalls, "I think in the house there were always guitars around and stuff – he played guitar too – guitars were always around. I was just intrigued by it really and he taught me a few chords. I learnt guitar first and then learnt the bass later."

He describes himself and Nat as "young kids with really long hair into horrible metal. I was singing for a bit and we were doing covers, singing Nirvana songs and Rage against the Machine songs and stuff like that. I was singing and then we needed a bass player so I played bass and sang as well. We both sort of picked it up and he taught me things and I taught him things and then we just started to play horrible metal riffs in the bedroom. Just singing and just being stupid really!"

Like Nathan, there is something a little fey about Iwan.

Perhaps it is something to do with his very slender physique and nimble movements but he gives off an air of subtle Cornish/Celtic mischief.

Today both he and Nat still seem as boyish and playful as they did when I first encountered them many years ago. This quality can only have been accentuated back in those early teenage years.

Back then, Iwan also played a lot of sport: "I did Judo, football, cricket, rugby and sort of week nights we were really busy and I met Tom through doing all these different things and then he ended up drumming for us and we were sort a three piece then. We were just pissing around really – it was like along with football and sport and everything, music was just something that I did. I didn't really take it that seriously, I just enjoyed it and enjoyed listening to it. We used to rehearse in Nat's garage at his Mum and Dad's house."

As is entirely normal at that age, the feeling that their music-making was basically about having fun is strongly echoed by Nat: "I don't know why we were doing it really. That's a question that I'd like to have answered myself. I suppose we were doing it because we could and we were doing it because we thought – well, maybe we thought it could one day become something but I don't think we had those aspirations. I think it was more about just being around a loud raucous noise – it's exciting for a thirteen year old kid, you know? So we were getting together twice a week and obviously we weren't drinking or anything like that. We were just clean-living young kids making a big noise. You know how it is where there's a certain age where you kind of fall into music completely head over heels. You've got posters on your wall and all that sort of stuff and you don't go through that stage again. That happens once when you're in your teenage years and we were lucky that we were able to play instruments at the time to kind of replicate what we were hearing."

At this point young Nathan's bedroom walls were adorned with "a poster of John Barnes – I had a poster of a Ferrari. Ashamedly I had a poster of something like Sepultura on my wall," he pauses and corrects himself "No, not ashamedly – I still have a soft spot for all that kind of stuff. When you get into something you tend to seek out the most extreme form of whatever it is you like so one thing leads to another and you end up right at the end and then you have to reign it back in again. So I kind of went right the way through guitar music until I got to the really super heavy stuff – but I was still only a kid you know, it was understandable. I think Nirvana were probably the first band who came along and really slapped me around the face and said like this is just as intense but this has got heart and passion and soul which maybe the other stuff hasn't – less calculated – more about the feeling and the vibe."

Iwan has some peculiar memories from this time of playing their songs at his school assembly:

"It was like eight in the morning and we would play really heavy metal to kids and we'd have our school shirts on and we were allowed to wear a black t-shirt, like a shit metal t-shirt," Iwan laughs. "We could take our shirts off and do that for the time we were playing but looking back it was weird really. Really weird, but the weirdest thing was that there was a band called Infiltrate that we knew and they were a really, really heavy band – they were like grown men – they were thirty odd – and they played in the school assembly just because one of the guys used to go to the school! And the kids were all like – tiny – looking at these giant men playing really loud metal!"

Another key character strays into the frame at this point. He occupies a special space in the inner circle of the band, both here and in later times. His name is Mickey Smith. Mickey grew up in a small fishing village in West Cornwall called Newlyn. Like Nathan and Tom, he had a deep love for both the sea and music.

"I've always been involved with the sea from a young age. It was tough at times, I guess we were struggling for money and my Mum was working so hard on her own to look after two kids – myself and my sister Cherry," Mickey explains. "My 'dad' was completely useless, but my mum always made us feel totally loved and solid and worked mega hard to make sure we didn't want for anything. We have always been a proper little trio. Eventually she got a better job as a teacher and we moved to Penzance. It was here she started dating a musician named Al, who became my kind of father figure, and I picked up music around him. He had me out playing in his blues band by the time I was ten, playing all around Cornwall, in different line-ups, on guitar, drums or bass, then playing in London and on some trips to the Canaries. It was a funny little time to be growing up through my early teens. I kind of lost the plot a fair bit, but I guess that helped me later on when all the kids at school were catching up, I'd already been there seen and done it all kinda thing. My mums been so supportive of my creative pursuits my whole life, shes a legend."

Mickey is someone who, in the few times I've met him, is like a breath of fresh, clean air. Bright-eyed and spirited, with an appetite for fun and adventure he injects an immediate buzz to activities, yet he also has a peaceful serenity about him. As he was involved in the local surf and music scene it was no surprise he soon crossed paths with Nat, Iwan and Tom. Mickey has a vivid memory of first encountering the boys: "I was playing at a jam night for old blues cats in a town called Camborne. I must have been thirteen, and I remember clear as day these three young punks walking in, Nat Iwan and Tom, with Iwan's Dad, Clive, behind them," he recalls "and they looked like they wanted to tear the place apart, like it was war, them against the rest of the room or something. Then they got up and launched into a ferocious *Bullet in your head* by Rage against the Machine, with Nat doing all this crazy shit on the guitar and Iwan screaming down the mike, Tom with his top off on the drums. Then they launched into *Aneursym* by Nirvana and it fuckin' blew my head off man, changed my life forever. I was listening to Guns and Roses *Appetite for destruction* at the time and loved it, but I'd never experienced anything so raw and aggressive live, especially from kids my age. I was there playing the blues with my little bandana on and then those lot turned up and I was never quite the same again. I was like – that's what I wanta be doing, so I did! I started playing in all sorts of bands, death metal, punk, anything with energy like that, it just lit me up."

It's interesting to hear Mickey speak about what an inspiration the boys were to him because I strongly feel that equally, he has been an inspiration to them through the years, especially in terms of following your dreams and taking the plunge, literally and metaphorically into that ice cold ocean where you never know what's coming next.

During this period Nat, Iwan and Tom hadn't actually engaged in songwriting. "It was more about just killing times and having jams and stuff. The writing didn't really start until we came across Gary," explains Nat, “and that was when we were maybe sixteen years old or something – sixteen or seventeen. The first time we played with him was the first time we realised that we could be something more than three blokes having a laugh”.

If you believe things happen for a reason...

Unlike Nat and Iwan, who as I've described, look slightly anomalous when placed in a Manchester setting, Gary, struck me as though he'd found a home when he arrived up North, despite being no more Northern in origin. It's not that the others haven't put down roots and it's not to say they necessarily *feel* they don't belong, but Nat, especially seems to need to return to 'source' on a regular basis and I suspect Iwan does as well, perhaps to a lesser extent.

It's not that Gary blends into the Mancunian way anymore easily. He has something of the Dickensian street urchin about him, the gaze of the perpetual outsider, but despite this, he seems like he has decided this is where he belongs. And a sense of belonging seems important to him, which is understandable when he speaks of his nomadic early years:

"I'd moved a lot, I went to something obscene like, fourteen different schools and never really had a… you know when you've got friends who talk about old school friends – like friends I've got in this area they sit around and they talk about "remember the time when you were fourteen or whatever". I find that like fucking "wow!" It's something I secretly covert, because I never had that."

Gary Briggs was born in Walthamstow, London on 17 September 1977 but as he explains, "I was there, I wasn't, I grew up all around the country really, spent a lot of time in Northampton, a lot of time in Grimsby, Cleethorpes and then moved back to London and lived in Islington, Notting Hill Gate, Woodford & ended up in Cornwall in St Ives."

The reason for Gary's upheaval is not entirely clear, but a large part of it stems from the aftermath of his parent's divorce when he was seven years old:

"The estate we lived on at the time, the council decided to re-house my Dad and his new wife on the same street and for my Mum that was really too much to deal with, you know?" Gary explains. "So there was an element of not wanting me to be round my Dad – I mean my Dad is a really good guy and by today's standards he'd be considered normal but at that point he liked to smoke and do his thing which is something my Mum was kept away from. Obviously stories filter back and my Mum is this really straight, kind of classic law-abiding English woman which is something I love her for. She's so kind of naive to subculture and everything else that goes on... so I think certainly a lot of it was to kind of keep my Dad guessing and she probably wouldn't thank me for saying that but I think unfortunately that's the truth."

From then on until his teenage years, Gary saw little of his father but, naturally, he missed him:

"I don't know what it is, it's something you can't put your finger on – it's that sort of parental bond, even if you haven't really grown up with them it's always there. I just wanted to see my Dad." When that longing got too much he basically ran away one day:

"I turned fourteen and my mum had long since moved away from where my Dad lived and she took us back to the area where my Dad was staying to visit one of her old friends and I knew the area really well. I said to my Mum that I was going to the shops," Gary recounts, "and obviously as I knew the area she had no reservations whatsoever or any idea that I would do what I was about to – that was like, sneak off to my Dad's and knock on my Dad's front door, and my Dad was like "Fucking hell, what's going on here?" and freaked out a bit because I was full of – well, cocky as you are at that age and I just said "I wanna live with you"."

On hearing this, it wasn't difficult for me to imagine the teenage Gary standing on his father's door-step with big, imploring eyes and his story, though delivered in quite a breezy manner, tugged on my heart-strings. I sensed the hurt and original feelings of abandonment ran deep and had seeped into his psyche, even if he did sometimes dress things up with an air of nonchalance.

The police arrived once Gary's mother found out but eventually his father did get custody of him and he ended up living with his father which ended up being in St Ives, Cornwall.

Gary says that it was his Dad that really turned him onto music when he finally moved in with him but he also recalls as a young child sing-songs around the piano with his mother and sister. His mother was quite an accomplished pianist and a big fan of musicals:

"She pestered me for years to learn the piano and I was never interested. I wanted to play the guitar. Obviously when you get older you think, "I'm not doing that!" he laughs at the memory.

"When he finally got custody of me he sat me down in my sister's bedroom – she had the best stereo – and he had a list of songs that he said that he'd been compiling and he wanted me to one day hear. I know it sounds like absolute bollocks but it's the truth. He sat me down and there was like a list of pages of songs that he wanted to play me. Songs like *Comfortably Numb* by Pink Floyd and all sorts and that was where I got my real sort of love of music from because, though we had a record player at my Mum's it was a lot of Carpenters records and Ralph McTell and that kind of stuff."

Before his fateful meeting with Nathan, there had been a not entirely serious foray into forming a band for Gary: "Not long after moving in with my Dad, there was this guy called Duane that used to bully me. I had my first guitar and had my bedroom window open and I was struggling through – probably something by Led Zeppelin or Nirvana and he could hear it out the bedroom window. I could hear his voice out the window and I looked out and there was Duane! I nearly shit myself because he was a bully, y'know? We got talking and he bullied me into starting a band in which he was the singer and I did everything he said because he was a bully," Gary chuckles dryly. "We were called Hooligan's Haircut – that was my first band – I wouldn't even call it a band it was a horrible noise – we had this drummer called Richard Burt and we used to rehearse in his attic and his Mum used to hit the trip switch when she'd had enough. We were only allowed to rehearse for 40 minutes a night and as soon as it over-ran the power would go off and that would be it – all sent home! But it was, y'know, something you do…"

When Haven were officially launched many years later, their press frequently focused on the legendary first meeting between Nat and Gary which allegedly took place in a second hand record shop in Penzance called *Days gone By*. The story goes that they both had their eye on an album by the psychedelic San Francisco band Quick Silver Messenger Service called *Happy Trails*. Neither could quite afford it so they went halves on it, bonding strongly over the deal.

They say never let the truth get in the way of a good story but at the same time, a biographer has a duty to delve, dust off discrepancies and attempt to present as accurate a narrative as is possible. So, though it would be nice to totally authenticate this story I think it has an element of myth to it – though, in my view, myths almost always have an element of truth to them so like many things in life the actual truth lies somewhere in the middle. Let's just say, Gary and Nat's first meeting *could* have happened exactly as described. Both were aware of each other prior to the Quick Silver Messenger Service encounter. Both also seemed to have some level of admiration and curiosity about the other. Gary and Nat were both regular visitors to *Days gone By* and their paths did look destined to cross in a place such as that.

"It used to be called *Alladin's Cave* – it was kind of the same thing. *Alladin's Cave* kind of morphed into *Day's Gone By* and ended up purely a record shop," explains Gary "You know at the time you start learning the guitar and I think to kind of escape the fact that you're not really very good you buy effects pedals to kind of mask what you're doing and there was this wah-wah peddle in there and I remember pawning a few of my Dad's Zeppelin albums for that. I used to go in there a lot and I used to see Nat hanging around the place and he was someone who I was very aware of who he was – I didn't know him but he had a good way about him. He's very different now to how he was then but he still had that instant likeability. He had it even without speaking to him – he's got that – energy about him, hasn't he?" "Warmth?" I suggest "Yeah, warmth," agrees Gary, "and you get that without even talking to the guy and I thought he looked cool as well… in a kind of Cornish way!"

"I've got sort of vague memories of being sort of aware of Gary – I can remember the first night we spent together more so than the meeting to be honest," Nat admits. "I'd seen him around, I'd seen him at college, I'd seen him at gigs. I thought he was older than me actually and he was from St Ives and St Ives and St Just people are very different. And I could see that he was very St Ives – they're kind of more image conscious, and probably much more 'street' than we were in St Just. We had fucking like red drain-pipe trousers on!" Nat collapses in laughter, "I wish I hadn't said that now! But Gary was – he had much more, I'm not saying this is for the better but Gary was much more aware of how he presented himself – all that sort of stupid shit. But that probably was enforced on him by being thrown into a new school and you've got to like fit in – so he's aware of himself so much more whereas I just grew up amongst people I knew."

So, it seems the pair had been subtly checking each other out for a while but somewhere along the line a conversation started.

Gary had been reading about and listening to Gram Parsons around this point. Parsons had praised Quick Silver Messenger Service which led to Gary wanting to check them out. "You know when you find something that you haven't got enough money for and you're in a shop – what do you do? You stick it in the Z section – you stick it behind ZZ Top cos you're pretty sure no one's gonna wanna buy a ZZ Top record," Gary chuckles. "So yeah, we actually met and when we met we were talking about this record – his record collection was like kind of adopted record from his Dad's and obviously with a smattering of his own buys and it was, I wouldn't say identical but damn near identical to mine. So we were saying about this band and there's a record in that shop and that's kind of how it happened really.".

Gary and Nat clearly ht it off right away. Nat recalls the first night Gary came to his parent's house:

"I remember going up into – at the time it was my brother's bedroom – and we had a couple of guitars and we had some dope and I don't think we had any skins – these are all the relevant things somehow that stay in my head! So we were rolling hash into rizlas but we had no tobacco. He sang a Pearl Jam song on his acoustic and I remember having the goose-bumps and all that and it just felt really right, you know? And he was a good lad – I knew he was troubled but at the same time he was probably one of the most polite of my friends to my folks – he made his bed in the morning and all that!

But I knew that he was a handful. It was an immediate thing really with him – I knew that he had something to get over and he had something to get off his chest which the three of us didn't have. Me, Tom and Iwan kind of – well, I can't talk for the others really but I grew up with a very happy life and a pretty stable family and I think I can talk for Tom being the same and perhaps Iwan as well – though Iwan did actually move from London down to Cornwall so he had a bit of unsettlement. Gary had been hopping from one school to another and his parents had split – I know that happens to the majority of people but that obviously gave him an edge that we just didn't have because we were just happy go lucky."

If Nat, Iwan and Tom needed Gary's edge, then it seems clear Gary needed their stability and encouragement. Nat goes on to say, "I think he felt a security with the three of us. I think he felt like he was walking into something that was quite secure and quite caring and I think he might have recognised that. I think he might have felt a safety element in it – I really do – it was an embrace for him that we wanted him to show up every week and we were hassling him – he had these songs that we wanted to play. It was quite a big moment – quite a big thing actually."

Meeting the others certainly had an impact on Gary who says, "If you believe that everything happens for a reason, then maybe… maybe it's got to be more than just dumb luck that we met. When I met Nat and when I met Iwan, particularly when I met Nat, that's not to say that I'm not as close to Iwan, because I am, I'd throw ,myself in front of a grenade for the guy but when I met Nat things started to make sense in a way.

Later on, me and Iwan actually became really close, we used to skate-board. We both love hip-hop which is something Nat didn't really get and Tom didn't really get. I used to love it – I just used to really like the words and the way they put things together. We got on really well, we used to travel all around the country going to skate parks. I was crap, for me it was just like another fad but Iwan was really good at it.

We got on really well but I remember us falling out massively one night we were staying at my Mums friend's house. Bear in mind we're not in Cornwall anymore, right? So McDonald's is readily available and we're only young, seventeen or whatever. We'd had McDonald's three nights in a row and I wanted it again – and he didn't because Iwan's always had a real health thing about him and it kicked off big time! "Not having McDonald's again tonight!" I've got a lot of respect for Iwan though, an awful lot of respect because his drive is unbelievable – the motivation and all that is faultless. It really is. He's just the type of guy you need around because given half the chance I'll have a kip anywhere and he's not like that at all."

Introducing Gary to the trio seemed to change the dynamic quite radically in the sense that suddenly they weren't just jamming or playing covers but beginning to experiment with writing original material.

Gary remembers the set-up when he first visited Nat:

"He said come to my place which is out in the sticks and I went out there and I stayed for about a week. It's not a farm but it's kind of like in the middle of the moors in St Just. He's got a brilliant family, really beautiful people, dead creative family. His Mum and Dad are both artists in their own right – and we just hung out – his folks were creative people so the idea that their son was making music with his friends, albeit in their house, very loud and not the most kind of relaxing music, but yeah they were well up for it so I went over and he introduced me to Iwan and Tom. I'd already met Tom at a party about two months before that and I had no idea so that was cool. And Iwan at the time was singing – they were a three piece and they were a really good racket but it wasn't really my thing. It was really heavy, kind of dirgy – kind of bordering on heavy metal which to me was like hilarious.

I had a bunch of songs – well I say songs, that's quite generous – they were like four chord little ditties – little tunes with words here and there I think they were taken back a bit that instead of coming in and saying "D'you know *Come as you are*? I was really keen to… probably a bit ego-driven in a way, I was like "Play this!" It worked, worked well, they were into it and I was kind of enthusiastic about singing and not so enthusiastic about playing the guitar. Don't get me wrong, make no mistake, when I met Nat, Iwan and Tom they were all really prolific at what they did – and I'm the guy that says he can play the guitar but in actual fact can't really so it was amazing to hear three guys playing, accompanying something that I had in my head and doing it justice, not just doing it justice doing it really well so it kind of worked. We all had that buzz and I just thought straight away this is what I want to do."

So, the first embryonic, incarnation of Haven was starting to take shape with rehearsals in both Nat and Iwan's houses. At this point they were nameless. Once they began to play local gigs which happened quite quickly they were known as "Blew", apparently after the Smashing Pumpkins record *Blew Away*. None of them seem enamoured with that name now, yet I can imagine it being quite apt given their proximity to the sea and the way the wind can blow along the coast, combined with, perhaps, a sense of being tossed along by a quiet sense of destiny. Other connotations are equally plausible, but at any rate, this was the name they went under for the next couple of years.

"We took Penzance by storm!" jokes Nat.

In many ways, the band were pioneers of the Cornish music scene as at this point, in the mid nineties, no local tradition really existed for breaking new bands or following in any ones footsteps. There was no such a thing as the well-trodden gig circuit you find in cities like Manchester, Liverpool or London where there is a well-defined map of progression or ambition.

"It's not a good place to gig really," considers Iwan, "but there was two places we used to play which was *Boisin's* and *The Dolphin*. There's a lot of drinking in Cornwall it just used to get quite out of hand a lot of the time. A few times this guy called Bob who used to work at *The Dolphin* said pretty straight up, "You're not playing again," and then changed his mind because he was making so much on the booze. We did it regularly, played sort of nearly every week."

Looking back on this period where teenage hormones were obviously running riot, Mickey Smith comments "Gary was the only bloke in Cornwall who could probably actually sing, and I started going to see them every Friday in The Dolphin. Those nights were classic, huge fights while they were playing, proper brawls, amazing stuff for a kid. They were called *Blew* then and it was raw, but every week they seemed to get better and better, refining what they did down to proper songs, which no-one else was really doing.

We were just writing fucked up death metal, but these guys were writing melodies and songs, and the girls all loved it of course! I was still into my punk and heavy gear, and so were Nat and Iwan really, so they played in a few bands with me – Bog Filler, Fukkas, and Gary played lead guitar in one of our bands while I sung/shouted, which seems completely ridiculous now, that was called Kung Fu flu. Bog filler were even on John Peel alongside Blew, 'well worth the £2 entry fee' said the man himself. Hilarious times man!"

This reference Mickey makes to John Peel relates to a Channel 4 programme Peel compiled that ran at the end of the nineties called *Sound of the Suburbs*. "It was about music made in remote .places," Iwan explains "He came down and spent the day with us. He came to a gig we did with our friend Dominic Payne's death metal band called Bog Filler! They were also in the programme." The programme featuring the boys was broadcast in March 1999 including their track *In C* – a blustery belter of a song, with screaming guitars and that sound of wistful wilderness easily detected in their later music all rolling chaotically but charmingly around in the mix. Peel also went on to play the recording on his Radio 1 show and Iwan thinks he played a second track *Falling Down* as well.

According to Gary, their very first gig was "Daisy Lock's eighteenth Birthday and we opened up with *Drain You* and I don't remember what happened after that but it was, y'know, good fun, rapturous applause due to cider-induced hysteria! The thing is you've got to remember, we were barely seventeen and we didn't care – it was all about having fun and it was just about finding our feet."

The boys all went to the same college, with Nat and Gary going to the same lessons mostly. It seems clear that academia or any kind of orthodox career path was not beckoning any of them, though Iwan went so far as getting offered a place at Cardiff University later on and Nat considered the idea.

"I wasn't interested in getting any qualifications or being anything other than – I dunno…" Gary muses. "I wanted life just to pass me by, I didn't care, I knew just as long as I filled every moment of it with something that mattered to me I didn't care about anyone else's kind of guidelines. But everyone else seemed to feel the need to finish college. Me and Nat led this kind of thing where if we both stayed at college neither of us would get a qualification because we just kind of encouraged each other in the wrong way and I decided to drop out. The day that I went to the head of year to drop out he said something like – "We must have a telepathic link cos I've just signed a letter to send you to say that you're not welcome at our college any more," or something pompous like that.

I started A-Levels but I didn't finish. I didn't enjoy any of it at all. I didn't enjoy it because I was doing Politics, Psychology and French. French OK, French is French, you can't start making your own French words up, right? Politics and psychology, if you ask me, correct me if I'm wrong, are largely governed by opinion and I just kind of got narked with people telling you something and that's how it is. I always thought education was about asking questions. Someone once told me you've always gotta ask questions, you've got to question everything, question authority, question everything. That's how things get done but it didn't wash. I'm not bothered because I'm not arsed."

Nat suspects that at this point Gary had greater ambitions than he did. Nat was enjoying the band and enjoying life and not especially thinking about where any of this might lead:

"Gary might have been thinking this could be something. I'm sure he was glad to be involved in something and I think perhaps he had visions of what could happen in the future whereas I never did. I really never did. I'm totally truthful in saying that. Well, to be honest it's part of my character, I don't look further than the end of my nose really. I don't plan and it's probably my downfall but it's probably my strength at the same time. I never think about tomorrow ever! I look after myself and I get on with it but I never think what's the plan? What's gonna happen in five years time? It fills me with dread to do that and that's why I don't. It absolutely scares the shit out of me!"

Tom was also, at this point, drifting along and quite enjoying the ride. Iwan says he thought it might possibly go somewhere though seemed to be being very practical and keeping his options open. With Gary, I get the impression that though he wasn't making any specific plans or straining to get anywhere fast, that he had big hopes and half expected something to magically fall from the sky and land in his lap! Strangely enough, he still gives me that same impression today. And perhaps he had and has good reason to.

Blew were building a reputation locally with large groups of enthusiastic college kids turning up for their gigs. I get the impression that image wasn't hugely important to them at this stage, if ever, arguably, though Nat recalls a gig at The Dolphin where Gary shaved all his hair off with a razor beforehand. He giggles at the memory, describing the skinhead Gary as pretty scary: "We'd play like ten of our own songs and a couple of Nirvana songs or whatever. And it was earning us a few quid, but more so it was just about having fun and getting together with people we knew and all that stuff," Nat comments. "We had a song called *Falling Down*, a song called *In C* and a song called *Bitch* – that was our anthem at the time and it was a song with a kind of upbeat beat – shit really, but it was good at the time!

We weren't thinking about record deals or releasing music – we were just sewn up in our little scene and we were lucky enough to be part of it and the hub of it, if you like, one of the young bands that everyone wanted to go and see. And though we were OK we weren't that good! But maybe we had a certain chemistry you know? It ended up always as a good night. It was an explosive night. We weren't like trashing our gear or anything but I remember there was a few kids that always used to come. There was often bloodshed. There was one kid in particular, I won't mention his name but I remember one gig he was running down the road and kicking the windscreens of about fifteen or sixteen cars. The police ended up showing up at our gigs but it was a small town you know? We weren't inciting violence in any way. We were just doing our thing!"

Very few songs survived from those days, making it into the official Haven catalogue. Songs that date from the Cornish era are *Change Direction* and also, *Say Something* though these were the results of a more intense song-writing period that took place when the band started rehearsing at "Kenny's Place" after having met Joe Moss. *Kenny's Place* was also the title of a song. But who *was* Kenny? Iwan explains:

"This Cornish guy, a really old bloke – bit of a drinker and his house was attached to my Mum and Dad's house. It was quite a big house but because there was so many storms half of his house blew away and caved in so it was like, in the end, he only had one tiny little room so he just moved into that one little room and that was it – didn't have a toilet, didn't have anything and just lived in that one room with just a bucket as a toilet and this huge massive Nicam TV," Iwan laughs at the image he's just described. "He just used to sit there and drink Caffrey's and when my Mum and Dad moved there he was there, so the person who was selling the house said this person was there – and my Dad said it was fine, and just ended up in with him watching football and got on with him really well. It ended up that, well – when he was about to die – he said to my Dad "I'll sell you this for – whatever". My Dad said "Yeah" and bought it off him for next to nothing and we (the band) moved into his little room and it was called Kenny's Place. We wrote *Say Something* there and a lot of the old stuff – we used to write constantly – that's all we did really – because no one had any work really, we just used to concentrate on that. My Dad was really into it – wanted to give me as much help as possible. Kenny's Place is now – my Dad's made it into a big sort of guesthouse area so my Dad's doing well with that. It's like a kind of B & B… so there was a lot smoking and drinking and we had people up there and lots of things going on – it was a good sort of time really."

A certain other figure had become involved in the band's development. This was Joe Moss. Moss, first manager of the Smiths, was based in Manchester. An old friend of his, Helen Davies, who had relocated from Manchester to Cornwall was the serendipitous link that brought the band to Joe's awareness. Gary had started renting a flat in St Ives where Helen used to live with a spectacular sea view. He speaks of her with great fondness:

"I really liked her, I still do – I think the world of her. This flat overlooked the cape – twenty five pound a week and it was just the best place in the world to live! She used to live there and believe it or not, I know it's a cliché, but this is the gospel truth I used to leave my key in the front door. No one's gonna rob you down there and if they did someone's gonna find out about a few hours later and they'd be hanging over a mine-shaft! It was like martial law down there. And I used to come home from work and I'd find her sat in my armchair looking out the window, smoking my dope, y'know? She was very musically minded and loved helping people out – she was an old friend of Joe's ex-wife and of Joe so she said to him you should come over and meet these boys because he happened to be on holiday there."

Joe followed Helen's suggestion and met up with the band and listened to them play.

"We went to this great little studio, in an old stone cottage in Penzance and they played three songs for us," Joe recalls this first meeting. "It was obvious that Gary had a good voice and Nat was potentially a really good guitar player. I met with them each time I went to Cornwall, which was about every two months. I also got to really like them as people. Truth is though, if they had lived in an uninteresting place we would have lost contact. I really do love Cornwall and the surfing and where they lived was very special."

The band's general consensus was that Joe wasn't that impressed with what he heard:

"We just played him a load of covers which he must sort of gone at the time "Er, oh great! Brilliant!" just like one new song maybe and all these covers," laughs Iwan, "but then we sort of badgered him really we just kept ringing him and we became friends. I think he loved it there as well in Cornwall and he came down a lot. We just kept showing him stuff and it just sort of grew from there. He was really busy with Marion so we weren't sort of expecting anything really."

According to Gary, it was Iwan who was really instrumental in keeping Joe in the picture. "He just hounded the poor guy until… well, we struck up a real friendship. He started coming down regularly, he bought my first proper guitar, gave us a four track," Gary remembers "He'd come down with all these amazing tapes. As I was into the Messenger Service and The Dead and he'd come down with these fucking like amazing live recordings that we'd never heard before and we'd sit around drinking wine and get stoned. It was never spoken about, we never really said… I mean, we knew that he was a manager and we had a rough idea of what he'd done but we had no idea to what extent."

Gary says they never, at this point, raised the question of Joe becoming their manager. In their typically modest manner, the band felt that might be a bit intrusive or cheeky. "We just like hung out and I just buzzed off the guy because…" Gary considers, "Well, he loved talking and he was as passionate about music as we were and he was just a fucking great guy to hang out with."

My perception when meeting the band in later years is, that Gary and Joe shared a particularly close bond and it was common to see them deep in one-to-one conversation at some bar or other. Nat mentions, "Joe had a hell of a lot of conversations with Gary about words. They used to drive off and have a stop and have a glass of wine and a spliff or whatever and they'd be talking about lyrics and stuff. These conversations I wasn't really a part of that suits me, you know, that's not really my thing."

When I asked Joe about his favourite memories with the band it seems to be the Cornish period that he looks back on with particular fondness:

"My favourite memories are from before they moved to Manchester. Lots rehearsals in Iwan's barn on the cliffs and plenty of wine drinking on the cliffs, the best positioned rehearsal room ever," Joe comments. "Nat's dad took me canoeing in Mounts Bay at sunset, after I had been working with the band, that was an amazing although frightening experience. Table tennis tournaments in Gary's flat at Cape Cornwall were good fun!"

However casual Joe's involvement may have been, his influence was starting to seep into the band's collective consciousness and it seemed to ground them. Even though they had taken their song-writing seriously before Joe's arrival a new sense of focus and purpose was beginning to emerge. Nat feels Joe had an important impact on his guitar playing also:

"He came to me and he said "Right! You're banned from playing chords. You've got two guitar players so why should you both be playing chords?" Joe had started to express his appreciation of Jerry Garcia and those guys who could just play beautiful melodies around the vocal and it's not pinned down, I'm not playing a C chord and then a D chord – I'm just floating around a melody, you know? Complementing the melody" Nat explains "And credit to Joe, years down the line I think that is probably my strong point – being able to pick up the melody and do stuff around it. That came directly from Joe and it was such an obvious thing but at the time me and Gary were just playing chords together!"

Years later Joe is obviously happy with how Nat's style developed, remarking "Nat is a really good guitar picker, I'm a big fan of his playing. I love riffs and picking, there's too much aimless strumming in most guitar music."

So, Joe continued to advise and spend time with the boys but was by no means their official manager. They did however, have a minor dalliance and spot of trouble with another manager:

"We had a weirdness with a management contract that we signed and then we wished we hadn't," admits Nat.

"I think he managed the Sisters of Mercy or someone," continues Gary "He was wrong from the start and we all thought – or not all of us, initially – well, I certainly did, Nat did, didn't like the guy in the slightest. It was weird but this guy – he kind of said the right things and he wore a suit and all that but the guy was a chancer – no doubt about it. Yet we ended up signing this management deal with him. He was really not good at all, not creative in any way. I remember one of his first suggestions was like condoms with our name down the side... d'you know what I mean?" Gary cringes.

"I had to pretend to be mental," Nat breaks down in laughter. "I felt railroaded into it a bit, but that's the nature of it. It's difficult at the best of times to make a decision between four people and since this decision came about and I went along with it, I don't blame anyone else for a second, but at the same time as this was going on I was in contact with Joe a lot and I thought this thing was crap – it was like small potatoes and what Joe had on to offer was potentially quite promising. So we triedto like defunct this contract but I had to pretend to be insane. I didn't get certified – but I spoke to the guy a couple of times and I definitely came across as insane!"

Gary remembers spending about a year pretending the band had split up in an attempt to dissolve the contract. "We pretended we'd split up so we could get out of it. Honestly, it was unbelievable!" he remembers "We wrote this letter – the letter implied that I'd lost my mind – I know, it sounds really ridiculous now but at the time that's what happened!" It's not clear how many of the band pretended to be insane, but one way or another they managed to escape from the legal entanglement with this dubious manager and continued working on songs at Kenny's Place, with Joe somewhere in the wings.

For a place as quiet and supposedly un-newsworthy as the west of Cornwall, life had its fair share of dramas. Gary found himself living in a house run by the "local Mafioso" for a short while. One night, a man was trying to escape from the house and kicked the double glazed front doors out from the inside in a panic. The scene resulted in Gary being kicked out by the top mafia man he was renting from. Luckily, he wasn't homeless for long. "There was a caravan that was on Iwan's Mum and Dad's property and I moved there," Gary mentions. "I was there quite a while. Obviously it was all about the band and making it work so I needed to be near them."

Iwan recalls having to make a decision around this point about whether to go to University or take a year out. "I had a place – I was going to do geology at Cardiff because I had a friend in Cardiff and at the time I was really into skating as well and I knew all the sort of Cardiff scene of skateboarding – like Matt Pritchard and all these Dirty Sanchez blokes and I'd been hanging round with them a few times. I was gonna move up there because I had a best friend called Ed and he was like the best friend that I'd known for years and I was going to move up with him and all them lot. I think then, though, we got the support for this Bluetones gig and we had another couple of bits in the pipeline so my Dad sort of suggested I should take a year off and see what happens. I think he said something corny like "Study rock or play rock!!I think he'd had a few glasses of wine!" Iwan laughs "So I was going to do geology but I guess it was just something that you just do, don't you? So then I thought I'd take a year out and then it got to the point where I was still a little bit unsure after a year but I thought just leave it. If I ever want to re-apply I can, so I ended up sacking the sort of education thing and concentrating on music and Joe was getting more involved."

Across the great divide...

May 1999

On the top of the ruins of an old Victorian hat factory in Tib Street there is a sculpture of a horn at the gateway to Manchester's Northern Quarter. It plays a significant role in the next phase of the band's history. An artist named Nathan Kemp had been commissioned by Manchester City Council to construct this work. He happened to be a neighbour of Nathan Wason as well as a close friend of his father.

Kemp finished the sculpture ahead of schedule. He had an idea that the band were considering a move out of Cornwall and got in touch, telling them the hotel he'd been in still had over a week's rent paid on it. Literally and symbolically he offered them the keys to a brand new start.

Gary felt it was too good a chance to miss: "I was like "listen, we've got to fucking go." We said to Joe this is what we're intending to do and he was like "yeah, great idea". So we scarpered… just like that! I mean, he phoned us on Thursday and we were gone by the Saturday."

Nat remembers Iwan being equally keen to break out of Cornwall but says of himself "I wasn't too bothered, I was quite happy in my little niche. And Tom – was a bit like me – but we were up for it, we did want to take the band further." The boys were driven across the country from St Just to Manchester by Gary's father "in the back of transit van – horrific journey full of shit," laughs .Nat "We went up there on the premise of being painters and decorators – going to paint this sculpture. We got in this gaff and it was complicated getting the keys – and getting accepted in because they knew we were full of shit – we were saying we were builders or whatever… and we obviously weren't but it was in the centre of the gay village in Manchester."

As far as I'm aware the exact location was a building that used to be the Dominion Hotel in Princess Street.

Although Iwan and Gary hadn't been living with their parents prior to the migration up North, for Nat and Tom it was their first move towards an independent life-style away from the safety net of the family home. It seems the experience was both exhilarating and scary.

"There's some funny stories because I don't think we at first knew it was a gay area," Iwan explains. "I remember Tom walking down the street – I think we'd realised but maybe we hadn't told Tom! And Tom was going "Hey, everyone's really nice round here, aren't they?!" And they were all winking and everything and Tom was going "Great, I really like it round here – they're all so friendly – look at these guys!" There was the four of us in the one bedroom. We had to share a double bed, me and Tom. It was really funny because there were loads of builders outside. We're slap bang in the middle of the gay area and there's all this banging going on outside and I just went "Will you fucking shut up!" to the builders outside the window. Obviously they saw Tom in bed like that and they all went "Oooooo!" I couldn't really say anything," Iwan laughs, "I just had to shrug it off. It was a complete culture shock, though, we didn't really know what was what and we were smoking a lot of weed as well – scared to go out of our hotel room to get milk or anything. Joe got us into smoking this really strong grass – that was first signs of us smoking serious skunk which I can't even smoke now – knocks my block off and we were smoking stuff like that and stuck in the hotel room – scared to go out and meet people!"

Having no knowledge of the city and no-one to guide them, they were left to their own devices whilst at the hotel. Nat remembers feeling the fear quite strongly:

"Everything scared me! If we'd run out of milk at half nine in the evening and we had to go to the shop to get a pint of milk two of us would go!" Their arrival coincided roughly with Manchester United winning the treble which may explain why venturing out was more overwhelming than usual. "The streets were full of big, bellowing men! It was weird you know – bizarre!," Nat continues, "I suppose we were thrown in at the deep end and we got to grips with that sort of soonish. We were drinking in all the wrong pubs. We were like – "Let's go out!" So of an evening we'd go to Piccadilly Square and go and drink in the Goose on Piccadilly! Go and have a few pints in there. We didn't fucking know where to go and then we'd go from there cruising round the bars in Piccadilly Gardens thinking that that was Manchester. We were just completely spun out by the whole thing, excited and kind of freaked out. The aim was to get a gist of it and I remember Joe telling us we had to see town on a Saturday because it's really buzzing and full of life. We went in on a Saturday and I was scared! It was as busy as the daytime and I was actually a bit afraid. I thought I'm gonna get robbed here. I think I had it tatooed on my forehead… like 'MUG' or 'NAIVE' or something because every single scumbag in town approached me. It was obviously the way I stood, or looked, or something!"

Fortunately, Joe soon introduced the boys to a safe haven on Oldham Street, a music bar called *The Night and Day Café*, frequented by musicians and an arty student crowd. It served food and coffee during the day and transformed into an atmospheric live music venue after dark.

"Joe said "Basically this is like headquarters – this is where our kind of people hang out!" and I remember three of the staff, maybe Kelly and Tash and a couple of others coming up to us and having a bit of a tease because we were the Cornish boys that they might have heard about because Joe was in all the time. So, we got ourselves a coffee and we felt we had a little safe spot again. We had our hotel room right in the middle of the gay village which was a safe zone and we had Night and Day in the Northern Quarter and everything in between was like Mordor!" Nat giggles.

The transition from south to north is one I made myself some three and a half years later, only I was leaving a city with such a marked pace, density and dysfunction that by comparison, for me, Manchester was like slowing down. It allowed space to stretch your arms to their full span, far less transience and anonymity, an opportunity to breathe a little deeper, even if the air was still laced with the same blend of carbon monoxide, grease and grime of everyday urban living as London.

Coming from the tranquillity and predictability of Cornwall, certainly for Nathan, Tom and Iwan this sharp jolt of culture shock required a period of mental adjustment. Gary, being less of a stranger both to city dwelling and upheaval, was likely less startled by the experience and I get the sense that he was beginning to assume the role of leader, not in an egotistical sense, just because, consciously or unconsciously, all groups tend to elect a leader.

When their stay in Nathan Kemp's hotel room came to an end there was no suggestion of going back home. After two weeks in Manchester the gang wanted to stay, as even at this point there was an awareness that here lay real possibilities of launching the band and making something of all this. They needed a new base. Having no other source of income other than whatever the government provided through Jobseeker's Allowance, there were limitations in where they could live. By the time they had to get out of the hotel they hadn't secured any other accommodation so Joe Moss allowed them to cram into the top room of his house on Brownsville Road, Heaton Moor. This was the start of the band's long and continued association with this little known suburb of Stockport.

Heaton Moor is one district of the Four Heatons, a South Manchester suburb that borders Levenshulme and Reddish on one side and Burnage and Stockport Town itself on the other. "The Moor," as it is affectionately known is a peculiar place, deceptively normal at first glance, almost quaint with its predominantly red-brick Victorian houses and the row of shops, bars and cafes adorned with pretty glass canopies and wrought iron railings. If you spend any time in the Moor, however, you will likely become attuned to what I can only describe as its supernatural energy. A black shadow flits by so fast. You blink. Did you imagine it? When exiting Heaton Chapel railway station which dates back to 1852, how many times have you felt *sure* someone is walking behind you only to look back and see a street that is empty yet clearly pregnant with presence. Many locals of the area have told me tales of hauntings in various houses dotted around the Moor. Those tall and beautiful trees talk, whisper secrets of the past, then catch their breath when the wind pauses…history hangs heavily on every corner. It's all too easy to imagine the ghosts of galloping highwaymen and carriages clattering along Heaton Moor road at the dead of night.

I mention all this because coming from Cornwall, a land equally ,steeped in magic and mystery perhaps Heaton Moor's charming strangeness felt comfortable to the band. I mention it also because I get the feeling that the area operates like some kind of mystical vortex that catches those who come here with dreams and whips them up into forms that manifest, or at the very least become more vivid and urgent. Or perhaps the band just ended up in Heaton Moor for no other reason than Joe Moss happened to live there.

Staying with Joe was only a short-term measure and finding a new home happened quickly. Gary recalls that he and Tom saw a notice in the Post Office window for a two bedroom flat on 104 Heaton Moor Road. They arranged to meet the landlord, claiming to be brothers and posing as chefs looking for work in local kitchens.

Gary's not sure himself why they felt the need to pretend to ,be brothers "I don't know why we did that. We said we were from Cornwall and we've got different Dads, that's why we look different!" Nat is equally baffled as to why they pretended to be brothers, "Why? I don't know, just to complicate things!"

The landlord must have been convinced that Gary and Tom would make suitable tenants as they completed the paperwork and he handed them over the keys. The pair moved in and waited a week or so before Nat and Iwan joined them in order to avoid arousing suspicion though quite why they were behaving furtively remains a mystery even to themselves.

From this day forward for several years the flat became the place not only where the band lived but where they worked and created the bulk of the songs that ended up on their first album.

Gary and Nat shared a room and Iwan and Tom shared the other. It doesn't sound like comfort was really a concern as they didn't even have proper beds according to Nat:

"Gary had the bed base in our room – I had the mattress. Iwan had the mattress and Tom had the bed base in their room. A hell of a lot of stories go with that place, but also huge amount of super good fun."

Gary agrees "It was a fucking hovel. It still is now. I was in there the other night, this guy I know has moved in there. But saying that, it was the most creative time we ever had. We had a drum kit in Tom and Iwan's room and in me and Nat's room we had a multi-track thing and we had amps all around the house. We used to sit in every night just taking ecstasy and recording music – it was awesome. *Between the Senses* was written there. It was a great, great time."

Iwan shares fond memories of the times they shared in this first flat. He remembers that the day he and Nat were sneaked in and they were finally all together was the day that Manchester United won the treble which would have made the date 26 May 1999, just days after Iwan's twenty-first birthday.

"We were sat down like – "here we are now" and there were loads of cars going past beeping because United had won the triple," Iwan says. "There was quite a lot of space but it was a bit like *Terry and June* with lots of kind of flowery carpets and all sorts. There was a little serving hatch from the kitchen. We were chuffed. That house turned into a party house really and we ended up meeting all these kind of old blokes from around Heaton Moor. We were really shy when we first moved up. We were scared to ask for anything."

Just around the corner from the bands new abode lay Shaw Road, which is now lined with restaurants, bars and an unusual parade of shops. In 1999, it wasn't quite as vibrant as it is now though many of its present establishments were there in some form or another, even back then. One of these establishments was the Blue Cat Café, which opened in 1996 on the site of what had previously been a TSB Bank. Danny Donnelly was inspired to open a music bar in the area as nothing similar existed, even in nearby Stockport.

Danny wanted to do something that offered an alternative to the local pubs where the live music programme consisted largely of dull covers bands and Elvis impersonators. The café bar had been open for a few years before the band became residents of Heaton Moor. At the point they arrived, Danny ran regular jazz nights, had a semi-resident band called The Removal Men along with a few other regular performers. He wanted to expand his live music repertoire and as the band needed to make themselves known, they gravitated naturally towards the Blue Cat Café.

Joe suggested to the boys to try and get a gig at the venue, even though he himself wasn't familiar with place at this stage. Iwan remembers walking back and forth past the bar many times, glancing in the window, before getting the courage to give it a go. "It took us about a week, I think," he laughs.

All the band seem to clearly remember first walking into the bar.

"There was no one in there," Gary recalls describing the place very differently to how it is today. "It was horrible, it still had the old bank front on it and it was half the size it is now. It was all white and it had this horrible snide-looking stencil of a cat's face on the wall. No-one in there at all."

Danny, himself, has a vivid recollection of the boys first walking into his bar:

"It was a Sunday night. They came in, obviously quite sheepish. I think it was Nat who spoke first and asked if I put bands on, saying they'd come up from Cornwall."

Nat remembers nervously walking in the bar and them asking for a gig and Danny's response being "What day do you want to play?" So, their first gig in the North was arranged as simply as that.

"What struck me was the lack of arrogance with them," Danny comments "but at the same time, confidence – an unusual combination, really. I can read people really well, having worked with the public for so long, and I could tell these guys meant business."

They did and business soon began.

"If you're trying to pull the wool over his eyes he'll know in a fucking second," Gary confirms Danny's perception "and he knew – he could see – well this might sound like we're blowing our own trumpets here but he could see how passionate we were about things and he could see that we had drive and we knew what we wanted to do and we had a vision. And he believed in it."

During their early visits to the Blue Cat Gary remembers Danny selling Gambrinus bottled lager that was out of date though, of course, Danny told them it wasn't. "You opened it and thought hmm, ,that smells funny," Gary grins "and Danny would say, "Well it's Czech lager. It's meant to be like that." That was the blag. "Czech lager always smells a bit funny!" and we just got talking." It wasn't long before the band struck up a firm friendship. Gary continues, "I actually started working there first, behind the bar. I lasted quite a while. I think I'm the only lad who's never had the sack! But we had some good times there, some really, really good times and the great thing is, it's still ongoing. It's the one place that I know I'll never get barred from." Though Gary was correct about being only the male member of staff never to get fired at the time he made this remark, I must mention there has since been just one other! This is extremely rare.

The venue became both their local and a place to play and develop their live set away from a judgemental audience of journalists, critics and the knowing faces who frequented the city centre circuit.

This was an important factor and something that Joe insisted on, playing regularly in what was basically a quiet suburb where they could relax and gain composure and confidence, where word was unlikely to leak onto the serious music business radar.

"We were just kind of the background and that's exactly what we wanted," Nat says on the early Blue Cat dates. "The Blue Cat became our first little testing ground really, a testing ground for new songs and it was good. Also, Danny gave us his garage which was small and cold but Danny all along, Danny was the opposite – he was warm and big hearted, you know? Anyone who knows Danny, if you're Danny's friends he's more than bighearted – if he doesn't like you he's a complete arsehole – he wouldn't mind me saying that – but he is – you're one or the other."

This same garage, still used by Gary and Nat until recently, has undergone some renovation and become a self-contained little studio, but back then, it was just a cold garage with a threadbare carpet, no toilet and no sound-proofing. However, it was handy and affordable and it was just around the corner from the band's flat.

"I think the Blue Cat was a big deal for us," Nat continues. " It was really what helped us. I think Joe held us back for maybe ten, twelve, eighteen months before he allowed us to play in Manchester. Really, that's how it was. It's like your Dad not letting you out to play! Fucking great! I suppose Joe doesn't piss around – he doesn't fuck about with half-arsed bands – he only wants it to be fucking great or not at all."

Iwan also acknowledges the importance of the Blue Cat gigs and the initial difficulty of finding their place in the grand scheme of things in the early days. "It took a long time really," he considers. "We'd done all these gigs at the Blue Cat – I mean we were going into Night and Day a lot and trying to meet people – it was really hard at first. There was a whole different scene going on and we were just from a totally different place. At first it was weird, I think the first year I lived in Manchester I hated it really – I really didn't like it all and then after that I really started to enjoy it and to understand it – but in the first year there was so much stuff to get on with – getting a house and sorting money out – because we never had any money – we were really skint."

When the band first dared walk into the empty Blue Cat, in suspense-laden saloon-scene Western style, the only thing they didn't have, besides money, was a name…

If music is your Haven...

The details of the first gig at the Blue Cat are fuzzy. Danny remembers the band being billed as Blew (the name they went under in Cornwall) and says he has a poster to prove it. The band insist they had to come up with a name quickly as they had actually been nameless for a while.

Also, due to licensing issues, Nat says, the first few gigs had to be acoustic though soon Danny ignored the whims of Stockport Council and let the band play fully plugged in and loud!

Either way, launching themselves as a live act in a new town meant coming up with a name, and a name, like it or not, soon becomes meshed with your identity.

Haven.

The word is synonymous with refuge, harbour, safety and home-coming. A gentle, yet powerful word that makes you feel warmly at peace, yet there's still a feeling of being close to the elements and having the freedom to either hideaway or set sail. There are various press reports suggesting the band called themselves after the famous Haven Holiday Camps, many of which are in Cornwall. As a group of deep thinkers who take their artistry and creative path seriously, I don't think they would consciously have chosen to name themselves after a holiday camp. Still, with the knowledge of where their origins lay, they must have guessed the association could and would happen.

Regardless of who chose the name or where the idea sprung from, it's a name that truly matches a quality of their music and resonates with themselves as people. It is comforting but with vast vision, familiar and welcoming like the twinkling harbour lights after a choppy voyage at sea. The waves, the spray, the breeze are almost audible and palpable in Haven's music. To me, it's truly a perfect name for the band.

"I don't exactly remember when we became Haven – finding a name is really really hard," Gary thinks, "largely because none of us thought – well, we believed we'd get a record deal or we'd never have moved to

Manchester but I think there was an element of just out and out wonderment that everything just happened and it was hard to take anything seriously – it really was." It's easy to understand how it felt this way, as though things were magically unfolding like a fairy tale, as that is what seemed to happen the minute the band set foot in Manchester. Regarding the name again, Gary gives the official spiel "We had this room upstairs in the Night & Day – to get to it you had to walk down Spear St – which is a really fucking horrible street with a scaggy drug vibe to it. You're running the gauntlet a bit to get there, especially if you're leaving late at night but the minute you shut the door and get upstairs and start playing music you feel really safe. The idea of the name came from the feeling that we all had together and that's as true as it gets. It was like that."

Perhaps it's also tied in with the feeling of coming from the serenity of somewhere like Cornwall to the inner city, as Gary goes on to say:

"I mean, Nat was born and bred in the countryside – when me and Nat met he used to think I had this really negative outlook on life. He would just talk to anyone – and when they'd nicked his wallet and his shoes and his bus fare home, he'd still have something nice to say about them! He used to think I was just an eternal pessimist and I used to think that he was outrageously naive. We've learnt a little bit off each other as the years have gone on – I've kind of chilled out a bit – my faith in humanity is marginally restored. I think he's become a little bit more aware. So it's good, it's two way traffic."

The room that was their haven, of which Gary speaks above the Night and Day, was the rehearsal room they moved to after they left Danny's garage to which they would return at a later date.

Iwan similarly struggles to pinpoint exactly when they became Haven but echoes what Gary says about the feeling of a home-base where you could settle and shut out the nasty vibe on the street. "I know it's a bit blurry," he says, "but we had a gig at the Blue Cat and we had to have a name. We obviously struggled with a name for a while. We had a song called *Haven* – in Cornwall. We just kind of went through everything. It was hard work. We had a list of possible names and we ended up liking that name. I always liked the song. I don't know if anyone else liked it and I can't even remember what it goes like, but it was a good song.

Gary had moved everywhere – that was his life really – I mean my family weren't as bad as that – we moved a bit, but the name Haven, it kind of meant a sort of home thing. A bit corny but that's it really!"

So, Haven were settling into a new life, playing at the Blue Cat, rehearsing in the garage and working and partying in the flat.

Looking back on this era now, the band have fond memories but they also acknowledge there was an element of absurdity attached to that period. They seemed hell-bent on making their lives more complicated than they needed to be, but perhaps a key factor in that drive was their economic situation.

"We were very skint, paying our rent from our giros. We didn't even have housing benefit – we got housing benefit years later," Iwan states. For whatever inexplicable reason Gary had told the landlord that he was Tom's brother, it was assumed that they were brothers by some locals around. "People across the road would be going "oh those brothers are throwing bottles at each other! I wish they'd put some clothes on! Draw the curtains!" Nat giggles "Somebody had ripped the curtain rail off and slung it out the window," explaines Iwan. "We had no curtains and people were just looking right in at us – they must have wondered what the hell is going on in there!"

Perhaps the daftest thing of all was the fact that they only had one set of keys to enter the building with. Getting another set cut was considered above their budget and everyone hoped one of the others would tire of the inconvenience and arrange for a second set. Though they scratch their heads a little about it now, at the time, they didn't seem too bothered about climbing in and out the bathroom window when they were locked out and keyless, even though this climb was somewhat hazardous..

"It was an ordeal," laughs Nat "You had to get on a shed and you'd carry up this wooden pallet and that would get you to a certain height where you could get to the window sill. Then you'd like swing yourself up to the window and it was only the top tiny bit of the window that opened so you'd be leaning with your entire weight over a piece of wood and then a great big sheet of glass so if that snapped you'd be fucking chopped in half! Your legs would fall outside and your body would fall inside – and you had to do an army dive into the toilet!"

Iwan and Nat have an armful of funny stories about life in 104

Heaton Moor Road. "I remember the police coming round twice," Iwan recollects, "I think the first time we were locked in – I'd jumped through the bathroom window and I think the keys were in there to open the door then I sat on the carpet watching TV and the police man came around and saying "is this your house?""

Nat and Iwan were always under a cloud of suspicion because they weren't officially registered as tenants like the other brotherly duo. No post ever arrived in their name. The policeman didn't believe that Iwan actually lived there and ordered him upstairs. "He said, "right before we go upstairs what's in this room?" And I went "Pants! Pants everywhere!"" Iwan breaks down in laughter. "In this room, loads of recording stuff and the policeman opened the room and went "oh my God!" Pants everywhere, pants on the drum kit! And then the other time I didn't have the keys so I couldn't open the door and I remember the policeman being outside going "get out, come out" and I was opening the letter box saying "I can't let you in -I have no keys" "You're a robber then aren't you?" "No I live here honest but if you wanna speak to me you have to climb through the window!""

Any half-hearted attempt to live a more 'normal' existence was speedily crushed while the boys shared this flat.

"We always used to be out of it, every night," Iwan says. "Four blokes in a stinky room! I remember sometimes thinking I'll have a good sleep tonight, just have a quiet night and then there'd always be someone… like even sometimes all three of us would fall asleep and then Tom would come back in from the pub and we'd all end up getting up drinking again."

Another comical episode occurred when a visitor overstayed his welcome.

"We didn't have any friends when we first moved here so we'd be in the boozers and we'd be happy to invite anyone back – like really horrible old blokes," Nat chuckles. "One time this guy came round and none of us liked him," Iwan remembers, "Gary just went up to him and stared him for ages and then picked up a guitar and just smacked it right above his head into the wall." This was Nat's guitar which was useless after that dramatic event. "The guy was a real intellectual and we were talking about bands and rock and roll and what rock and roll is, this and that this and that" Nat explains "and Gary thought "I'm gonna fucking scare the shit out of him!"" It obviously did. The irritating intellectual scurried and a big dent in the wall remained.

Over time, naturally the boys began to make a few real friends locally, as opposed to unsavoury characters that latched onto them at during last orders in the nearby pubs and bars. One of these, who remains a lasting friend, is Jamie Colgan who shared some of their subsequent journeys in the years that followed. During the period that the band occupied the upstairs of 104 Heaton Moor Road, Jamie resided above the bakery on the corner. This was the building that later transformed into the slightly swanky Bakery bar but back then, was an old-fashioned, flour-dusted functioning bakery.

"I was at the window looking out over my yard," Jamie recalls. "I used to listen to a lot of music and get stoned. I noticed these weird, skinny, long haired guys. Eventually, I went and introduced myself to, I think Gary, outside the Plough and I think there was some ecstasy involved and we ended up going back to their gaff and writing *Out of Reach* that night – or the lyrics to it. A great friendship started between all of us and I eventually started hanging around with them."

Jamie's presence was helpful in more ways than one as Nat explains:

"When Jamie met us we were certainly aware of being the new little gang in town and we all walked around together. We were in hyper creative mode and were writing the best part of the first album in our shitty little flat, using plenty of stimulants to get us there. Jamie experienced first-hand a lot of that creative process and in return… we used to get shit in the pub with people elbowing us and nudging us and not getting served and all the rest of it – but when we walked in with him, suddenly they were leaning over the bar trying to give you a drink!"

In this own words, Jamie says he became like a slightly older brother to the band. He had local knowledge and reputation and smoothed the way for them. He was a good presence to have around and when things finally did take off for the band a little further down the line, Joe Moss invited Jamie on board as tour mananger.

As mentioned previously, Heaton Moor seems to be a magnet for the supernatural and strange. The flat had an edgy vibe and Iwan and Nat both felt a sinister presence resided there with them. "I was scared every time I went upstairs and across the hallway – that's the bit that used to freak me out," Nat confesses. Iwan told me of a horrible experience he had one night where he woke up with a jump, feeling there was a dead body lying beside him covered in blood. He leapt out of bed in terror. It's not that there literally *was* a dead body there but it was a vision, an impression that felt terrifyingly real. Iwan was prone to "seeing things" as a child, sometimes when he was ill, in those kind of childhood delirium attacks that happen to many children. "My parents had this big mirror in their room and I remember seeing some guy that was all dressed in gold and looked like Elvis Presley in the mirror looking at me once," he says. However, this vision in Heaton Moor was no childhood nightmare and though Iwan readily admits they were all doing too much drinking, on this particular night, he hadn't been and the experience understandably freaked him out.

There are other stories of Iwan being placed in a cardboard box by Jamie Colgan, and this box sliding off the roof of a car. The truth is, the band were probably not behaving any differently to students who go to University for the first time and are free to amuse themselves without parental control. Nat himself makes this point:

"Kids go to university and go mental – and even though we had pretty decent parents so we could do all of that. We didn't have to hide anything from our parents but that was the first time that we had to look after ourselves properly." Joe Moss was around the corner, and as far as what they did outside the band was concerned he didn't intervene. When it came to their music, however, that was a different story.

It was at least a year before Joe considered them ready to play their debut gig in Manchester. They were booked to play at the Night and Day, which was by now familiar territory. They'd hung out in the bar numerous times but playing there was a big step forward. The potential audience were likely to be more discerning and expectant than the locals of Heaton Moor. Timing was important here and Joe knew it.

"We were so ready for it," Nat says, "and I remember Joe saying "I think I'm gonna pull it cos I don't think you're ready" And us thinking "Fuck! What do we have to do? Fuck!" But you know, credit to him again – every time Joe frustrates us and he does often. He frustrates you by holding you back but then you look back on it and with hindsight you have to thank him for it every time becuase he's done it for a reason that you didn't see at the time cos you were so eager."

Iwan remembers this period in a similar way, "Joe said if you're gonna play in Manchester you've got to be ready cos you don't want someone to review you and then you get a shit review and then that's what everyone knows of you. So we did God knows how many gigs at Danny's – we got better and better and more people started coming there and we just started to kind of develop a life because before that we didn't really have a life. We were just kind of imposters sitting in the corner with straw hats! We didn't have any direction. We didn't really know what to do with ourselves and then as soon as we got the flat and Danny was across the road and it all really started to develop and then the next stage was doing the Night and Day."

Once the band were finally let loose on the Night and Day things really speeded up. They were quickly offered a residency there. At this point they also moved from Danny's garage to their haven above the venue.

"By the time we did hit Manchester we were shit hot," Nat grins. "We played once and then we played like eighteen times and got a load of record companies up. They all came up here. We used to wine and dine them in the Indian down the road, near to Joe's house. It was convenient for them! That was a funny time – you know, just meeting people and talking to them and knowing that you're not gonna go with them, knowing that you have already got plans with someone else but going out with them because you know you're gonna get a free piss up. Strange times!"

Down to the sea again...

The sleepy life the four had known in Cornwall was becoming more and more distant as the pace began to accelerate in Manchester. Haven were beginning to attract serious record company attention and getting signed was now viewed a matter of course. They had still only played in the North but A & R scouts seemed quite happy to head up to Manchester to witness the young musicians Joe Moss had hovering excitedly under his wing.

At least one of the band was uncomfortable with what was happening though, and had been for some time.

"You know when you get this vibe from someone?" Gary asks "I'm sat at home, 104 Heaton Moor Rd, and we've been here over a year now and I get up every morning and there's a vibe about Tom. I always think I'm a bit sensitive to this, maybe because I've moved so much but there's so much stuff that's said without being said." Gary feels Nat was so close to Tom that perhaps he wasn't picking it up as he brought it up with Nat almost every morning for about a month, his concern that something was wrong with Tom. According to Gary, Nat felt he was over-reacting and reminded him that Tom was the quiet type and that's just the way he is.

But Gary wasn't the only one who was worried. Iwan, of course, shared a room with him. "It was horrible really," he recalls. "I knew that there was something not right. I remember my Dad saying when we all moved up "One of you's gonna come back" I didn't want to think that would happen and I thought "that's bollocks" you know? That's not true but he was right. Tom didn't enjoy it really. All this time we were dead serious into it. We wanted to write good songs and there's certain things you have to do to do that. He was becoming really weird as normally he's like a really happy person. In Cornwall he was really happy. He was a surfer and he likes to do what he likes to do. He likes to get stoned and do his own thing and as it started to get serious we couldn't sort of sit there telling jokes totally stoned! We had to focus. The gigs just started to get ridiculous, just so busy! It was just stupid at some points. I remember there was a time when there were girls fainting and there was an ambulance outside the Night and Day and all these Japanese girls fainting. We still don't know if they were faking it! We were meeting record companies. It was kind of the best time and the worst time because all this time Tom was backing out of it and seeming like he didn't want to do it."

By his own admission, Nat suggests he was too close to see what was happening in many ways "Tom got quite ill actually. Because I saw him every day, I guess it's like a child growing, you don't see a child growing in front of your eyes when you see them every day. You see them every now and then you notice but Tom was growing quite ill in front of our eyes without us realising. Tom wasn't the type to moan about anything."

The illness Nat speaks of is unspecified at this point but he admits that they were all doing too many drugs and not eating properly. This is also something Danny at the Blue Cat observed, mentioning that the band seemed to exist on a humble diet of potatoes bought in a shop on the Stockport Road.

However, what happened with Tom is unlikely to be have brought about purely by a lack of nutrition. Sometimes, when we don't speak up, our body tends to speak for us and it seems an illness may be what our soul resorts to when we ignore its pain. One particular day, Tom had stayed home as he didn't feel well and the others were out working. Danny remembers him coming into the Blue Cat saying he felt sick. He looked very ill too, Danny thought, realising it was important to get him to get to a doctor or hospital quickly.

Gary and Nat both describe an identical scene when they arrived home and found a note on the table where Tom had scrawled "Appendix – hospital – fuck!"

Alarmed, they rushed to hospital where Gary remembers, "We walked in and he was lying there. I've got a photograph of this, it's horrible – three of us stood around his bed and he's got a morphine drip going into his arm and he's this horrible shade of green." It turns out Tom's appendix had burst.

His mother was notified and came up to Manchester to see him. "Me,

Tom and his Mum were in this hospital together and Tom was out of his face on morphine," Nat recollects. "I was upset and he was upset – he was crying and I said "as long as you're leaving…" – because he'd already made that decision to leave the following day in hospital. I said, "As long as you're making that decision based on the right reasons then I'm more than happy for you to go – not for a second will I try and make you stay in this band and live in this life if you don't wanna do it," but he was out of it you know? He said, "I don't like this morphine, it makes me feel sick" and all this sort of stuff but he assured me that he was making the decision based on the right reasons and I believed him."

As Tom began to get better Gary had a similar conversation with him: "I said "Tom, listen, you don't wanna do this anymore, do you?" And he said "No" and he looked me in the eye and he said – not being melodramatic, but he was like "I've been waking up every morning for the last two months trying to find a way to tell you that I don't wanna do this anymore" And I respect him for that and I'll tell you why, because he's the only musician I've ever met that's done it purely for the love of it. He didn't like it when we started meeting industry people and suddenly there was an opinion that we were supposed to consider and the only opinion that mattered to him was mine, Nat's and Iwan's."

Tom decided to return to Cornwall and go back to the life he loved. Nat comments "Tom's not the type to stay in a situation that he didn't want to be in. I suffer from sticking around things that I don't necessarily want to be involved in but I often find that – if I could only have a little bit of Tom's kind of willingness to just up sticks I'd be out of this situation but I can't – I feel obliged to stay and all that stuff."

It takes guts sometimes to follow your heart but it's the only route to an authentic and happy life. The band are all still close friends with Tom and speak about how happy he is now fishing with his father's fleet and living with a woman he loves in Penzance.

He was sorely missed though – and not just on a personal level. Everything was happening at once for Haven and they had a prime slot to play at the IN THE CITY festival not to mention an invitation to support Badly Drawn Boy on tour. He had just won the Mercury Prize so this was a high profile tour. Iwan remembers the first time they met Damon Gough which he believes was the day after he won the prize:

"We were sat down in the Night and Day. Joe knows him really well so he'd said "I've got this band". We rehearsed upstairs at this point and he (Damon) said "D'you want to play me a couple of songs?" I think we played *Til the End'* to him and we might have played *Out of Reach* or something like that – only a couple of songs but he went away and he said *Til the End* was his favourite song and he still says that every time we see him. He must have told his management and told his record company that he wanted us on tour with him. We didn't have a deal and it's pretty unusual for an unsigned band to get a tour like that. So we were like "Brilliant, we're gonna go on tour!" Our first tour is with Badly Drawn Boy but we didn't have Tom."

Being handed this tour on a plate was obviously a fantastic opportunity for the band but it felt bitter sweet when a dear friend was out of the picture. Finding a new drummer was vital and there was no time to waste if they were to keep their planned engagements and answer the call of the rock and roll siren that rarely beckons more than once…or so I've been told.

Banging the Drum...

Jack Mitchell was born on April 28th 1981 at Withington Hospital, Manchester. The family resided in Cheadle Hulme where Jack spent his childhood and teenage years. From a very young age music provided a focus and anchored him to some degree when his parents divorced a little later.

At the tender age of four, Jack remembers listening to his older sister Lucy's tapes in bed, mixtures of chart music and bands such as the Beatles coloured his dreams.

Keeping the beat was possibly in his bloodstream as his father, Peter, was a drummer, belonging to a band called *Ank*, who had been produced at Stockport's Strawberry Studios by Kevin Godley in the seventies.

"With my Dad playing it was perfect because there was always a kit around for me," Jack recalls, "and it's not easy for anyone to start playing drums because of the money involved in getting a kit and because of the noise and stuff. A lot of people wouldn't want a kit in the house so I was lucky."

He always gravitated towards the drums though he did also learn to play guitar.

At school, Jack was fortunate to have an inspirational music teacher named Mike Harris:

"A really cool guy – I'll always remember him because he wasn't your typical school teacher, he'd just let you learn what you wanted to learn so if you came in and you'd heard this song you wanted to learn he'd let you do that – I think these days with school lessons you have to learn what they want you to learn which is a shame."

Jack gives a touching account of the effect his father's drumming had on him following his parent's divorce:

"Dad was looking after me – I was nine – Victoria was thirteen and Lucy was seventeen at the time so Dad basically looked after three kids – went to work, cooked, cleaned – got us up in the morning for a long time. I remember when they first split up I remember listening to… my Dad's way of dealing with it and getting over it was hammering drums – just belting them. I don't think I've ever heard anyone play like that. He was getting out all his emotion. You hear drummer's play and you think "that's amazing" but they're not going through that emotion that my Dad was at that time. Still to this day, I don't think I've ever heard anyone play like that. I couldn't really work out what he was doing. I know I was only nine but I remember sitting in my room thinking "Jesus, this is amazing!" And he's never played like that since. He still probably could but yeah, it was the emotional thing. He is an amazing drummer but hearing him at that time he obviously had a lot of things going through his head."

It's easy to imagine the impact those sounds may have made on young Jack and pounding drums himself was surely a healthy and positive way to release his own feelings. Music was much more than therapy for Jack though and as soon as he was old enough he joined a series of local bands. The first band was called *Drowned* and another had the lovely aromatic name of *Coffee*. Although nothing came of either outfit, they were composing original material and featured Jack's guitar playing as well as his lyrics. He still has recordings of these early efforts. In many of the conversations I've had with Jack over the years it often strikes me that he has a sweet sentimentality regarding the work he has done as well as a real sense of excitement as he travels each rock and roll journey. It's refreshing and endearing that he hasn't become blasé about the music industry and his place in it and this positive attitude has certainly helped keep him afloat.

Instead of attending Sixth form College in Cheadle as might have been expected, Jack decided to travel to the College in Marple, figuring that it was an opportunity to make new friends. This turned out to be a smart move as here he got to know a guy named Asa who was working with Aziz Abraham, who at that time had ex-Smiths Mike Joyce and Andy Rourke playing in his band.

"Asa told me Mike Joyce was after a drum tech" remembers Jack "I was only about sixteen or seventeen at the time. Back then, when he said *The Smiths* I was probably like 'who?" because I was too young to appreciate them. So I always remember that phone call and going "oh yeah, I'll do it" and then I went round to Mike Joyce's house and the first time I met him I called Mike "Andy" and Andy "Mike"!

I remember them looking around like they were thinking "Where did we get this guy from?" It was all good and I went on tour with them supporting Paul Weller and stuff in the Royal Albert Hall. I mean I wasn't playing but it was an experience."

Asa was involved in a small record company called *No Label Records* who had recently signed the band *Tailgunner*. This was Mark Coyle's band. Coyle was the producer of the first Oasis album *Definitely Maybe* and seventeen year old Jack was in the right position to land a job as their drummer. Tailgunner embarked on a four week tour which was a wonderful chance for Jack to get his teeth into some serious drumming but he remembers the tour being a little fraught in places. "I was seeing a girl at the time which made it a bit tricky because she was on the phone every day because she didn't understand – and I didn't really understand." There was a lot to understand and things were moving quickly. In contrast to the other members of Haven who spent many years honing their art before casting their musical pearls before the industry, Jack was forced to find his feet whilst still a teenager and was earning a modest living as a full-time musician straight from sixth form college.

Tailgunner's guitarist, Eric, quit the band after the first tour and was replaced by Phil Cunningham, formerly of Marion, who quickly became good friends with Jack during the six weeks of the second Tailgunner tour. "He told me all about Marion and Joe Moss ,and the whole experience he'd had," Jack explains "all the ups and downs and then right at the end of the tour me and Phil went on the piss for about two weeks! We were expecting to get about two grand each for this tour so we thought we may as well go out and have fun – but then we got a call that the label had gone bust and there was no money coming, so we were like "Oh no! What can we do?" We were in hundreds of pounds of debt. It was a real bad time. It was before Christmas as well."

Meanwhile, in another corner of Manchester a replacement for Tom had to be roped in. Otherwise, Haven would have to turn down the support tour with Badly Drawn Boy not to mention their *In the City* slot. Still reeling from the recent loss of their friend and drummer, it was a stressful time.

"When Tom was in hospital people were saying things like "oh has he left the band?" you know?" remembers Iwan. "Can you imagine how bad that sort of time was for him? It was obviously bad for us but I remember my Dad saying that when he left his band it was worse than leaving your girlfriend. He couldn't listen to music for a year. He didn't listen to any music, didn't buy any music, he just couldn't do it. So, on top of that and then getting ill and everything it was a weird time. We were on the point of getting a record deal and it felt very strange. We carried on with this girl, Becky. That was a very strange thing as well, suddenly having a female drummer."

Becky had been playing in another band who were friendly with Haven and was swiftly drafted in. "We did the ITC gig and we did quite a few gigs afterwards and they didn't work out," Gary comments. "Just personalities and all that kind of stuff – nothing to do with the fact that she was a girl."

The band's *In the City* slot was at Atlas, in Deansgate and attracted the attention of the influential Seymour Stein. "It was packed inside and we had a good three or four rows of people deep .outside looking in," Gary enthuses "After the gig, Seymour Stein made a point of being stood outside with Joe and showing everyone that he supported it. He wanted us to sign to his label. I remember hearing voicemails he left on Joe's phone. I remember feeling over the moon because it felt like we'd won the war!"

Danny of the Blue Cat clearly remembers the buzz of Atlas gig as he went down with his daughter Georgina to support the boys and realised this was the moment – they were about to be signed. It was all pretty much on the table, both a publishing deal and a record deal.

Though Becky had been brought in for that gig and the Badly Drawn Boy Tour it was on the understanding that she wasn't an official member of the band.

"She's a shit hot drummer," Nat says, "and she did that tour with us with Badly Drawn Boy. This was just before our record deal, so we owe it big to her as well for jumping in last minute and doing this tour with us. It didn't work out between us and her, for some reason. To be honest with you, the soul just was torn out of the three of us because Tom had just left. We were the last gang in town, we felt invincible, we felt we were all part of the same thing and then suddenly one just went and Tom – he's a real comfy guy, it's hard to explain – he was always sat there in the flat with a spliff. He was always there and reliable and he was suddenly not there anymore. For me, Iwan and Gary, we came to realise that what we were doing was more than four friends having a laugh; it was actually – or it certainly became a career thing and it's got to continue whether or not the personnel are still the same. We had a really difficult stage. I remember it probably being the most argumentative period we had. Me and Gary fell out a few times and we very rarely fall out, over things like who's going to be the drummer. It was really difficult for us."

Iwan echoes much of what Nathan says regarding Becky:

"She was good – she was a strange girl, a lesbian. It was awkward because I had to teach her all the songs and I mean I felt sorry for her because I – I just didn't really wanna know! When you look around and see your friend is gone and then you look at someone totally different – it wasn't because she was a girl or anything. There were a few gigs that were really rough and I had to really train her up because we were the rhythm section so I had to put more hours in to try to get her right. It was just really hard then, going to see Tom in hospital and then doing these gigs in London to try and get this deal. She was obviously buzzing because it was clear this band were on the point of getting a deal whereas I was like – it was probably one of the most surreal times of all – being on such a cusp of being signed but knowing that one of your gang members is not there – it was awkward really. I mean we got it sounding good but there was still that underlying thing that Becky was kind of a stand in. It just wasn't right, you know? We all sort of knew that really we needed to sort something out. We had to tell her. I mean she wasn't with us for long and I don't know how gutted she was or anything."

So following the tour, the task of telling Becky her services were no longer required fell to Gary and Joe at a meeting in *Love Saves The Day* in Manchester's Northern Quarter. They explained as nicely as is possible that it just wasn't working out and that they were still getting over the loss of Tom.

On the dotted line...

The year 2000 was racing to a close and so were the record label negotiations. The winner of the bidding war was the mighty Virgin Records who wanted to sign Haven to their brand new fledgling off-shoot label, *Radiate*.

David Boyd who ran the highly esteemed *Hut* label wanted to emulate *Hut*'s success with a new label. According to Gary, Boyd headhunted Jon Chapman who was working for the legendary *Island Records* at that point in time. Somehow, it came about that Chapman signed Haven as the first act to *Radiate.*

"In theory it was a great idea because it had all the financial clout of Virgin and a sort of independent cool at the same time," comments Gary. "It seemed like the perfect home. We had all the attention and no other bands. It was all about us!"

The deal certainly appeared to offer the band more autonomy than would have been possible had they landed in one of the other major label nests.

On the 18th December 2000, the boys accompanied by Moss, travelled down to the record label's west London home to sign their contract.

Despite the flow of champagne, Iwan remembers the signing being emotional for the wrong reasons. During the proceedings, the news of Kirsty MacColl's tragic and untimely death broke out. At that point of her career Kirsty was signed to Virgin and Iwan remembers the obvious upset in the office:

"This guy from Virgin who knew Kirsty really well had to go on the radio to do a talk about her and Johnny (Marr) knew her really well and did a lot of stuff with her. I didn't realise at the time how well Johnny knew her. We were about to sign and this guy came in and he was basically crying. It was really weird because it was our big moment, really". For Iwan, it felt like getting a high and a low together and was not dissimilar to the bitter sweetness he'd felt when success became apparent at the same time as Tom's departure. "There must be something about us where that seems to happen. God, I hope we're not going to get one next time!" he ponders in the summer of 2006 when I conducted this interview, and the band were once again looking for a new label.

Nathan remembers the champagne glasses clinking and the feeling that at last they had reached the magic point they had worked so hard towards for several years. At the same time he remembers a bizarre conversation taking place beside him, between Joe and Gary:

"Joe was telling Gary about these Jersey Royal potatoes! And you like boil them, and they're the best potatoes you ever had! Literally like!" Nat declares. I can well imagine this, as I recall a crazy night in the Blue Cat some years later, where Joe was waxing lyrical about a selection of vegetables he'd got from Unwin's Greengrocers, which he had cooking at home. The talk was so mouth-watering that he asked Danny if he could go and fetch the vegetables and eat them in the bar. Danny and Joe are probably about as eccentric as each other, so nobody minded.

"Typical Joe, talking about boiling potatoes in mint!" Nat shakes his head at the memory.

As it was approaching Christmas, Nat remembers raising a glass and then going to catch a train to Cornwall for the holidays with a big smile on his face. "Getting on the train with a record deal was a really big thing for me at the time. I was full of pride – absolutely bursting with it." So, Nat and Iwan returned to Cornwall as local heroes. Gary remembers having vague plans to go to France with Joe but instead he and Joe ended up getting drunk together in London. And the bells were ringing out for Christmas day!

As that ceremonious spilling of ink was taking place at Virgin HQ, accompanied by its strange gastronomical musings, strangely enough I had hatched a plan to start a record label with my close friend, Viv. The idea had been swirling around gently in my mind for a little while and once I'd found the right band (which I believed I had) the decision was cemented once the band in question agreed. So, in December 2000, Viv and myself, devoid of any laminate passes or illusions of having A & R women grandeur, found ourselves in the Barfly in Cardiff making an agreement with a band then called 'Tommy and the Chauffeur' to put out a record. This has repercussions that will follow.

The bells were ringing out loud and clear, we just had to listen to their message and learn to de-code it…

Last gang in town...

One night at the very tail end of that year, Jack Mitchell and Phil Cunningham were out having a beer. They were both feeling the pinch as the *Tailgunner* tale had wrapped itself up and there was nothing visible on the horizon but the dawn of a vacant new year. At this point Jack had begun working in a pizza takeaway shop in Cheadle Hulme for two days a week. This same shop also employed Sarah Harding before her *Girl's Aloud* fame, according to Jack.

Phil took a call from Joe Moss while Jack sipped a drink over-hearing interesting snippets of conversation but not realising the ramifications of this call as he heard Phil say "Yeah, I do know someone," and hang up, turning to his friend. He told him Joe was looking after a band called Haven who needed a drummer. He mentioned that Haven had a record deal and Jack began to feel faint butterflies and a sense of new direction began to open up.

Jack had an awareness of the band as though he lived in Cheadle, having gone to college in Marple, he had many friends scattered around the general Stockport area. He'd hung out in Heaton Moor from time to time where he'd picked up snatches of local gossip about this band, Haven, who had come up from Cornwall.

"I remember seeing it in the NME that people are going to love Haven as much as the Smiths," Jack recalls, "so I thought this was amazing!" A meeting was quickly arranged with Joe Moss at Town Café Bar on Heaton Moor Road and an audition swiftly followed. Jack says he remembers the audition vividly.

"I was really nervous because when you go for an audition with a band and they're already signed you think surely they're gonna be seeing lots of other people. I got the impression that they actually didn't – I think it was just me that went for the audition, there might have been a few other names in the hat. I found it very hard because when you've not played with someone before it's hard to just come in and put your own feel to it, especially when all their songs were already written. It was nerve wracking! I found it hard work and I didn't actually think I played that well."

Following the audition the band went with Jack to a pub in Oldham street. "I knew straight away that we were all going to get .on," he observed "Even if they turned around and said "it's not gonna work out". They were really nice lads and I thought I'd definitely see them round or whatever but it was like literally the next day they phoned up and said can you come in again?" Following another session, Jack found himself in *The Elizabethan* public house back in the moor where Gary announced "Here's your first wages, you're in!"

Although Jack was, even at such a young age, a highly competent drummer, I don't think it was his drumming alone that landed him his place in Haven, but that he had the right personality and temperament to mesh with the existing members who were still slightly raw from Tom's recent departure.

Nat explains "We lost our drummer and we were devastated we didn't know what to do. We messed around with other people and we ended up with Jack and he was brilliant. He was a great drummer and all that but I think more than anything he was constantly trying to have a laugh. Me and Gary get quite serious and Iwan also gets wrapped up and serious about what we're doing so Jack's kind of the element of well, stupidity really! We knew that it was right and it was so exciting to be a four piece again and yeah, and I suppose from that stage onwards we felt like we were kind of a band again and we were having fun and it was back to how it should be. None of us forgot about Tom. We felt like, now we can move on. Tom didn't wanna do this. Jack wants to be in *Rhythm* magazine, you know what I mean? Tom never did. He wants his own pair of signature drum sticks! So he was the man for the job."

Iwan echoes Nat's sentiments closely, "We kind of knew of him vaguely. We knew Phil pretty well and he'd given us nothing but good reports. We were chuffed when Jack came because he was this breath of fresh air. He's kind of like a natural joker. We would talk about everything dead serious whereas he would just take the piss – he just diffused the seriousness out of everything. Obviously he had to do a sort of audition thing but he was a good bloke really and we felt a bond with him. The other thing is his Dad's a drummer and he's always bought like drum magazines, stuff like that, which made me think "Geek!" – but also made me think that's his thing – that's important to him – he wants to be a drummer and it's an ingrained thing so from there it started to get really, really good!"

Gary remembers Jack being really nervous at the audition and not really understanding why, "When we were looking for a drummer he was undoubtedly the perfect guy," he says. "He's got a big personality – a great guy to party with and – he's a really caring guy, as well."

Jack is a few years younger than the others but I don't think this is the reason for his playfulness, rather, that it is just inherent in his nature. He was and had exactly what they needed, an injection of humour, a pure and joyful love of music, a grace and an ease that allowed him to not just enter the inner circle of the band but to immediately be part of it. Jack's arrival helped restore morale and get things back on track. It's not easy to join a gang as tightly knit as Gary, Nat and Iwan undoubtedly were, but as well as his typical drummer's ability to make light of things, I've always found Jack to be a sensitive soul with a great listening ability. He was the missing piece of the jigsaw necessary for Haven to set their ship on sail again.

Delighted as Jack was to be on board, he soon found himself thrown mercilessly in at the deep end. Plans were afoot for Haven to record their first EP *Til the End*. This meant five days of rehearsals before they left for Heliocentric studios to do the actual recording. This left Jack with less than a week to learn from scratch all the songs for the EP. "I actually remember that week being one of the hardest weeks of my life! In fact I think it probably still is! Even to this day!" Jack laughs, "So intense! Me and Iwan used to go in and rehearse and play some drums for hours before we even got Gary and Nat up. We'd have played for three or four hours and then we'd get Gary and Nat in and then we'd play for another three or four hours so it was really intense. I remember seeing Phil one night and I was absolutely exhausted. I had a bit of a funny turn and he was like "Are you alright?" I just remember feeling really ill and I had a bit of bad stomach – I think I might have even got an ulcer or something because I remember at one point getting this really severe pain in my stomach. It was after that first week. And I was thinking 'Jesus! This is what it's like being in a band!' – feeling sick and knackered all the time!"

This trip to Heliocentric Studios was Haven's first official recording as everything prior to this had only concerned demos and potential b-sides. This was the real thing, so expectations were high.

The producer who'd been assigned the job with Haven was Mark Wallis who'd worked previously with acts such as The LA's, The Go-Betweens and also The Smiths, a band who seem to be curiously linked with Haven, tenuously and not so tenuously again and again.

The experience was challenging for everyone but it was especially hard on Jack for the reasons already mentioned.

"He was alright, Mark Wallis, but he gave me a bit of a hard time to be honest, bearing in mind I'd been in the band a week," Jack recalls "We'd been doing live takes to a click to a song I'd only played literally maybe four or five times – it takes a long time to gel with anyone but in a week it's hard. I remember just going into take after take after take and I was getting blisters on my hand. So was Iwan on his fingers from playing bass. It was really quite a weird vibe – I don't mean a weird vibe from the lads, but Mark Wallis."

A combination of factors seemed to be conspiring to make Jack uncomfortable. The pressure that Wallis put him under may have been due to a deadline in studio time set by himself and label boss, Jon Chapman who was present to witness his first *Radiate* act record their first EP, his first release. According to Jack, Chapman was sitting in the studio all the time with his arms folded.

Sleeping arrangements were a bit tense as well. There were three beds in one room which Gary, Nat and Iwan claimed banishing Jack to the other room which he had to share with Joe Moss. This was slightly daunting for the new drummer. "Yeah, the bastards! After a hard day in the studio I had to get into bed with Joe! Or not *into* bed with him – but you know what I mean?!"

Jack admits he came away from the Helliocentric session "feeling a bit down about my own ability …I remember Mark Wallis saying to me "You need to go home and listen to some more music and practice playing with the radio." And alright, I wasn't amazing but I had confidence in my ability. He shot it right down in that week." There were moments where Jack even wondered if he made a mistake in joining the band, longing for the comfort of being at home, hanging out with Phil and perhaps just signing on the dole. Luckily he found the stamina and the mental discipline to ride it out. Even though he was suffering he was aware he had a great opportunity here. Texts and calls from the outside world wishing him luck and congratulating him reminded him of that.

Iwan was aware of how tough it was Jack, "I mean he knew us but he'd not known us long enough to get thrown into the studio like that – you know, it's hard work. We were a little bit worried about the track at the time – that it was a bit rough but it was actually really good if you listen back to it now. We did all that and we got a lot of interest through that EP. It did get on the radio."

Although the *Til the End* EP failed to chart this is by no means unusual, even normal, for a first release from an unknown band where a publicity machine hasn't quite cranked into gear yet. The finished EP featured four tracks and was released that Spring. It contained the heart-wrenching title track as well as *Beautiful Thing, Speakers Corner, and Feel Your Way.*

What strikes me most about the title track, aside from the obvious emotional impact of the lament, is its unconventional structure. The song is devoid of a chorus, verse or intro in the traditional sense yet it hangs together in a kind of shaky, precarious beauty. Gary's vocal ranges from fragile to forceful, dipping in and out of this futile journey with the skilled subtlety he excels in, while Jack and Iwan create a pounding platform of pain with drumming and shuddering bass, all collapsing into release when Nat's guitar chimes through at the close, dispersing the tension like ribbons of blossom blowing away on the breeze.

It was a limited edition with only 1000 copies being released. As the band's first physical record it was an exciting event when the records turned up at Joe's house.

"I remember going round and getting mine because they send like forty to Joe's house and I got my ten," Jack recalls happily. "We went out and got pissed that night – I remember walking down Heaton Moor Road handing them out to people "go on here you are – here's our single – have one of these!" thinking that you never know, in years it might be worth a lot of money. I remember that single, when we were at our peak doing really well, I remember it was going on ebay for maybe ten or fifteen quid at a time".

After Heliocentric, there was subsequent band business in London and despite being skint, the boys made the most of it. Any money they did get they spent necking beer and checking out bands in places such as Camden's *Monarch*. One night, in that particular slippery-floored venue, Gary accidently knocked over somebody's pint.

"This guy swung for him, whacked him on the nose!" Jack reports "There was a big skuffle where the guy grabbed him and put him in a head lock. I think Iwan gave him a few digs but it was a real bonding experience because Gary got hit and straight away my reaction was to grab him – I don't condone any violence but it was like I'm sticking up for him – I think that was quite an important night for us."

The gang spirit was alive and well and it's clear from talking to the band on numerous occasions how much they looked out for each other and cared for one another. Jack had found his place in the group and their bonds would only grow stronger as they worked and played together throughout the clearly plotted itinerary Joe and Virgin had created for them. The whole year was marked out ahead, with the recording of their debut album taking the prime slot in the early summer. Single release dates, tours & promotion were constantly being woven around the campaign. There was a lot to be excited about.

This charming man...

Johnny Marr already had a presence in the Haven story. There had even been some recording of early demos at Revolution studios under his supervision when Tom was still in Manchester. Joe and Johnny's relationship extends back to Marr's teenage years and he subsequently became the Smith's first manager. Moss and Marr always remained close and still are to this day.

Gary remembers first being introduced to Johnny in the *Night and Day*, "Hanging out with him was always brilliant, always creative," he smiles. Gary was also struck by Johnny's accommodating manner and ability to put you at ease "even though in the back of your mind there's always that voice going 'It's JOHNNY MARR!' He's a great guy".

Iwan and Nat both remember first meeting Johnny at his house. Iwan explains "We met him when we went to Revolution (studios). We had to pick his Hammond up, stick it in the van and go to the studio. We were all stuck in the back of the van and we turned up at his house, opened the van and saw this beautiful house and a nice summer's day. So we dropped the Hammond off and that's when we met him. We were only there for about an hour and then he said to Joe he wanted to record in the studio straight off." This is how the original demos which were instrumental in the band getting a record deal came about. "That started the relationship with Johnny," Iwan continues claiming that Marr soon said he wanted them to do a studio album. "It was good in Heliocentric but we needed a producer really. With Mark Wallis – it just didn't work out, but with Johnny, because we'd met him a couple of times and started to become friends it was great!"

Nat comments on the speed of the learning curve they all shot along with Marr in the studio: "Every minute, every time we're around Johnny, still to this day, to be honest, you learn big lessons quick and fast. That's how he is – he's an inspiring bloke and he works fast and *he* gets very inspired – he's so excited about music – I've never met a person more excited by music than Johnny Marr and he's been around it for so many years! But you can play a few chords together and he can get all giddy about it and that's inspiring in itself, to be around that, you know?"

Perhaps, Marr manages to remain enthused because he is coming from such a sincere place and is doing exactly what he loves to do without getting caught up in the baggage of his past, that so many of his contemporaries seem to obsess over. He brings a fresh approach and the his numerous and frequent recordings and collaborations bear testament to his unusual versatility and ability to be so fully immersed in his creations, yet to be able to move on at the speed of light to whatever's round the next corner. I can't imagine him ever allowing anything to stagnate or to be half-hearted about anything he does.

The band entered Clear Studios (Johnny's home recording space) in the early summer and recorded the entire *Between the Senses* album in a whizzingly intense two and a half weeks. Listening to the album, I've always felt it had an otherwordly quality, a sense that it had been conjured up by a sorcerer and his four apprentices in a dark Cheshire cavern. This could have something to do with an NME article that mentioned the recording in a very esoteric manner, referring to the use of crystals in the studio. Gary is quick to point out that there was nothing "weird" going on but equally quick to acknowledge that the place had an wonderful feeling of natural magic

"It's just supremely creative," he says about Clear. "It's just got that vibe about it. The minute you get over the threshold you feel like you've got all these ideas that are just screaming to get out."

As a producer, Marr also had a talent for recognising people's gifts, hidden or not, as Iwan observed: "We all had different personalities. Johnny brought out singing in me and I didn't think I could sing. I mean, even Nat sings on it. He just brought everything out – as a band obviously, but everyone started to do all different bits they might not normally, and we all realised that you could carry on recording something that might be used for something else." The speed at which the album was put down is probably partly to do with this process that

Iwan describes, that things were being utilised in all sorts of imaginative ways. Gary mentions that they also had another room with a four track outside the studio where stuff was happening simultaneously to the stuff happening in the studio. It sounds like it was all woven together very intuitively, with an enormous amount of enjoyment involved. "There were lots of late nights and lots of laughing, you know?" Gary says "We'd get in at eleven in the day and we wouldn't leave till two, three, four in the morning."

Iwan was equally inspired and considers the weeks at Clear to be the most creative time they ever had collectively: "It was unbelievable. So much going on – we had enough for another album. All the b-sides were done too in no time, it was just amazing." I asked Iwan if he thought this was because it was the first time that they been given this kind of freedom and it was a the natural result of all the creative energies that had been bubbling away beneath the surface, which were now given a chance to fully bloom. Iwan puts it more down to be driven and inspired by Johnny, feeling Marr's involvement to be the true catalyst. "He's just a workhorse really," he says "I didn't realise anyone could work that much, especially after everything he's already done, you know? Because we sort of think "Ok, right, that's done" and sit back in our chairs but he just constantly works. We all got on really well and he started giving us advice and he started asking advice on his stuff. So, we were dropping ideas into his stuff and it was just brilliant."

Of course, many of the songs were already written before the band ever entered Clear but they also found time to create some new material from scratch. This seems to be the case with the last couple of tracks which are more experimental, less destined for daytime radio but breathtaking in an enchanting kind of way.

Iwan agrees, "A bit spacey, aren't they?" and goes on to tell me how he sneaked some atmospheric vibes onto *Keep on Giving In* without telling Gary:

"It was recorded on this old Acard thing, which we still use now. Gary just recorded that himself and each day we would come in and I added a weird sort of – I didn't even tell him – because I listened to it and I thought "ah, this is fucking great this!" I'm not going to put like a big heavy bass line on it. So I ended up doing this sort of delay thing on it so it sounded kind of like a cello. I don't think I ever told him. I think he sort of knows it's there. I sort of added that and built up the track and then we got the track on the computer and ended working on it from there. *Keep on Giving In* and *Holding On* – it's such a good end because everything's kind of reached that peak. It's like six or seven in the morning and whatever you've done, you can put it on… really late night music."

Jack remembers worrying slightly about his connection with Mike Joyce when they started working with Johnny, in case there were any lingering problems since the infamous Smiths royalties court case. Needless to say, there was nothing to fear, as Johnny was "cool with it asking how he (Joyce) was," Jack mentions.

Joyce did advise the younger drummer to make sure he got something in writing though, as now that a studio album was being recorded with a major label it was only sensible for any musician to have a contract. Jack didn't like to pester but felt he needed to keep asking Joe if something could be done. Eventually, Moss organised a contract to be drawn up at Virgin which was sent up to Manchester for Jack to sign. Now, he finally had peace of mind on that front.

Between the records...

Hot on the heels of the band completing the album, the second single *Beautiful Thing* was ushered out, lovingly encased in one of the oil spattered canvas-like sleeves that artist David Moss, Joe's son had provided for the both this release and *Til the End*, back in April. The arrival of this CD brings me full circle to where I came in, sitting in a pub in London's West End, holding one in my hand.

Strangely, enough, Radiate had now released two Haven singles but there seemed nothing else in the pipeline with other artists.

"Radiate itself was a good little label but it never hardly existed really, other than us," Nat comments "there was no other bands on it, I dunno whether Jon Chapman was too picky. He never signed anyone else. We were his first act and we were waiting for a bit of competition – not wanting it, but you kind of need it – you needed someone else to be signed to that label to spur each other on, never happened."

There were releases by Brighton band *Eighties Matchbox B-line Disaster* in the next few years during which the label was active but I can see why Haven felt as though they were completely alone. Like most things in life, it had its benefits and its pitfalls. They were given free reign with artwork and perhaps a slightly false sense of security that it was one small and therefore closely-knit family and in many ways it was.

Unfortunately, *Beautiful Thing*, also failed to chart, not that charting is the only or most valid bench-mark with which to judge how well a record is received. In terms of Haven being recognised, the process seemed quite slow, and perhaps a little disappointing considering how strong those first two singles were.

Looking back on it, years later, Gary considers the dynamics that were at work:

"Unfortunately, he (Chapman) had this kind of – he had this real lack of ambition, it was almost like, if we sold a million records it wouldn't be cool and as a result all the promotion and everything you want a record company to do they did by half because they thought it was better that way. That was the problem or that's how it seemed to me. I don't mean that to sound bitter – but it was kind of obvious. We did our end of it and made a great record. Don't get me wrong, I mean it was successful to a point but it could've been handled a lot better. It did OK but there was a lot of – how can I put it? Everything was like....it's not cool to seem like you're trying. I just think it could've been a lot more. It could've been a LOT more. And they were excited about getting a top 40 single – I wasn't – I mean top 40 – not good enough, know what I mean? That ain't down to us, that's down to them because you know you've got to be realistic, we all know how it works. If you do your job – if everyone does their job and maximises what they're doing – it isn't just about how good the record is – well ultimately it is, but under the surface it's about how hard it's kind of worked."

I think one area of coverage where the band seemed sadly absent was the printed music press. There were only a handful of articles in the NME and next to nothing in the monthly glossy magazines.

They received the odd mention in the local Manchester press or the Cornish press but I feel Gary is right to say the push they needed wasn't there.

On a positive note, the band were included in an NME article published in October 2001 which placed them in the Top 10 up and coming guitar bands.

"I remember Joe making a really big deal about that," Jack recalls "The Music and The Coral were in it and I forget who else but it was the first big piece we had." The NME journalists responsible made the trip up to the band's rehearsal room at The Night and Day. "That's one good thing about Joe," Jack continues, "he always used to make sure he got them up here. He got the A and R and press up here – a lot of them don't wanna go out of London." The NME gave the band a big sheet of white paper which was pinned to the wall and was for them to scrawl on it whatever they wished "We just got spray paint. They wanted something representing us," Jack remembers.

Haven chose to spray 'THERE IS NO SOLUTION OUTSIDE LOVE', an André Breton quote on the wall, complete with the band's name and some splashes of colour. The piece also contained some unattributed quotes such as "Haven are like a Beckham free kick!" – which Jack says were supplied by either Gary or Nat. He mentions that he and Iwan weren't too keen on interviews "In those days, I was probably a bit shy."

A third single, the uplifting and irresistible *Let it Live* was released in September. There's a remarkable story attached to this song, which is a true testament to what a positive, life-affirming anthem it is. The single was play-listed by Radio 1 but during that time the catastrophe in New York, referred to as 9/11, occurred. In a time of enormous tragedy such as this, it's usual for radio stations to revise their playlist and sometimes not much is played at all as a mark of respect or if deemed insensitive.

Gary explains, "We had to fight like fuck to get *Let it live* as a single. They didn't want us to release that. We just wanted to put that out because we thought it sent the right message out about what we were about and interestingly enough, not something that I'm proud of, but when 9/11 happened *Let it Live* was the only single that *Radio 1* played because as you probably remember they had this policy where they weren't gonna play any singles – it wasn't right – but they played that. Hopefully because they kinda got it and understood the sentiment of the song and in many ways, I'm not proud of it because it's such a fucking horrible disaster, but in many ways it's nice to think that something's recognised for what it is."

It is an extraordinary song that feels like a thunder storm is brewing and explodes before it glides into that ecstatic chorus where the sun bursts through and a rainbow should surely manifest, delicate but stunning, powerful enough to make you feel like the roof is going to lift off – especially when it's played live.

Speaking of which, the touring that Haven did in 2001 and into the following year was incessant. They certainly got to know all the regular small to medium venues up and down the country.

"We toured and toured like every other band does," Iwan laughs, "all the shit holes – all the toilets!"

Jack points out a memorable gig that happened at the Adelphi in Hull, strangely enough, on the fateful day of 9/11. They had a portable TV in the van with them and as they pulled up outside the venue earlier in the day to unload, Jack recalls the disaster happening on the screen as they all sat huddled in the van in shock. For whatever reason, the gig that followed that night was a highpoint in his mind and the crowd were full of delight. He noticed they were beginning to build a fan-base, sometimes seeing the same faces beginning to repeatedly appear at various locations. They were even beginning to draw the odd groupie and at that same Hull gig: "There was this mother and daughter combination in Hull and they told us they'd been shagging him and shagging him – urrgh!" Jack winces with a giggle, "Oh God, I remember them coming in taking pictures of us and trying to put their hands down our pants! And telling us how they got on the Cooper Temple Clause's bus and all that and we were like "woah!" – but yeah, we did start to notice a certain fan-base."

There was even a promotional trip to Paris that December, though Iwan couldn't make it because he was attending his sister's wedding in Las Vegas.

For the most part, the band seem to look back at this period of time fondly, despite spending so much of it in the back of a van, but the camaraderie was strong, they were young, fit and healthy and the future looked dazzlingly bright with their album set for release early next year.

Between two worlds

Seven months or so after I sat holding the beautiful thing that was Haven's second single, their debut album *Between the Senses* was officially released. As Iwan said, it was a small hours of the morning kind of record. I have a vivid recollection of staying at my sister's south London flat shortly after this record came out. It was a slightly strange time in my life where everything felt quite transitory. I was sitting up late one night, on the floor with my back against the bed, in the dark, with *Between the Senses* on the CD player. It may sound like a cliché but Gary's voice literally sent shivers down my spine. I was completely absorbed in how almost angelic his singing was and how this was not fully being noted by the world! There was such a haunting feel to the album and that night particularly, it seemed to be transporting me somewhere on a deep soul level. Without wishing to over-dramatise the impact this record can have, I do think it has an almost supernatural vibe, or quite simply, it has the power to take you away.

I played the album infrequently but anytime I did, I marvelled at its beauty. Life seemed particularly frantic. Running the Manic Street Preacher's fanzine, *Terrible Beauty* which I'd been doing for six years felt like a full time job, even though I already had a nine to five day job on top of that. More and more, I just had this desire to get off the roundabout. Deep down, I knew I had to fold the fanzine and reclaim my life. Being a fanzine editor had become more like a counselling service for distraught Manics's fans. I wanted to leave it all behind and I wanted to do what I said I should do, start a record label. For some reason, I knew this meant, for me, getting out of London town.

Between the Senses entered the UK chart at 26 and went on to sell somewhere in the region of 100,000 copies. The critics were relatively luke-warm about the album's merits, with a few being quite enthusiastic. The album was rapidly assigned its place in the loose category of indie Brit-pop. Although, there is no real need to force any record or artist into a particular genre, I don't think this album sits neatly in that field by any means. Listening to it now, in 2010, what jumps out again at me is this almost mystical quality the songs have and I feel it's essence is closer to the soft, searching sixties folk movement of Laurel Canyon than the in-your-face swagger of much of what is now considered Brit Pop.

The band seemed to straddle two worlds, and truly inhabit neither. Even though they were based in Manchester and were respected within the local music scene, they were usually referred to as Cornish. Even their art work could be considered a bit peculiar for its time, with its tactile, earthy hues and thoughtful smudges.

The cover of the album is a painting of a publicity shot of the band taken by Tom Sheehan, re-worked in rich, deep oils by David Moss. It was sensual and spiritual at the same time, leaning towards the psychedelic, but grounded and measured enough to co-exist within the climate it was born into and not be considered too leftfield for mass appeal.

On many levels, life was changing for the band, now that they had an album on the racks in most record shops within the UK and release dates being planned internationally. They were by no means rolling in money but they had enough to enjoy themselves on a moderate level and keep a roof over their heads. This is often the stage in some artist's lives where they go off the rails a bit, finding the rock and roll ride, increased recognition and attention, coupled with the drugs and drink so readily available too overwhelming. Somehow, although there was much partying and fun to be had, Haven seemed capable of keeping their feet on the ground. Nathan finds it hard to say how his life changed and he didn't feel it was really that different on a day to day level

"I feel like it all just came to life a little bit, perhaps all of the hard work had kind of paid off a bit. I can't really remember what changed, though I'm sure it did. You're only doing what comes naturally to you. I suppose the record deal might have affected Gary more than anyone because Gary had been the one that had been particularly skint due to living on his own for all those years, whereas we'd all been living with our parents. Living with your folks you're never gonna go without a meal, are you? Gary was living on his own for a long time and also they're his words – so his words were being published and his story as such was being bought. So it probably had more of an impact on him, even though it had a huge impact on me – but I think it was expected. To be honest, I never expected anything other than getting a record deal."

Gary, as lyricist and lead singer was probably under a little more scrutiny than the others. He tended to take the lead in interviews and slipped into the role of spokesperson with seeming ease. Perhaps this was partly because the words of the songs were all his own and the others felt it was his place to tackle the questions the press presented to them. Having said this, as the band gained confidence they all chipped in at interviews. They all had something to offer, which was usually served up with a nice dash of humour.

I asked Gary if he ever felt over-burdened handling all the lyric duties, as it is a huge task.

"Not a burden," he considers carefully. "You have good days and bad days, don't you? I hate it because it feels like the only part of it that needs proper dedication. Most of the other stuff just kind of happens, you know? Music just happens, the trouble with words is you've got to be really careful with what you're saying, and you've got to have something to say and what if you haven't got something to say? You're gonna get judged because you haven't got something to say. I've kind of loosened up about it, I'm kind of with Marc Bolan on that in that it doesn't really matter, just talk a load of nonsense! Who's gonna question it?" he jokes. "No, I don't mean that …. I really don't mean that! It's all about that big line, but you can get caught up in it because if you say it's all about the big line as long as you have one big line it doesn't matter what the rest of it says. There's too many kind of schools of thought on it. I try to just let it sort of happen."

I think more credit is owed to Gary for his lyric-writing than has generally been acknowledged. There is pure poetry to be found within many of his lines. His lyrics are never too complex to get in the way of the music but they have a grace and symmetry that is not easily achieved, though often taken for granted.

His writing can also take on clever twists and turns such as the craftily duplicitous line "Believe me now, I'll only lie to you" in *Say*

Something. I think Nat has a point when he says it was Gary's story that was put out there and many of the interviews conducted throughout Haven's history seemed to unearth tales of the singer's nomadic childhood and accompanying angst. Not that I feel he was intentionally aspiring to the tortured artist persona, but the hint of that, I'm sure, helped rather than hindered interest in the band and authenticated their sensitive sound.

Following on from the album's release the band continued to tour. They were scheduled to play at all the major festivals that summer.

Their fourth single to be lifted from *Between the Senses* was *Say Something*, which quickly became and probably remains their most popular song to date. It was certainly the song that received the most radio play, consequently peaking at number 24 in the UK charts. *Say Something* was considered catchy, far less cluttered and curious than the releases that preceded it. Quickly, it became the song that the audience demanded at gigs and proceeded to go wild to when it was played. It was that smiling monster of a song, that most bands develop, the one they can't get away with dropping from the set-list without an uproar.

Having the single b-listed by *Radio One* suggested that Haven were finally making their mark and though not exactly house-hold names, many people were at least dimly aware of them. The fact that they were being played regularly on national radio with this particular single was possibly the real breakthrough point and Jack remembers a moment when this really hit home. At this point, he was living in Didsbury with Jess, his girlfriend at that time.

"I remember some builders working next door," he says. "It was shit because I wouldn't be getting in till three or four in the morning and then they started at half six or something whistling, radio blaring. Then there was one morning when I thought "I recognise that tune," and it was *Say Something*! And all the builders were singing along to it and that's when I thought "Fucking hell, I've made it!""

Another heart-warming account of sudden awareness that Haven had entered the dizzy world of rock stardom is told by their friend Mickey Smith. Around the same time that the band migrated up north, Smith also left his native Cornwall to "chase the waves in Australia." He worked there in a surfer's paradise, building a reputation as one of the finest surf photographers of his generation. "I'd obviously spoken to Iwan on the phone a bit and kept in touch, but I came back two years later, got on my plane looked in the in-flight entertainment mag and there were the boys, looking funny as fuck in big flares with big hair do's" Mickey exclaims. "Then I got off the plane at Heathrow, jumped in a taxi and Gary's voice is blaring down the radio, I was like, fuckin' right boys, yes!"

Having a hit on their hands the band were psyching themselves up for their first *Top of the Pops* appearance. Unfortunately, that didn't quite happen. Gary explains, "We were robbed by Incubus with *Say Something*! I tell you we were! *Say Something* was coming out and they (Incubus) had a record coming out and the powers that be decided that Incubus were bound to go in higher than we were, right? So the night we were meant to record *Top of the Pops* they had a show at Wembley so they pre-recorded their *Top of the Pops*. Then, when the midweek's came out we were like kicking their arse big time but unfortunately because they'd pre-recorded theirs they decided they'd just go with that anyway even though by rights it was our spot. So, it was just one of them little moments in life where you have to just go "ah well fuck it – hope we get it next time" and we did with *Til the End*".

Though I don't remember catching the band's one and only *Top of the Pop's* debut at the time I've since seen the footage.

Nerves were on edge, with the performance being live – but playing live went in Haven's favour, as they clearly *did* know how to play their instruments and carried it off admirably. Gary made limited but effective eye contact with the camera, emitting a sultry moodiness that was compelling to watch. Nat looked a little like he had wandered onto the set by accident, had been thrown a guitar and got completely wrapped up in playing it.

Iwan and Jack both seem sprightly and fresh-faced, loving every minute, in their element.

I've also got a vivid memory of Jack's Mum showing me a text he sent her when they were about to play which she'd touchingly kept in her message box, it being such a historical moment.

For the best part of March and April 2002 the band were on the road, and this time they had a proper tour sleeper bus. Times like this can make or break a friendship; when you're thrown together in a heap, cooped up 24/7, on stage, off stage, sound-checking, eating, sleeping, drinking, morning, noon and night.

"This was our first real taster of living together for four weeks on a bus," Jack laughs, "like waking up opening your curtain and seeing Gary looking back at you – or seeing Iwan's arse in his bunk! Urrgh! Or Nat's feet poking out! But I think the worst thing about those buses is the crew. You wake up in the middle of the night and you've got this like, chorus of snoring and farting and smelling! Ah it was awful! It actually gets quite intimidating but once you get in your bunk it's like a coffin – once you close that curtain you're in your own room!"

The crew tended to be the same for most of the tours over the next few years. Despite the difficulty they caused with his sleeping patterns, Jack thinks it's good to stick with the same people: "We had Peter Carroll on guitars for a long, long time and then we got his cousin in, Brian, to do my drums," he says. "We did try and keep the same crew because it's like people you can trust so it helps having the same people around you. But obviously as well, the budget was so low we had to try and have the cheapest people so we ended up with some big fat guy who didn't have a clue on sound who'd turn things up when he didn't mean to!"

A character named Hippo was frequently tour manager and Nat mentions that he seemed to configure the tour dates to suit his own life and plans. This meant that, as Hippo lived in Milton Keynes, the band ended up having a day off there, which, with no disrespect to Milton Keynes, was probably not as potentially exciting as a day in somewhere like Glasgow or London.

A day off in Milton Keynes proved memorable for Jamie Colgan, however. Jamie and Nat tell a tale of encountering two very attractive, but in their eyes, "mature" older women at the hotel bar. A lot of flirting and fun ensued involving Jack impersonating Rod Stewart and serenading them. One of the women apparently turned out to be a former Miss Scotland which Jamie proudly mentions he later took upstairs.

As with the majority of rock bands there are numerous hints of various exploits in hotel rooms that I have chosen to omit. My feeling is this gang were by no means squeaky clean and probably fall into the category of naughty when they felt they could get away with it, but not in an insensitive brutish way. Sex, drugs and rock and roll tend to feature on the same menu but this book is not an investigation into the seedy underbelly of Milton Keynes or anywhere else, so I've decided that what went on behind closed doors should probably remain there.

Big in Japan

Late April 2002, Haven made their first trip to Japan.

It was a journey they'd repeat at least five times together. Their experience from the moment they set foot in the land of the rising sun stepped things up several notches from when back in the UK. Although they had certainly begun to develop a small but loyal fan-base in Britain, the welcome they received from their Japanese fans was a special brand of haven-mania, that was exciting and flattering, even if a little surreal at times.

Fans greeted them at the airport, waited for them in hotel foyers laden with gifts, cameras, screams and adulation. This even culminated in screechy-braked car chases and being enthusiastically followed through streets.

As Iwan points out, if it was like that everywhere they went, in every country, it would have been freaky but as it was just one place it was fun, "I remember we had one girl chasing us down the street and then when the car stopped at the lights she got a chance to say what she wanted to say she couldn't breathe," Iwan remembers, "and we had to drive off. I felt really sorry for her because she'd legged it for that long and she was about to say something really important and we had to just go "Sorry!" and pull off. But the Japanese thing was just crazy, really – it's a different world – like *Bladerunner* or something."

Generally, in their own polite way, Japanese fans tend to be more passionate and demonstrative then their British counterparts. For some, travelling the world to watch a band that really move them is not out of the ordinary and it's often been the case at Haven gigs in the UK that the front row is made up of mostly their Japanese followers.

"We've got a really good relationship with the Japanese audience," Gary comments. "We've played good venues there. I like it – I like the place – everyone just wants to have a good time. It's like in this country, certain cities you go to, everyone's really up for it and certain cities the audience is like "hmm, impress me". You don't really get that in Japan. That's not to say they're not discerning. There's a common myth that Japanese audiences will jump up and down and clap at anything but that's bollocks. They're probably more discerning than anywhere else – I think that's probably down to their honesty and their sort of togetherness."

For Jack, the first Japanese trip is etched in his memory because it happened to coincide with his twenty-first birthday. "When I heard I was going to spend it there I was a bit gutted because I thought I'd be spending it with Jess, who was my girlfriend then," he recalls, "but then I thought, hang on a minute I'm gonna be spending it 6000 miles away in Japan! It was amazing because the record company after the gig bought me a bottle of champagne – sang me Happy Birthday!" Jack had a chance to celebrate with Jess on his return for yet another reason, "We'd just done *Top of the Pops* the week before we went. We'd recorded it but we still weren't sure whether it was going to get shown or not," he says. "I remember Joe getting a call saying we were going to be on it. I think the day we flew back it was on, so as we were flying back so I couldn't text anyone to let them know. I know my Mum and Dad were getting texts out to people saying we were gonna be on!"

For Nat, all the Japanese trips have merged into one happy blur.

What sticks out for him is the varying seasons "You go over there one time and you're all like wooly hats and scarves," he laughs. "You go back and it's just absolutely roasting! Incredible place. Japan, it's kind of where we go and we feel like we're living the life, you know? They go a bit crazy. They've been good to us."

I think it's true to say that Japan holds special memories for all the band to this day and it would have been easy for them to take their experiences there for granted. I've never encountered anything even close to arrogance with any of them though, and I think they were stunned and delighted at the response they received there. "I don't think you ever get used to it really unless you're a really big band and you go all the time. When you come back here it's like a straight drop down really. They're just really responsive," Iwan says. "The interviews we did as well were really interesting with the reviewers talking about certain songs – really interesting sort of interviews – and crazy people – unbelievable – when you come down in the lift and all these girls are waiting and you're signing peoples things that you've signed already – it was a complete new thing for us!"

There was a one particular return trip from Japan which is, perhaps, not so fondly remembered. It was a peculiar event to say the least. It's a long flight, especially for a smoker and Joe seemed to be feeling the strain. Jack recalls that he and Iwan were sitting beside Joe, and Gary and Nat were across the aisle with a stranger in the third seat. Halfway through the flight, according to Jack, for no apparent reason Moss suddenly started hurling insults at the band's song catalogue. "He just started slating us for no reason at all," Jack recalls. "Saying things like "Fucking *Say Something* is shit!" I actually find it hilarious now but at the time me and Iwan were sitting there thinking what on earth is going on!" Jack could see Gary and Nat both pretending to be asleep and keeping out of it.

Once the rant was over, Joe returned to normal and the incident was never mentioned again.

Here comes the sun...

That summer the band performed at practically every festival happening in Britain and Ireland, including the mighty *Glastonbury*. "*Glastonbury* was pretty special because, you know you go to *Glastonbury* as a punter and that's the one festival everyone asks you if you're doing. If you say yeah they're impressed – if you say no then you've still got a bit of work to do," Gary smiles. "That was really great, you know? I've got a video of it at home – I look really nervous – that was mainly because of the wind – I swear to God it was that windy – I was singing down the microphone and you just hear your voice go "hoooooorrggooo" down the stage, it's really bad. It's kind of ridiculous – how can sound be like literally blown away from you? It's weird!"

Gary was gaining more confidence as a front man with so many performances under his belt. He says now that he doesn't really get nervous anymore: "I used to, but not anymore, not anymore, because I just think well what's the point you know? I got nervous when it was about "we've got to impress so-and-so from this company" and that used to put me off. As it went on I used to say "Joe, I don't wanna know who's in the audience" because then you don't think about it too much. Yeah I used to get really nervous."

It sounds like Nathan had some particularly colourful experiences at the festivals. Highlights included riding on a giant pink snail with Gwen Stefani as well as a close brush with the law following a trip to Ireland where the band played at the *Witness Festival*. In his own words, Nat explains:

"I'm completely ashamed if anything, but we did the *Manchester Move* festival and then went to *T in the Park* and did that and on the same weekend – that was Friday, Saturday and Sunday we did *Witness Festival* in Ireland and from T *in the Park* we didn't go to bed. Well, me and the drum tech didn't go to bed – stayed awake on the ferry boozing all night and we were playing at twelve in the morning at *Witness Festival* and we were first thing in the morning on stage. We came on and we all just did a load of MDMA and before I knew it – a few things happened – we were with the Cooper Temple Clause and we were going totally fucking nuts and then we got on the ferry back to England. There were loads of bands on the ferry. We were in the back kind of lounge and according to the others I was asleep and I just stood up, really fucked up and said "Right, where's the toilets?" and someone pointed to the door where the toilets were and I stood up and walked over to the bar and got my dick out and pissed on the bar! I got arrested by the police when we got to the other side because there was loads of families and stuff and it was indecent exposure – not violent conduct – disturbance of the peace – drunk and disorderly – I had three different charges!"

Jack remembers this scenario well:

"I was completely sober – well, not sober, but relatively sober and Nat was curled up on a couch in the bar and he woke up so I was like "Nat, d'you want a drink?" So I went over to the bar to get a water or something and next minute I turned round and he was having a piss next to me at the bar and I remember thinking "oh God!!" and there was that band, Hoverstamp, an American band and they were going "oh Man! You dirty bastard man!" And then he literally got back on the couch and curled up again!"

That's what festivals do to you…

The next adventure gleaming on the horizon for the band was a trip to America. This would be a lengthy trip lasting for around three weeks and taking in towns and cities where they had no profile at all. It was an exciting prospect but before they set off, a hurdle annoyingly appeared on their path. Radiate/Virgin wanted some reassurance there was a second album with some potential hit singles on it in the pipeline.

"I suppose once you get a record deal and you go on tour, your head's all over the place," Nat comments, "We always pretended that we were writing songs but we found it really difficult . Other than sound-checks where little bits that come out you can actually commit to songs. To commit to songs, we found really difficult so we had a load of good ideas, a load of good music but we didn't really have any proper songs!"

Joe informed the boys that Jon Chapman of Radiate was coming to Manchester to have a listen to the new material he assumed was coming together for their second album.

Panic flushed through the band and they congregated in their space, which was now back in Danny's garage behind the Blue Cat Cafe. With some chemical assistance they summoned up some inspiration to get something decent down they could play to Chapman to assure him they weren't resting on their laurels and it was worth sending them to America and chalking up the plans to record a second, not-so-difficult Haven album.

"There was quite a few sort of hangers on or mates or whatever – I don't know – can't really remember who they were," Nat struggles to remember, "a load of people in there as well and we all got really, really high and then – Gary just sort of sang these amazing melodies over I think something like sixteen or eighteen of our little ideas – really, really beautiful stuff and then the following morning we had a CD with 18 songs on it!"

Jack had some prior engagement which he can't now recall that night so wasn't involved in this marathon session but he remembers getting a call from the others early the next morning:

"They were still up – you know, fucked – and they were like "come over – listen to the stuff we've done!" and it all sounded really amazing. I remember them all sat there at half eleven in the morning with cans of Fosters in their hands and I was, like, sober thinking these songs are top!"

He also recalls Jon Chapman appearing to be thinking they looked a completely exhausted and intoxicated mess, but the important thing is the songs were standing up.

When I asked Gary about using drugs to assist in the creative process some years later, it was this particular time that he recalled:

"We used to take a lot of ecstasy. It was a great drug because it made you really keen to write you know? I remember one night Jon Chapman from Radiate, who was their main boy, was coming down to check out what we'd done and Joe had given us a bollocking a couple of days before saying "where are the new songs – you haven't got any!" And we were like "Shit, he's right though really". I mean we had a lot of half-arsed ideas and we sat up in the garage for a couple of days, you know, eating a lot of pills and having fun and out of the fun we managed to get a lot of really good songs together," Gary explains. "I'm not saying we wrote them all but we had a lot of ideas and we just kind of… very workman-like mechanically recorded a lot of demos and they were good, you know? I've still got a mini disc to this day with all of them on – songs like *Tell Me* was on there *Have No Fear* was on there and *What Love is* was on there – and a whole bunch of stuff that never really went anywhere but it – I think, for us anyway, it's the one drug that you can be creative with. Coke don't work, I don't really enjoy listening to music if coke's on the menu and that's a bad thing. And beer obviously, well, you know what happens when you get drunk? You start thinking you're Neil Diamond!"

Nat expresses similar feelings about that night: "We didn't abuse drugs, we used drugs creatively," he comments going on to make the point that sometimes the presence of drugs and alcohol led those around him to think that he wasn't doing serious work, which in Nat's mind was a misconception. He recalls some nights when they were working late in the garage and his girlfriend would call to ask when he was coming home. "When she called at two in the morning I'd say I'll be back in a minute. I knew I wouldn't be back in a minute, she knew I wouldn't be back in a minute but she didn't think "Oh fuck it, he's not coming, I'll go to sleep." She'd phone me back an hour later and I'd say I'm really sorry I'll be back in a minute and that's kind of how we did things, like we were naughty boys doing what we were doing – but we were working on a record and we should have been allowed to just get on with it, but because there were drugs involved it was considered not work. It's a good point really because rehearsing, writing and being in a group is all work but there's beer involved so there's this perception that it isn't, but it is. Something phenomenal happened that night because we had fuck all to show the record label and when he arrived in the morning we had eighteen songs – it's like doing your homework on the bus on the way to school!"

This highly productive night that paved the way to many of their future songs seemed to mirror the spirit with which they left for America. Nat remarks that several of the songs even made it into their set across the Atlantic, such as *Tell Me.* "It was one of those nights where it all connected," Nat smiles. They were now about to connect with a new dream in another continent, a trip that shook their souls, dizzy highs and some sobering lows were just a transatlantic flight away.

Stars, Stripes and sticking out from the crowd...

Haven flew into Atlanta where they had the best part of a week to get over their jet-lag and adapt to the American way of life, before boarding their bus for the long string of gigs twisting along the road ahead. Somehow, drama reared its head within hours of them stepping off the plane. The boys had checked into their hotel, showered and then despite some minor disorientation due to the long flight, they were keen to go out and experience what Atlanta had to offer. They had a guide called Dennis who chauffeured them about, pointing out the best places to eat, drink and hang out.

The band who were booked to support Haven, Division of Laura Lee, had also touched down in Atlanta but there was little interaction on that first night. Jack has a memory of both bands sitting in the dressing room, sizing each other up. Their drummer, Hakan, had the unfortunate experience of being separated from his belongings, "My luggage got lost at arrival in the states, I spent most of the time on the phone calling KLM to try to get hold of my stuff so I don't remember meeting them (Haven) that day. There is a memory that still sticks from the first days of that tour. I remember wondering why they had brought their own PA. Moving this around must have been a pain in the ass!"

While Hakan was trying to locate his luggage, Iwan and Jack found themselves in a particularly dark club. Iwan recalls Jack admiring some girls and wanting to strike up a conversation with them. As he stepped forward to do so, he tripped flat on his face due to the dim lighting. As the girls in question looked on in faint amusement, Dennis came running in. Iwan describes Dennis as "gay and really camp. He came running in going "Oh my God! Nat! Nat!" It was just really funny the way he ran in and at the time I didn't realise how serious it was."

Jack remembers being flat on the floor and hearing Dennis shriek "Nat's being attacked!" Iwan and Jack stumbled out of the darkest club in Atlanta, onto the street in confusion and worry. Jack says, "We missed the actual attack. I just saw Nat on the street with his head covered in blood and that was pretty scary really – especially a head injury or something like that, and in America. The bouncer was the biggest thing I'd even seen in my life – not just fat – absolutely enormous – I remember thinking – the first thing I thought was "right let's go and have him!" but then I looked at him and I thought "Jesus…pretty grim!"

What had actually happened was that Nathan, being jet-lagged and dazed and a little drunk had urinated somewhere that he shouldn't have and the bouncer, who they later discovered was appropriately nick-named 'Trauma' had beaten him up because of this trivial offence. By all accounts it wasn't just a single punch but a serious beating.

Iwan remembers urging Nat to get himself checked out. However, Nat, being the sort of person who doesn't make a fuss, said he would be alright and retired to bed, bloodied, hurting and distressed.

Curiously enough, the boys remembered Joe's precognitive warning before they left; a warning that Nat felt was directed personally at him. Joe reminded them that they were no longer in their own back-yard and would have nobody looking after them. "He said the second you stand out of line and stick out, someone is likely to do you one. And that's exactly what happened on the very first night," Nat sighs. "Maybe it's good it happened on the first night anyway and I – well, I didn't let it taint the rest of my time over there. I got stuck in with the best of them – but it left a long lasting thing with me for sure. I'm not a fan of violence. It's the worst thing."

Joe was on the phone to check Nat was alright. He also remembers a concerned Johnny Marr giving him a ring when he heard the news. Johnny told him, "Nat, you're better than that. You shouldn't get into these situations." The words rang in Nat's ears. This was a reality check. This wasn't Cornwall or even Manchester. This was the United States of America and he knew he needed to keep his head screwed on the right way from now on.

This was the first time the band were away from home for an extended period, away from Joe, away from girlfriends, swapping the cosy red brick of Manchester for the vastness and craziness of the American dream. Perhaps this meant there was a greater temptation than usual to go off the rails. Gary describes his time in America as "Really good fun – we went for two months between the two albums, pretty debauched – I picked up a few bad habits."

Nat speaks about the Barney Hoskyns book, *Across The Great Divide* which is a biography of The Band "Discovering The Band, that was a real big moment in our sort of musical growth," he comments, "and *Across the Great Divide* is basically a very factual statement about exactly how they all met and how they got into it. It was hard work for me because I'm not a great reader but it was a fascinating story about their time with Bob Dylan and Screaming Jay Hawkins. We were lucky enough to experience a little bit of America when we toured. It was nice to read about these guys that were doing it so long ago and talking about the same places, same beaten tracks."

Haven rode across these same, dusty tracks in a tour bus, sometimes driving solidly for two days at a time. "That was a big lesson for us, you know? A big learning curve," continues Nat, "being in each other's pockets for that long with no escape, you know? We had day rooms every now and then where we could go and have a wash. This was the first time we'd experienced the vastness of the country. We'd put the gear in the van and then be driving for days through the Rockies or something to get to the next gig – a really incredible experience. We sort of learnt how to go on stage drunk as well!"

It seems that up to this point the band had a strong work ethic, a kind of unspoken rule that they could, by all means have a drink or two before a show but were always careful to be professional, to be sober and coherent enough to play their instruments properly and have their wits about them on stage. According to Nat, that ethic went out the window during the American tour: "When we were in America we really did get drunk on stage! We did it for our own enjoyment more than anything else because we didn't think for a second we were gonna go there and smash it so we thought let's just have a really good laugh. Joe wasn't on every date – he was there but he wasn't. I can't remember rightly…" Nat ponders the uncertain presence of their manager, "I don't think he came to every gig so we were kind of like kids playing without their mum or dad being around. We all kind of let loose a little bit and it was really good, you know? To experience going on stage with much more of a party head on then going to do a job." Nat remembers playing

Philadelphia where they became aware of the reputation of the Philly steak, which is "apparently world renowned." He laughs at the memory of Gary comparing it to an English roast on stage, weighing up the merits of each and drunkenly telling the audience "We don't need your Philly steaks, we've got roast beef!"

Division of Laura Lee put on a riotous performance each night.

"We're in different genres, which kind of came through as a bit strange to the audience I guess," comments David from the band," but personally, we were a perfect match. We made very, very good friends with them. And I, in particular love Britpop and everything that Haven did. But in a way I feel bad about destroying their sets! Honestly, we were doing our thing, which included smashing our gear at the end of the shows. Our songs are a bit screamy. And you can imagine how they must have felt to go on after that!"

Hakan agrees but also feels it was more interesting that the bands had different sounds, "It was a cool setup! Having two similar bands tour together is so boring."

Throughout the tour both bands really gelled and enjoyed each other's music. David remembers a couple of gigs that stood out: "Salt Lake city where Gary smashed his guitar. NYC for being all corporate, with stiff music buisness people all over the backstage area." For Divsion of Laura Lee, trashing their gear at the end of sets was traditionally the norm. It seems that Haven also adopted this habit on and off whilst on this tour, though it was something that they stopped once back on english soil.

Jack admits that much of his memories of the American tour are "a bit of a haze because we spent most of our time off our rockers to be honest – not playing, but just afterwards because the journeys were so long. We'd have a day's journey so we'd think what are we going to do after the gig – we're going to get smashed but being on a tour bus for so long gets a bit depressing after a bit. We were on it for five weeks – did a gig, got really drunk – after a while, it gets to you." Perhaps part of the problem was also that they were playing to audiences who, for the most part, had no idea who they were and Jack remembers several of the gigs being really hard because of this anonymity. "Apart from New York and LA where obviously you're going to get a crowd and places like Boston, Chicago – some of the other places literally maybe four or five people turned up," Jack shrugs, "and even those four or five people, you can see them looking at us like "what the fuck is this?" Some gigs you just think "fuck it" and just really enjoy playing regardless. Some of them you went out there and thought this is going to be really hard work."

It's hardly surprising that the band seem to struggle to isolate many specific memories of this tour because, like Jack says, there were few sober moments.

Jonas from Divison of Laura Lee confirms this:

"They were way more rock n roll than us. We were deeply into the Dischord back catalogue and used to be straight edge kids. We always toured with drug free, vegetarian bands and so on. I could not understand the amount of party nights that tour had. I remember walking backstage in Toronto or something, and I fell across some girl snorting coke from my hard-case. I was freaked out. I started drinking a lot myself but I think that was later, after we left for another couple of weeks supporting some other band. I guess I missed those guys. Me and David tried to cut our hair just like they did. We look dead funny on those old pictures."

Speaking about Division of Laura Lee many years later, Nat remembers them as being lovely guys and tells me that "We used to turn off all the lights in the dressing room and shout "Per Per Per" (at Per Stålberg of the band) to freak him out!"

Nat picks out their gig at the legendary Troubadour in Los Angeles as being the one they were most excited about "because of the amount of famous names that have been through that place but it was good all over. The only dodgy one maybe was the second gig which was Baltimore. It was just a weird place, with a weird vibe and we were playing at about half one in the morning and it was just not really working"

Hakan, the drummer from Division of Laura Lee, selects a gig in Denver as being memorable where the venue looked "more like a cafe. The audience sat down, very mellow night. Then, out of the blue Jack throws himself through his drum-set at the end of the show, with a huge grin on his face!"

As might have been expected Jack and Hakan hit it off quickly, "Put two drummers in a room and you get… yup you guessed it! Always had a good laugh with Jack."

David chips in regarding Jack, "I remember him for always repeatedly responding "Yeah yeah, fuck yeah!" to everything you said. AND for his drum stool with a back on it. SO posh, SO british!"

Despite the severe battering he had taken in Atlanta, Nat showed no signs of serious injury, though I sense the unpleasant event shook him up more than he was letting on at the time. It emerged that the bouncer who had done the damage had a history of serious violence. Nat didn't want to press charges against him though, preferring to move swiftly on: "I didn't do anything about it. I just wanted to – I didn't want any dealings with him, really," Nat tells me several years later, "a lot of people were saying you should do this or that and he did the same thing again – he's got a reputation for doing that sort of stuff and the kid he did it to has lost his eyesight so I feel like – I kick myself a little bit cos I think maybe if I'd have done something then this other kid wouldn't have had that happen to him. These are only things I've heard through other people. I don't know how factual it all is. He's on the run and I think he may even have been on the run before he did this thing with me. He's now either in prison or on the run."

Don't look back when leaving town

Leaving London, the waves of nostalgia were strong but the sense of liberation and adventure got the upper hand. It's easy to look back in fondness when you are miles away but at the time, the summer of 2002, I knew I had to uproot. To be truthful, it wasn't a difficult battle as the force propelling me north seemed to have a mind of its own and I recall, at the time, I didn't question it. Because of my long-term involvement with Manic Street Preachers, Cardiff may have appeared the obvious destination to launch a label from, especially when the band we were working with were based there, yet blocks and discomfort surfaced when that path was even considered.

Manchester beckoned. I've always had a soft spot for Manchester and had visited it enough times to know I could embrace a life there. Today, the city stands with many of its old industrial hulks no longer humming or clanking, but the past is still very tangible, as Victorian architecture rubs shoulders with Millennium glass towers and strange, elitist, minimalist shopping malls. However the buildings huddle, music still seems to be the oil that lubricates the city's soul. For that reason alone, Manchester was calling me. So, Viv and I decided we would launch our record label in Manchester. I had some worries that I would be viewed as a pretentious or interfering southerner, but I felt strong enough to ride that out, knowing that as long as I remained true to myself I could look anyone in the eye.

Because of the irrepressible scribe in me, it was unthinkable, after seven years of pouring my passions out in a fanzine not to have an outlet for the words I knew would surely stampede through my skull in the city of music. So, from day one, the label which we called *Urban Foxx*, had an accomplice, a publication called *Urban Scrawl*. This is the juncture where Haven re-enter the picture. Even when still in London and tossing around ideas of what we wanted the publication to become, Viv and I agreed that Haven should feature in Scrawl's debut issue. Some may have seen this as an odd choice, and would have opted for a more stereotypical Manchester band of the moment. I still knew very little about Haven personally, but I had an instinct that they would embody the spirit I wished Scrawl to carry… slightly quirky, passionate, yearning, worthy of mystical, magical writings on walls, whispers that creep into your consciousness while you sleep.

At this point, Haven had been accepted into the local scene and were generally viewed as a band on the rise who would go on to do many great things. They still had an outsider vibe in their collective aura, perhaps with the exception of Jack who was Mancunian, though I would argue he still shared their quality of being somehow "different" without trying to be. The city of Manchester may have been shaping their journey and reputation on some level, but there was another breeze that could be discerned, a playful breeze dancing through their stance, their speech, their hair. There had a strange purity in their eyes. They were not indoctrinated. They had minds of their own despite their reverence for the musical heritage thrust on them from their adopted city. Neither were they taking their success for granted. They were not blasé, even though clearly enjoying the offerings of the rock and roll lifestyle they were caught up in. They were beautiful souls. They were the boys I wanted on the cover of Urban Scrawl.

Our move to Manchester was protracted, due to finalising work contracts and finding a flat. Viv and I had no idea which nook of Manchester to head for initially. My friend, Jane, lived in Whalley Range and we ended up staying there for a few nights to get our bearings. Whilst still in London, I was already working on both label and zine, with our first release already being pressed by a half-crazy duplication company in London's New Cross, run by a man who began every sentence with the instruction to "Be Brief!" I also contacted Haven's PR company, Triad, around this time. Would they be interested in featuring in a new, cutting edge publication focusing on the Manchester scene? A guy called Tones said "probably", and he'd find out for me.

We rented an oddly shaped basement flat which we knew wasn't ideal but it was a base and we needed a base to launch from.

It was late October when we hit the motorway in a hired van for the North-west. Dramatic and furious rain pelted down on the M40. The downpour was so heavy you could barely read the signage but there it was behind a white wall of rain – Oxford – Birmingham – The North. A suitable soundtrack erupted from our stereo *There goes the fear* by Doves. We tore through the fear and I resisted the urge to look back on leaving town. London was history. Manchester was the city shrouded in hopes and dreams – anything felt possible and at the very least I felt I could have a fresh start.

Hours later, as we staggered through the doors of our new home with the final boxes from the van, my mobile started ringing – unknown number – "You wanted to interview Haven?" it was Tones from Triad. Yes, they would, yes, when they got back from America in November. That felt like a good omen. America?

Trauma, teeth and rock and roll: going west...

So, the Haven tour bus rolled on from city to city with Nat, though a little bruised, not suffering any obviously serious injuries from his brutal encounter with Trauma.

Despite being barely known in America, the boys were headlining the tour. Virgin must have pumped a substantial amount of money into this tour as Haven were fortunate enough to have their own bus, while their Swedish friends were squashed in a more uncomfortable mode of transport. "We toured in a van, trying to keep up with them," Hakan remembers. "We only travelled in their bus when we went to Toronto/Canada. Our crew didn't have the papers that we needed, so we had to leave them and the van in Chicago. We spent a little more than 48 hours on that bus. Awesome forty-eight hours! Could easily have been forty-eight days when I think of it."

Iwan pondered why it was that there was a general reluctance within the band to pay attention to health issues or things that might have gotten in the way of the schedule.

"You don't really want to do it," Iwan says referring to Nat ignoring his injuries. "You just want to carry on and sometimes it is important. What happened to me was the same. You just think it will all be fine." Iwan's problem began with pain in his mouth, which he assumed was mouth ulcers, exacerbated by heavy drinking. "I was in extreme pain every morning and I just hammered pain killers – ridiculous amounts of painkillers combined with alcohol as well – just being stupid really."

As many of us do, Iwan kind of hoped that if he ignored the pain it would go away. However, the body does speak to us, and if we don't take any notice it sometimes has to shout. The pain became so extreme that it started to spread across his face. He kept popping pills which took the edge off it, yet every morning, relentlessly it returned.

By the time the tour reached San Diego, Iwan was suffering too ,much

"I couldn't take it anymore. My eyes were watering and it was just awful," he explains "A horrible pain, it was my whole face now and it started to swell up. I looked a bit like a chipmunk! I didn't look good at all and I was thinking I have to do something – getting really worried – so I went to Jay, the guy that was managing us, and said "I've got to see a doctor or see a dentist or something!"

Why Jay didn't order Iwan to seek help before is a good question but then, it sounds like Jay was drug-addled much of the time himself. Like Nathan, Iwan has a tendency to grin and bear it. An appointment with a dentist in San Diego was arranged. There was something about this dentist that made Iwan wary from the start.

"He took an X-ray and he just made me feel uncomfortable," he recalls. "Jay said, "Let's just fuck off!" – and we just left – I just didn't like him. Someone like that is supposed to make you feel like everything is going to be alright and he didn't do that. He just went "I can't do it, man, because if I did this I might paralyse you!" He said that and I was like "What do you mean? What's the problem?" "Your wisdom teeth are impacted" and he said I can't do it because they're so close and they're so far up and if it goes wrong there's a nerve that could paralyse you or something!"

Jay and Iwan fled but understandably Iwan was growing increasingly worried. The dentist trip and Iwan's state meant the band had to cancel two gigs. The San Diego dentist had also given Iwan the chilling warning that if he didn't get something done in two days all his teeth could shatter.

"I never thought that could happen but I think there was so much pressure because they were so high up they were crushing my normal teeth," Iwan shudders at the memory. "We had to go to LA then and had to cancel a TV thing and these two gigs. It was horrible because I felt like it was my fault. I was feeling really bad by then. I was getting really bad headaches." There was no other option than to find another dentist. Luckily, this time, Jay found Iwan one with a better couch-side manner. "He was the complete opposite to the other guy," Iwan recalls, "he had a big white teeth smile and had pictures of George Clooney and stuff on the wall." The dazzling Los Angeles dentist to the stars told Iwan that he needed all four out but he would do two now and he could get the other two done when he got back to England. The procedure cost around two thousand dollars but it was an absolute emergency. Iwan trusted the dentist and said he'd do whatever he thought best. The dentist, in pure Hollywood style said "Hey! It's a Thursday – let's do all four teeth!!" Iwan complied.

"Looking back on it now it probably would have been better to just have done the two," Iwan surmises. He was put under a general anaesthetic as is customary when the wisdom teeth are impacted like his clearly were. "It wasn't the operation, it was the afterwards that was really bad. I couldn't eat anything. I don't know why it was so bad for me," Iwan explains, "I mean the guy said it was so far back that he couldn't get to them. I've got these four scars up there in my mouth and it took ages to heal."

Following on from the operation, Iwan found himself on a plane to New York. By time he got off the plane the stitches in his gums were coming open. As he found it hard to eat, he was losing weight and being skinny at the best of times, this was quite a concern.

"It was really horrible," Iwan says remembering phoning up his parents and being unable to stop bleeding. Autumn was collapsing into winter at this point and the streets of New York were a cold and unwelcome place for someone in the state he was in. In some part of Iwan's mind he was aware this should be a real high-point in his career with the band. They had a gig in the Mercury Lounge coming up and lots of press and promotion to attend to. Naturally, his physical state interfered with enjoying much of this.

"It was a fucking nightmare but I had to carry on," he says and that's what he bravely did. "I just really needed to go home. I just needed soup! It was quite funny because we did a Levi shoot in New York. I'd been chewing gum because the dentist said chew gum it would loosen it up a bit but I'd done it too early so I was just like chewing gum waiting for this photograph – just like get on with it – and then blood just started pouring down my face. They must have some pretty amazing photos of that somewhere – it just kept pouring out!" Iwan also remembers being in a New York subway with his mouth just swimming with blood. He had to spit it out on the floor. "I couldn't swallow it because there was so much of it and these people were going by watching me. I was trying to hold it in and I had to try and swallow it all the way to the hotel. All I wanted to do really was go to the hotel and my face was all swollen – but I had to carry on." It's hard enough to have to deal with the bleeding but I can imagine the countless eyes watching him as he walked through New York made him feel much worse, as though people thought he was some kind of delinquent English vampire who had over-indulged on this trip to the Big Apple.

Iwan had been prescribed Vicodin to help ease the pain and that did give him some relief. "I should've rested really but I couldn't rest. It was one of them things," he shrugs philosophically. Perhaps the Vicodin put him in a bit of a daze but somehow Iwan got through the ordeal. He stayed in the hotel as much as he could. Jack was sharing a room with him and remembers coming in drunk and finding Iwan in bed spun out on his medication.

"He'd be lying there going "J-A-CK!" Milkshake!" I remember going to the shop to get him Nesquick milkshakes every day or ice cream," Jack says gently, "I felt really sorry for him because we were all going out having a good time. I was coming in pissed into the room waking him up and he'd just nodded off."

Things did improve rapidly for Iwan when he got back home and was able to re-build his strength and take it easy.

The tour went on for five to six weeks, which, as Jack points out was a long time to be living in such intimacy and at times, on the road, cooped up in the bus he felt fed up. There were numerous highlights though, despite Iwan's teeth trouble and Nat's scare in Atlanta.

Iwan remembers some fun times with their Swedish support band, Division of Laura Lee, "They were doing pretty well over in America, so we were swapping over. They were all on our bus in the end – we ended up like going to Canada with them on the bus. They were brilliant, fucking amazing blokes and they smoked this stuff like snuff – it was like down in Cornwall, it's like chewing tobacco. They called it "snus" They kept going "Snus! Snus!" They weren't really heavy drinkers. I was like "that's horrible, that stuff, it could give you mouth cancer" or something. They would go "snus! no!" and shove it in the back of their mouths – they had a big pouch of it. Urrr!"

I asked Division of Laura Lee about this substance:

"It's not a heavy drug or anything," chuckles David Fransson. "It's more like a Swedish version of chewing tobacco. It's totally legal and everything. But if you're not used to it, it can make you feel real dizzy. I remember they (haven) all almost threw up from it in the beginning, but at the end of the tour they were all "Hey, got one for me too?" everytime I took one."

So, the bus and the beat rolled on....

Jack's friend, Phil Cunningham, was now a member of New Order. Both he and Jack had come a long way since the demise of *Tailgunner*. Phil's girlfriend lived in Los Angeles and Phil was there at the same time Haven were. Jack remembers that Phil set up some gigs for them with L.A band *Run, Run, Run* which the band remember being exciting occasions.

David of Divison of Laura Lee mentions a wild after show party at Jay's house in L.A that sticks in his mind, "I remember being really drunk already when I got there, and then I remember having a very deep conversation with Gary and then I also remember a post-it on the manager's computer screen saying: "Don't touch the motherfucking screen". Nice guy. Lots of coke around."

Naturally the band did their fair share of press as they criss-crossed the continent. Mostly, it was Gary and Nat doing the bulk of the talking. Nat mentions during their time in Toronto he and Gary were busy doing some radio show and Iwan and Jack had been landed with doing an interview on their own. According to Nat, this was a bit of a struggle. "When me and Gary walked in the door they just went "Ah right" and stopped the recording thing, rewound it and started again with just me and Gary!" he giggles. Gary, particularly, always played the role of semi-official spokesperson giving the standard story, with Nat slipping easily into the role of his slightly mischievous sidekick, both complementing each other in a way that makes good copy. Many interviewers are geared up to speak to the lead singer and lead guitarist and mistakenly believe the rhythm section have nothing to contribute. For the record, Jack and Iwan have some wonderful stories to tell but I think it's true that the pressure of a microphone and tape can induce more anxiety for them than Gary and Nat, but that's probably a lot to do with them not being as accustomed to it.

Nat recalls another interview in LA where "The guy said "So Jack, drumming wise who are your influences?" I know Jack really well and he does this thing with his hand when he's nervous," Nat says demonstrating a drumming with fingers on table type motion, "and I just went so-and-so and so-and-so because poor Jack couldn't get his words out."

There was also a special moment when they did their final show in New York City where Johnny Marr came on stage with them "It was part of the CMJ (college music jamboree) festival. It was our last night in America and one of our best!" Jack smiles.

Jonas Gustafsson of Division of Laura Lee summed up his experience of and impressions of Haven on this tour and he has the last word here:

"I had never really heard Haven before that tour started. I knew how their artwork looked from ads in NME. I was a huge fan of a number of British bands though and I had my hopes kinda high. We were stoked to be on tour with them. They had probably never heard of us. It was a cool line up with The Hiss, us and Haven.

Gary was the coolest cat. He wore a scarf, smoked a ton of cigarettes. His voice was top, even better live than on record I think.

I remember they had their own mixing board and mics and I thought these guys must be either super famous or super rich. I didn´t even have my own tuner. I was a bit worried that we would sound like crap compared, us using the house-gear and all, but it didn´t really matter since we´d always play ahead of them. We were awful anyways.

Nat always had this nice grin on his face. He seemed to be happy all the time. He was one of those dudes who could drain a bar and still look great. No sweat.

Jack was intense, I couldn´t understand half of what he was saying, it was so fast and with that accent. He was a laugh. I think he really liked the way we used to beat the shit out of our gear at the end of our set.

Iwan was a bit more calm than the other guys. At least that´s what I imagine. He seemed like there was no trouble in world. I believe he´d be a great older brother. He was my fave. Like George Harrison without the hippie bullshit.

They kinda grew on me as a band. As friends and to hang around with they were absolutely top. No doubt. They wore their jeans like perfect. Always been important to me how people wear their jeans. Seriously, very nice gentlemen right from the top of the tour, but musically it took me a few shows before I got it. They were too cool to ignore though and I started to enjoy their set, especially the groovy, noisy part before the last chorus of *Let it Live*. That was one cool song.

I sometimes wish we could do that US lap one more time. It was beautiful. I sure wish I could get a chance to get to know those boys again."

Remember, remember a night in November...

The first Urban Foxx release was scheduled for November 25. Having only just relocated from London, there hadn't been time to organise a proper gig for the band *Small Victories* who were the label's first offering. I wanted something to happen on the day though, even if it wasn't an official launch. Somehow, and I really have no idea how, I stumbled upon the Blue Cat Cafe who put on an open mic night called *Blue Monday* on the first day of every week. Even though the venue seemed to be off the beaten track, I felt a curious pull and so Viv and I went to check it out one mid-November evening to ascertain if it could be a suitable launch-pad for James Chant, the song-smith of *Small Victories* in two weeks time.

I'd never even heard of Heaton Moor before but that's where we found ourselves that night. An enormous, insistent full moon was waltzing through the clouds overhead and an air of inexplicable anticipation swirled in the ether as we set foot on Shaw Road. This odd cluster of bars, cafes and shops hung together, whispering like a half-released secret. The Blue Cat Cafe had a neon Krombacher sign outside. I warmed to it straight away as it felt unpretentious and quirky. Danny, the owner was flitting about in a faded yellow t-shirt that said 'Cuba'. That particular night, Danny wasn't compering 'Blue Monday'. The person who was, we soon discovered, was Chris Layhe, who used to play bass in moderately successful eighties band The Icicle Works. Viv and I bought a drink and took a seat. We agreed that this was the right kind of joint to invite James to come and try out some acoustic tracks when he got to Manchester. The acts that night were an eclectic mix, many of which I came to know in later years. We'd only been in the bar for twenty minutes or so before my eyes were drawn to a couple who had just walked in and were standing at the foot of the bar awaiting service.

"Oh My God! That's the singer from Haven. Gary. Yes, it is. Well, blow me down!" I muttered to Viv. My first time seeing Gary, I admit, was enchanting. He looked beautiful and somehow exquisite and there was a peculiar aura of familiarity about him. A hundred thoughts rushed through my head and I wondered why it was he struck me so, like an echo of the past and the future clashing simultaneously. I couldn't make any sense of it. I watched him pay for the drinks and walk by with his then girlfriend, Heidrun.

As he walked past us he dropped all his loose change on the floor at my feet. For some reason, I resisted the urge to help him pick it up.

The bar started getting very busy and I succeeded in tearing my eyes away from Gary and watching the acts. At some point, Nathan also arrived and I recognised him also. He seemed playful, good humoured and very natural, no rock star ego present at all. Later in the night, when the Haven boys had gone, Danny started telling us about his bar and his clientele. He seemed an interesting guy and an easy rapport built up. In some part of my brain, I was aware that he too had something uncannily familiar about him and so did Nathan. This strange sensation of déjà vu that hit me that night cropped up again and again as I embarked on my Manchester journey. There are some things in life that you just can't explain.

25 November 2002

Viv and I were riding on a tram through St Peter's Square when we got the call to say could we interview Gary and Nat tomorrow? At the Night and Day Cafe, at noon? We could and did but the night before we took James Chant, as planned, to the Blue Cat Cafe to perform three songs. There was a slightly edgy vibe in the venue that night. We soon realised that Gary, Nat and Iwan were all present. Another local rock and roll star had manifested as well, holding court at the bar was Mani, of Primal Scream. Loud, drunken conversation combined with bursts of hysterical laughter rose continuously from their end of the bar and I worried a bit that the noise would piss off James during his performance. It did and caused him to sing louder and louder to be heard! I wasn't taking much notice of the Haven boys this time, in fact, I was slightly embarrassed to be around knowing we were due to conduct an interview with them in the morning but then, they didn't know who I was, so that was OK.

This was the first time I had seen Iwan and at the risk of sounding repetitive, he also had that same unusual energy about him I had sensed from the others two Monday's before. It's difficult to pin-point what it was but generally I would describe the energy as ethereal. I had a vague notion that they could all be shamanic shape-shifters, not fully grounded in what we tend to call normality. That makes little sense as a passing comment but as time went on and I got to know them better this feeling never left. They were different.

James didn't want to hang around as he wanted to catch the train back to Cardiff that night. He scarpered, we scarpered and I vividly recall Mani's voice booming in my ear as we ran out the door "SEE YA!!"

James missed his last train from Stockport so had to stay the night with us. I awoke in mild panic in the morning, scrambled some eggs and scribbled some questions for Gary and Nat which were probably some of the most daft and random questions I'd ever brought to an interview. I was mildly disappointed that this wasn't going to be a full group affair but I knew from experience those often descend into cacophony. Viv,

James and myself rode the tram to Piccadilly and we headed for Oldham Street and James for the station to head back to Wales.

When we arrived at the Night and Day, Gary was reading a newspaper amid recent breakfast debris and Nat had popped across the road to Piccadilly Records to buy Jackie O's latest single. I got the impression, Nat, who always likes to try and please everyone felt a little pressurized into buying the record because the band Jackie O, were scattered around the bar, though it also happened to be a great rock and roll record so it was worth the investment. We ordered some coffee, and sat down with half of Haven. By the next round, the coffees had turned to beers and my over-riding memory of this interview was that we all seemed to be laughing almost as much as we were speaking.

Compared to some of the characters I've interviewed in my time, Gary and Nat were like a breath of fresh air. They were entertaining, frank, thoughtful and sweet-natured souls, residing on a wavelength I was very comfortable with. We talked about America as it was obviously still occupying large strands of their inner-world. It seemed as though they were having difficulty adapting back to the version of life that had existed before they went. Gary, in particular, gave the impression he had left a part of himself somewhere in the hissing, honking streets of New York City.

Then again, it may also have had something to do with the fact that they had been up half the night, drinking with Mani and watching Mel Brooks' *Young Frankenstein* which apparently, had them all rolling around the floor in hysterics. Neither Viv or I mentioned that we had seen them with Mani, the evening before in the Blue Cat for fear of coming across as loony, London stalkers.

One of the clearest things I noticed at this first meeting, was the deep, deep bond between the guitarist and singer. I remember them jokingly hugging each other and saying "It's a fucking love affair!" Danny at the Blue Cat describes Gary and Nat as being like "chalk and cheese" and I don't disagree. The ying and yang polarity between them seems to function in a highly positive manner. They needed each other, they loved each other, they understood each other and this seems to be the case before you even consider their creative relationship where I doubt they need to explain themselves too often. They are finely tuned to each other and I immediately felt that they could and did spend a lot of time together but never even began to tire of each other's company.

The interesting dynamic with Haven is that ALL the band appear to share a special one-to-one connection with each other, yet, they also fall neatly into two camps when it comes to, say, sleeping arrangements on the road, with Gary and Nat sharing a room and Iwan and Jack doing the same. They are all so clearly bonded, they fit perfectly together as a whole. I think their friendship would exist without the band, but with the band, I feel that creative chemistry accentuated the potency of the friendship. From the very beginning I noticed the solidarity between them and it was a beautiful thing to behold, such togetherness and playfulness. Refreshingly, they weren't embarrassed to show their affection for each other either.

When we'd concluded the interview, we asked if we could take a couple of photos as we wanted them on the front cover. They joked that the only cover they had to date was the front page of *The Cornishman* newspaper. Shockingly, as far as I know, that is still true.

Gary seemed to intuitively know we wanted an eye-catching piece of urban scrawl in the shoot and led us through the dimly lit bar and out the back entrance where we were forced to adapt to the fact that it was still daytime. The wall outside had been daubed with bright primary colours which he and Nat stood in front of together.

I remember going home in the November sunshine, feeling happy with the interview and happy to have finally met half of this band who'd been dancing on the periphery of my life for a little while now. I strongly felt we would meet again.

Boys next door

It was very early on that involvement with Danny and the Blue Cat Cafe began. Before Viv and I knew it, and I don't recall exactly how it came about, we'd all become partners in the label which caused it to morph into a slinky blue feline as opposed to a mysterious nocturnal fox. We'd discovered a new local band to work with, Desolation Angels. The Angels, as they were affectionately known on the local scene, had a shimmering, hauntingly beautiful body of work almost ready for release. I was particularly chuffed to be working with a band named after a book by one of my favourite authors, Jack Kerouac.

I was obviously aware that Haven lived somewhere in the Heatons area. I'd seen them around on a few occasions while we'd been in Danny's bar. It suddenly occurred to me to ask if they would be willing to play at the launch of Urban Scrawl, as the first issue containing Gary and Nat's lengthy interview was ready to be scattered intriguingly around the city. I have a particularly vivid flashback of this, in fact. I remember asking Gary if they might play, and hoping I didn't seem too cheeky. It was at this point, I realised that this man had eyes you could swim in! I remember him being immediately enthusiastic and scrawling Joe Moss's number on a Krombacher beer mat for me. He then hoisted himself onto Danny's bar counter and sat grinning at me, swinging his legs. In those days, Gary had a slightly naughty vibe about him and with those dancing blue eyes you could see how it would be easy for him get away with murder. However, even though he had that mischievous air he also had an intrinsic politeness, a true gentleman, appearing to have time and interest in everyone and everything which was a quality I admired. He seemed high on life and I felt a similar surge myself at this point. Things seemed especially colourful, vivid and alive.

Working closely with Danny meant it made sense to move to Heaton Moor to be in the immediate vicinity of the venue. It was the kind of place I wanted to live anyway, and in April 2003, Viv and I moved into 118

Heaton Moor Road, just around the corner from the Blue Cat. On the day after we moved, I was washing up in the kitchen dreamily looking out the window admiring Heaton Moor Road in the approach of Spring. Next thing I knew, I saw Gary, Nat and a third man I didn't know, turn in our drive-way. I heard a front door open and bang shut and thought "Oh My God! They must either live in this house or next door!" I didn't have a problem with having any of Haven as neighbours, but I was worried that when they discovered who'd moved in they would think of Viv and I as stalkers. I hoped that maybe they were just visiting the third guy, but deep down I knew at least one of them lived here.

Our fears were confirmed, when we were in the Blue Cat next time and Danny asked us where our new flat was. When we told him he exclaimed "Ah, next door to you!" to the bar-maid, who we later learned was Nathan's girlfriend, Emma. I prayed that Emma didn't think I was a stalker and wondered how on earth, in the whole of Heaton Moor we had ended up next door to half of Haven.

It was Nat and Iwan who shared the ground floor of the house next door with their girlfriends. I don't know why I felt slightly illegal, as if I'd had any inkling I wouldn't have moved into that flat, but we were completely clueless.

When they did come to learn that that those two Scrawl girls were neighbours they, at least, didn't behave warily, or label us as obsessive fans. Even if they viewed us as a little weird, I hoped they could see we were just harmless, music-loving folk who, by some strange twist of fate had wafted into the moor on perhaps that same breeze that ushered them in, four years earlier.

Around this point, the band had been given the green light from Virgin to go ahead with the second album. There was much discussion on who should produce the record. "It was the same old thing where we thought one thing and the record company thought something totally different," sighs Jack. "They gave us this big list of producers with the bands they had done and straight away Dave Botrill who produced Muse, and Dave Eringa who produced the Manics were the two that really stuck out in our minds." Naturally, it did occur to all involved to invite Johnny Marr to replicate his magic again on the new record but the general consensus was that some new blood in the mix would be the best approach. "I thought, we've done one with Johnny – let's see what someone else can bring to it," continues Jack, "I think Johnny thought that as well. Give someone else a go. Dave Botrilll came up to Heaton Moor to listen to the songs in the garage and he was really into them. He was saying straight away "oh I'd do this and do that" which was really good but I think somehow it turned out either he was busy or he had the wrong vibes."

Nat comments on how difficult it is to choose a producer, remembering listening to stacks of CD's at this point: "Sometimes it's songs you don't like and you're trying to listen to the production. We were sat there listening to loads of things like Feeder songs – and it was a case of "I can't say that I like it but is the production good?" I don't know, so it was a bit like that. We always knew that Johnny would kind of help us out and we knew we had a really good working relationship with him but also we wanted to kind of go off in our own right. I think the record company had a push towards Dave Eringa I think because he's had some pretty big records. He knows how to record a band – he's really, really good at what he does."

To rack your brain...

RAK studios can be found in the plush and pleasant environs of St John's Wood, in North London. A number of London's celebrated recording studios lie close by, such as Abbey Road and Air. I'd been in RAK on two occasions during my life as a Manic Street Preacher's fanzine editor and had actually interviewed Eringa there some years before. The studios seemed vibrant and informal, as well as a little mad and unpredictable, with characters such as the illustrious Robert Plant popping up out of nowhere when I had been there talking to Dave. It must have been a real buzz for Haven to begin their residency there and it seemed that Virgin Records were taking a more extravagant approach than they had with the first album recorded in those intense few weeks in Johnny Marr's studio. Haven were booked into RAK for around seven weeks.

On the surface, the making of the second album should have been an uncomplicated affair. Dave Eringa, a young, but experienced producer who had worked with the likes of Idlewild, Manic Street Preachers and Ash was at the controls. It was now just about getting some of those ideas down, making flesh and blood some of the metamorhpic phantoms of songs that had been knocking about since that all-night, ecstasy drenched session in Danny Donnelly's garage, as well as ideas they'd been working on, individually and collectively since. Before the sojourn to London, there had been some fruitful pre-production sessions at Clear, where songs such as *I am Leaving* and *Whatever feels Right* were born, according to Jack.

Assembled in RAK, all appeared to be going to plan musically and creatively, and socially this period is generally viewed as a pleasure peak of sorts. "It's probably the best time in my life," Jack says fondly, "I love it in London. There was loads of money flying about. We went to the bank and probably pulled out about a grand each every week! I just remember, literally – I had probably the biggest room there as well – I had a suitcase at the end of the room with an envelope with twenty and fifty pound notes in it. I bought four snare drums in that period because I did my drum bits and then when they were doing other bits – every now and then I just went out on the tube and went to a drum shop or a different part of London. I remember going to the Tower of London on my own one day and just doing stuff like that – it was just a really amazing time. We all were thinking this album is going to be massive and we were all dead happy with it and we had all the money in the world and all our girlfriends coming up – staying in this amazing apartment – it probably was the best time of my life."

For some reason, Gary, Jack and Iwan were accommodated in rooms above the studio and Nat was assigned his own apartment nearby; a grand, seventies style abode, complete with sauna. The only draw-back was that it was rumoured to be haunted. From what I can gather, so were the studio's themselves, so there was no escape!

It seems that the haunting stories were not just rumours either. Various unexplained phenomena occurred whilst the band were there. The RAK staff were quite matter-of-fact about it but the band were not quite as blasé. Nat says he "went to bed scared every night – really scared!" Iwan adds "to the point, you didn't want to lift your face out of the covers."

An event that certainly freaked Nat out happened one night when he was alone on the phone to his girlfriend, Emma. One story they had been told was that the building used to be an old school and was haunted by a mother and child.

"I was in the games room where it's got table tennis and computers and all that sort of shit – it was a massive great big room," Nat recalls, "Emma was being a bit weird with me, and then she ended up cutting the conversation short so, anyway I hung up and went to bed. And then the next day Emma said who were you with last night? All shitty with me – and I said I was on my own and I *was* on my own in the games room I fucking swear I was on my own! She said she heard a girl's voice saying "Sssh! Go to bed. Ssh! Go to bed" over and over – and I was like arrghh! It went straight through me! Fuck me! The Mum was sat with me on the couch – maybe talking to her daughter – maybe talking to me, but anyway, ,even now talking about it is giving me goosebumps" he shivers seven years later, "how weird is that? And I didn't hear it but she heard it through the phone. I mean *we* were taking drugs – but Emma wasn't!"

If there is any whispering on the album tracks it is inaudible but

I suspect having that kind of energy around must have an effect on artists who work there, even if it is purely subliminal.

As well as the phantom mother and child, the studio's were also playing host to The Libertines who were caught up in their second album agonies around the time that tension was running high between Carl Barat and Pete Doherty. The band mention enjoying hanging out with Carl and subsequent partying into the night.

There was a basement below the flat, which you could reach by descending a spiral staircase in the pitch dark as there was no light. Nat explained that they used to take turns going down and time each other to see who dared stay down there the longest on an exercise bike which was right in the middle of the basement.

"You just felt like you were being watched in the dark corners," Nat shudders. "It ended up, I had the exercise bike out in the middle of the road once!" Iwan laughs at this memory, "We were meant to be going to start recording and I went "where's Nat then?" and went to open the curtain." He discovered Nat outside on the road pedalling furiously on the stationary bike accompanied by Jamie Colgan, who was barking like a dog.

"Gary said all these people were going by with brief cases," Nat giggles, "and someone stopped and said "Are you on drugs?" and I said "Yes, I am! Fuck off!"

This must have been quite a sight for the residents of St John's Wood to wake up to, "It was about quarter to eight in the morning," laughs Jamie. "And everyone was going to work. I was barking and Nat was cycling!"

It all sounds a little pythonesque and this scene, in particular, feels as though it should be framed in a classic, seventies British sit-com where outsiders are loveable rogues rallying against the stiff upper lip of the suit and briefcase brigade.

The easy access to money fuelled the partying and living it up seemed the natural thing to do. Nat expresses some concerns about this in hindsight, "We were away from Joe. Joe is our guardian and we had the cheque book that we never had before and as far as we were concerned there was just like a bottomless pit of money in the bank and we were accessing it very regularly – and it caused trouble you know? There was just a real lack of commitment and concentration over the task in hand."

Having said that, Nat also adds that he feels they recorded "some of the best stuff we've ever done there and as a whole body of work we were ultimately completely pleased with it." Iwan adds that no matter how wild the parties were they didn't forget why they were there: "We just had an amazing time. We always did. The thing is, whether we're getting hammered or whatever, which has kind of died down since then we always got the job done. The album was great."

Or was it?

I've got no inclination to sit here in judgement on whether this album was, or wasn't "good enough" as my first answer to that question is "good enough for who?" Had the second album achieved commercial success I doubt its musical merit would even be challenged. Also, I have never heard all the tracks exactly as they were that summer, only the ones that made it to the version that was finally released the year after so it's impossible to comment on its strength or weakness at that point in time. Somehow, though, like a goal that's sneaked into the net by the opponent at the ninetieth minute, the album was snatched inexplicably from their hands while it was still warm on the mixing desk.

So, what happened?

It's never easy to wrap up a creative project to a deadline, but that's often what is demanded when a band is placed in a studio at the record company's expense. That deadline was fast approaching and luckily the majority of the work had been done. "We had to get the monitor mix finished by nine because we had to move out of the studio the next day – early in the morning," explains Jack, "so basically the only way to get through it was to stay up and get smashed, so we did that. Dave was really ill – he was there mixing and really out of it and then the next day I woke up about half six in the morning thinking "yeah, we've finished, we're moving out". From there, we went to Miloco in south London where we were gonna mix it."

Between mixing, the band also started rehearsals as they knew a tour would be imminent and most of the new material had never been played live as they hadn't gigged since the American dates the autumn before. The band all report being happy with the finished record and the mixes. "We heard the mixes and were sitting there dead proud. On the final day of mixing we had literally got three or four crates of champagne ready," Jack recalls. "The crates were being chilled and this was like about half two in the morning. We finished the last one and we were like "Let's get the champagne out!" and then Joe phoned up and I remember seeing Gary on the phone to Joe for maybe an hour maybe an hour and half."

Gary came back in, pale and pained. In a nutshell, Joe wasn't happy with the tracks. Jack was shocked and confused by this because Joe had been around during mixing and had commented that the tracks sounded as good as they could. So, this happening at the end was a big blow. "I remember that night going from one of the best to one of the worst in my life," Jack says. "I remember Jon Chapman had tears in his eyes and remember him saying "What's happened Jack?" and no one really had a clue – it was all a bit of a haze – and when Joe phoned up we then went down to try and change the mixes but you can't do ten mixes in three hours so it all just turned into such a nightmare. It was even worse for Gary and Nat. When they got back to their hotel room a carton of milk that Gary had left in there exploded in the room and it like stank – so they got back to that! We all got in from the studio on big downers and their room stank of cheese and sick!"

Iwan was equally gobsmacked: "That was pretty weird. I mean it was pretty strange because we were all happy with it and I think Joe just had a freak out – he just wasn't sure if it was right."

Strangely enough, when I questioned Joe about this point in time he doesn't recall the long phone call with Gary, or even not being happy with the tracks. Yet, it seems he must have had a problem, or somebody must have had a problem or the album would have been in the can. And sadly, it wasn't. It was up in the air.

The band returned to Manchester in something of an anti-climax. Plans for the single that had been chosen were under way and weren't pulled, but the fate of the album was another story…

Summer in the city...

If my memory serves me well, my first summer in the moor was the hottest that decade. Due to the majestic canopy of trees that line Heaton Moor road, the area has a distinctly seasonal, picture postcard quality, as these same trees, bud, bloom or shed, to become stark or snow-kissed. During the summer months when the foliage is gloriously verdant, the nights are soft and balmy and the air is laced with a heady, solar energy, it's a pure thrill to be alive. I remember that first summer fondly. Though still finding my feet in the north of England, I was enjoying getting to know both the city and suburb. One of the musical back-drops to this summer was the first taste of Haven's new work.

Viv and I had popped into the Blue Cat one afternoon for some business with Danny. One of the band had left him a promo of the soon to be released single *Tell Me*, housed in an orange square of cardboard – just that one solitary track. Oh, but what a bolt of pure intravenous rock and roll this was! It had a big dizzying sound, sizzling with adrenaline and a shower of dancing endorphins. I could also detect a healthy splash of testosterone in this hormonal cocktail, perhaps more than had been apparent on the first album. In fact, this is the record on which I remember Gary telling me he wanted to "sing like a man!"

It's not that they hadn't rocked out during *Between the Senses* but not as directly or with as much abandon as on this track. Yet, this out-pouring was precise, tight, hitting all the right spots in neon-flashing capital letters.

Danny lent me the CD to go home and burn. The intro reminded me a little of The Cult's *She Sells Sanctuary* which I couldn't resist digging out and playing the two tracks back to back for comparison. Perhaps very distant cousins…

Tell Me stood up as a classic rock record straight away. In more predictable times, it would have been immediately filed under "sure fire hit" but we lived, and live, in strange times…

There were a handful of tour dates in early July, including a high-spirited, if humid one at the Night and Day. Having not seen the band play live for over a year it was a buzz to be there and it was the first time I'd seen them play on home-turf in a venue so familiar to them. This particular gig is one I reviewed for Urban Scrawl where I scrawled enthusiastically:

"While sweat mingled with beer, mingled with smoke, we all melted and merged in smiling appreciation of the majestic, magic songs these walls have heard many times before. But then, early in the set Tell Me (current single) bursts out, pace quickens, more, drums tear off somewhere new and unfamiliar. I can't imagine Haven ever losing their ethereal charm, or the subtle, dream-weaving quality I see as one of their greatest strengths but something about the new tracks suggests a more earthy, grounded reality has crept in. They sound more direct, more in your face, more demanding – an edge that commands attention at the same time as it makes you want to jump around. This is restless rock and roll. These are men, not boys. This is home but it's also away, wide expanses of parched natural landscape suddenly straining to travel through claustrophobic, steaming city streets, never missing a beat."

I re-printed this extract from the review because it makes even more sense to me now, when I look panoramically at their story. Something had shifted in their sound and I feel it had something to do with their experiences in America, of growing up, and even growing apart a bit, finding their place outside the safety net of Joe's watchful eye and the times they had shared in the happy mad-house that was 104 Heaton Moor Road. For the most part, the new tracks were heavier, less floaty and enchanting than much of *Between The Senses*, but just as compelling.

In short, it sounded like Dave Eringa had encouraged them to play harder, faster, louder and that they had been happy to oblige, almost like they had been given permission to be more irreverent.

This even ties in with Gary feigning to smash the screen at the end of the *Tell Me* video, not a statement that would have belonged with any visuals on the first album. In fact, this video was very different to anything they'd done before. It was exciting, unapologetic, featuring an iconic, if straight, band performance of the track. Shot in black and white, the band are also dressed alternatingly in black and white, conjuring up those notions of good versus evil, angels and devils, temptation versus fidelity. This is probably the strongest video to date which I'm sure the record label thought would elevate Haven onto the next logical level in this great rock and roll game.

However, *Tell Me* was released without the ceremonial fanfare expected when a band who've made a popular first album briefly go off radar to make a new record return. It's hard to know if this was because Radiate/Virgin were a little miffed that the second album currently had a big, fat question mark hanging over its head and so weren't prepared to pump loads more money into promoting the single. Or it could be that the band were just plain unlucky because for whatever reason, radio generally chose not to playlist the track.

The single appeared to come and go, barely causing a ripple. During this period, the band spent time at Joe's house, listening to the tracks over and over, listening to opinions and naturally, in that kind of situation, everyone started to second guess themselves.

To this day, Jack still thinks the album was ready to go as it was. He remembers clearly feeling it was amazing when they checked out of RAK.

"Joe picked out things and the more and more he said it, maybe the more and more people thought maybe he's right," he comments, "and whether he was or not, the more he said it the more we had to take it – the more you heard it the more you get it in your head, don't you? We all had a copy of the album – the mixed album and we listened to it and listened to it and that didn't help."

Nat admits to not being entirely happy with the album, though is quick to point out that some tracks were some of their best.

"I think personally, and I think the boys would agree as well that some of the stuff we did with Dave is some of the best stuff we've ever done," he muses. "My own personal thing is that the first album as a whole is really complete and it's really soulful sounding and it comes from a lot of years of jamming and playing and also we were living together and partying a lot together and the music was really just part of our fun times. We'd take E's and sit around the flat playing those songs as that's how they developed and that's where the kind of soul comes from. The longer working relationships go on I suppose, you have your personal life and then you go and do your music and that's just purely natural but I think the second album as a whole doesn't quite match the first one. I think some of the stuff on there is better than anything we've done on the first album if you know what I mean? I think that Dave really captured the energy on some of the songs. Dave was more in his production credits – more to do with sound and energy and a certain vibe, telling Jack how hard to hit his drums – always encouraging Jack, saying "imagine your snare drum is David Sneddon's face!" because David Sneddon was upstairs and it got Jack hitting the drums so hard! Whereas Johnny pulls a song to pieces and puts it back together again. He's just got that musical genius type touch."

At some point in these discussions and analysis, Joe came up with the suggestion that the band re-record the album again with Johnny Marr at Clear.

This re-recording and re-consideration went on all over that summer. "We kind of went back to the drawing board," Nat says, "pulled the album to pieces, went to Johnny's, re-recorded a load and had a really bad time with it and we knew that we'd just spent a shit load of money on something that had been deemed, not not good enough, but not right."

There seems to be a general vagueness about what was considered "not right" with this record. Speaking about the album a few years later, with hindsight, Iwan says, "I love that album because it's kind of half and half – we were really worried about how they would go together – they sound good together even though separate recordings – it's good as you've got the sort of relaxed thing and then you've got the full on thing. RAK is such an amazing studio and I love that full on thing Dave did – but we needed to kind of soften a bit like with *Between the Senses* so eventually we kind of got there. I mean there's still things on every album that you don't like – that's just what happens. There are bits on there that I don't like at all but that's just the way it is. You're never gonna be perfect. There was a lot of things we weren't happy with but we had to kind of let it go. It was so stressful – we had to get rid of it – just let it go."

Smile like you mean it...

It took a gestation period of around nine months more before the album finally saw the light of day. It was, as though, a time of reflection was being enforced on the band as that July an unexpected and unfortunate interference entered Nathan's life.

The starting point was an earache which lasted all day.

"I never get ill generally, I never go the doctors about anything but the earache was so severe I thought I'll go to the doctor's tomorrow morning," Nat explains. "That morning I woke up and this thing had happened and I didn't know what it was. I phoned *NHS Direct* and explained the symptoms and they said they think it's Bell's Palsy. Then I went down to the doctors and they said yeah, that's what they think it is. It's hard for me to remember that very first two weeks as obviously I'm still dealing with it now and it still bugs me, but the first two months really I couldn't close my eye in the slightest it was completely open – this right eye and I looked really strange, really, really strange. I couldn't watch TV because it was too bright. I couldn't have the lights on in the house 'cos it was too bright it would hurt my eye. I knew nothing about it all really. I just sat in a cold, dark room with a flannel over my face for a good month or so. Couldn't do much, doing pretty much what I had to do, sitting generally in darkness playing my acoustic or whatever and reflecting. At this point I was told it could take up to six weeks to get better and I thought that sounded like forever – obviously if you're ill and someone says six weeks it sounds like forever." I had this conversation with Nat in 2006, three years after it happened and I was surprised to hear to what extent he was still suffering.

"I still have to sellotape my eye shut at night now," he reveals. "Can't shut it and all sorts of funny little things. There's no discomfort as such but if it's too bright I've got to look at the floor because I can't squint either and all that sort of stuff. It all – it all happened at once – everything kind of caved in at once a little bit including me. But Johnny was really cool, well, everyone was. All we had in was the V festivals. We cancelled everything and Joe just left it to me and said it's your call with the V festival and we decided to do it. Well, I decided I could do it because you're not going to get that opportunity every day are you? So we just did it and it was painful. My first gig in with a pair of shades I felt pretty cool and my fucking guitarist pout! I'd lost that as well. Gutted!"

Listening to Nat's experience with Bell's Palsy, I was struck that the psychological scars were as traumatic as the physical. By his own admission, and I certainly agree, Nat is a person who tends to face the world with a smile and it was heart-breaking to hear him admit he feels he lost the ability to give that gift to others. The phrase "a smile costs nothing" is true but what if that wonderful split-second reaction that can light up a room is suddenly swiped from us?

"You know, it's a huge thing. One of those things that really makes you think and learn about face value," Nat continues. "First time I've ever felt really sort of super self-conscious walking down the road. It's like every time I laugh I can feel my face go out of sync and I didn't like it all – I still don't like it now, and how valuable a smile is – just a smile can be almost a throwaway thing, you know? But to me it feels like the most powerful thing now because I can't quite get it together."

Nat explains how he couldn't lift his eyebrow and how physical mechanisms previously taken for granted suddenly required concentrated effort.

"I dunno if you can move your ears? Some people can move their ears" he stated. I told him I couldn't. "Well, if I say, try and move your ears your brain will be searching and trying to send messages and that's exactly how it feels for me if you say "move your mouth" and having to search, that's completely new to my brain it seems. It's really frustrating, it's like staring in the mirror looking at your ears and trying to move them. That's what it's seemed like for the last three years!" he laughs. "I get sad – every now and then I'll see a picture of me with a huge ear to ear grin and I think "Shit! I don't know if I'll see that again."

I assured Nat that he would as it's what I believe. He's someone who always carries a sunbeam somewhere, even if it's tucked away in a pocket.

Bell's Palsy doesn't always drag on for years, like it did in Nat's

With John Peel during *Sound of the Suburbs* in Cornwall (also featuring Tom Lewis– 2nd from right) 1999
© Iwan Gronow

Jack in Japan
© Iwan Gronow

Band with Danny Donnelly outside Blue Cat Cafe 2001
© Danny Donnelly

Backstage (touring Between the Senses)
© Iwan Gronow

Gary with Japanese audience
© Iwan Gronow

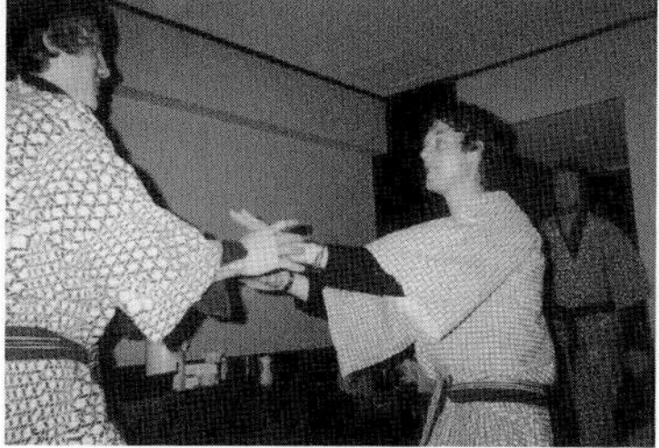

Japan hotel room
© Iwan Gronow

Nat & Mickey surfing the moor
© Mickey Smith

Iwan (American tour)
© Piper Ferguson

Nat (2006)
© Mickey Smith

Gary & Nat (back of Mickey's car) 2006
© Mickey Smith

Nat (American tour)
©Piper Ferguson

Iwan (2006)
© Mickey Smith

Gary & Johnny Marr (New York 2002)
© Piper Ferguson

During American Tour © Piper Ferguson

American Tour
© Piper Ferguson

Johnny Marr joins band on stage CMJ New York 2002
© Piper Ferguson

American Tour
© Piper Ferguson

Gary at Troubador Club,
Los Angeles 2002
© Piper Ferguson

Gary & Nat outside Tower Records (American tour) 2002
© Piper Ferguson

Jack (American tour) 2002
© Piper Ferguson

Gary & Nat at Night and Day Cafe – Urban Scrawl Interview 2002
© Vivienne Lindley

Mutineers
© Scott Kershaw

Strays - Cornwall – 2009
© Mickey Smith

case and it does make me wonder why it was such an intense attack. Serious supposed viral attacks like this are mysterious and difficult to explain, though there are theories linking the condition with head injury. It is possible that the beating in Atlanta played a role, and equally possible, as Nat admits himself it was partly stress-induced, or a combination. My feeling is that it was also because he was holding a lot inside – frustration, upset, a feeling of powerlessness which created a type of paralysis.

Nat was perplexed by the reaction to the RAK sessions: "We took *Tell Me*, full of confidence to Radio 1 and they said "No, we don't want to playlist it" And suddenly we were floundering cos that was our hit, so at that point we had to start thinking about maybe recording some more stuff that's – not make a compromise because we wanted it to work but, I don't know….we didn't see any change in direction from what we were doing before and I remember the comment was "We're not so sure about Haven's new rocky direction" and I didn't really see it, to be honest," Nat states, "and then this thing happened with my face and so I just sort of took a big step backwards. I was obviously getting far too anxious about everything."

Like many of us, Nat struggles a little when it comes to asserting himself or confronting an issue head on.

When I asked Gary to tell me something about Nat he brought this up: "Nat will do anything to avoid confrontation. He hates it! But he makes it worse for himself because he has to face things sometime. Everyone likes him – happy, jovial but there's another side to him – he bottles things up. Best friend you could ever have – if you are lucky enough to know him you don't need any other friends."

"My weak point is that sometimes if there's stuff to confront or if there's something happened between two members I'll always be the guy at the back of the room with my head down cos I can't stand it and I know that's a weakness," Nat confirms. "So I get away with stuff. If there's a couple of us going at each other and even though I'll probably have an opinion and everything I'll keep my gob shut so no-one can turn round and say fucking you did this – that's a bad point. That's definitely one of my weak points cos I don't often enough stick my neck out and I'm learning to – really, really trying to and it's against my nature I find it difficult but I feel good when I do."

Jack also remarked on Nat's tendency to hold back his opinions and how this may have played a role in the Bell's Palsy problem:

"I think Nat might keep things in a bit. Maybe that was something to do with his illness – when all that was going on with the album – if he'd spoken out a bit about what we thought – though I suppose it was the same for all of us. But now it's much better, if we were all to sit down together in a room Nat would be the first one to be honest about what he thought."

Regardless of what triggered Nathan's illness, it's clear it had a strong impact on him. When I asked him if he felt he'd changed much as a result he emphatically said yes. "I was never concerned about anything before…but I've cooled down a lot. You can't party twenty four hours a day!" Strangely enough, at that point during this talk Mani turned up and started talking about his recent rock and roll escapades with Primal Scream at London's Astoria. When he left, Nat and I both exchanged similar thoughts – that perhaps Mani was the exception and was as immortal as Keith Richards seems to be! This was 2006 and of course, now, Mani has been inhabiting an alcohol free body for extended periods.

Alcohol and drug abuse catch up with us all sooner or later, but we do all have different constitutions. It seems perfectly obvious though, that you can't cram your body with toxins day in and day out without doing yourself some kind of damage. Nat may have reigned it in a bit but it's all relative. From my observations he still enjoys a good party and lives life to the full. I don't for a minute suggest we need drugs or alcohol to do that either and embracing a cleaner life-style can sharpen our senses so that we experience the beauty of life more acutely. There's nothing like a natural high. This gushing, enthusiasm for life I sense from Mickey Smith is also present in Nat. Whether this comes from the euphoria of riding on waves, I don't know.

"Me and Nat are proper trouble together," Mickey laughs, "Cornish madmen of the highest calibre. I used to go and see the boys as much as I could over the years, they seemed like the only folk as mad as me, I could relate to them like no-one else, especially Nat, we're like brothers."

The sea continues to surge, it beats through the music on both albums.

You can hear it lapping gently on the shores or crashing in celebratory whooshes across the rocks…

After a second round of recording was completed at Clear studios, *All for a Reason* was finally ready for launch.

Riders on the storm...

All for a Reason was officially released in the UK in March 2004, accompanied by the only single that was ever lifted from it *Wouldn't Change a Thing*. A strange choice, I've always felt. Though a pleasant, inoffensive track in itself, there are in my mind, far stronger singles on the album, including the title track itself, as well as the oddly proud and tumultuous *What Love Is*. Iwan mentions there were also some excellent tracks that didn't make it on to the final record, which have now sadly evaporated into the mists of time.

I believe the band weren't especially keen on the chosen single. "It wasn't the best choice in my opinion," Jack comments, though adds in the label's defence, "but then to be fair to them they gave us the money to go re-record it and they could have turned around and said "You've already done it. Fuck off!" but they didn't – they turned around after a week of thinking about it and said "if that's what you want we'll give you it" – got to respect them for that."

It appears that the label were opting for the gentle and familiar with this single choice, rather than allowing the band to showcase their diversity. So, as the song itself declares, no reason to shake things up or inject new dynamics if all is comfy and cosy. However, often change has a habit of crashing into our lives even when we don't invite it, and though the record was in the shops, as it should be, on release day, there was an uneasy feeling around the entire project. Although there had been a perceived lack of promotion for *Between the Senses*, the campaign for the second album was virtually non-existent and given that the band had been low profile since the summer before, a promotional push was crucial at this point.

With hindsight, some years later, Gary states "We had a lot of issues with the second record, Joe had issues, our publisher had issues but no one from the label had any kind of critique or reservation with it in any way whatsoever. So, me and the band were in a bit of a sort of weird space because although we were kind of confident of what we'd done when there's an air of…" he pauses, collecting his thoughts – "When you've got people around you that you trust saying "listen we don't think that's very good" you kind of start to doubt your confidence and this was really, I think, looking back the first time I thought there was something wrong at the label because they were a little bit kind of blasé about it. Dave Boyd's words were something like "You've made a great contemporary record" and we were like "oh that's great, Dave" and then Daryl, our publisher at the time didn't think it was good – not all of it but bits of it. Joe wasn't happy with a lot of it so we were like well "Fuck!" it was an issue, you know? And it went on and it was about to come out and there was a real noticeable kind of lack of promotion from the record company."

Some of the band were also unhappy with visual aspects of the record. They all make it clear that up to this point, they were very happy with the psychedelic aesthetics of David Moss, which lent all their previous releases a unique and instantly recognisable identity.

For this album, there was disagreement about the chosen image. It's a murky, mysterious sleeve that looks like it's been dragged up from an ancient ship-wreck, stained and battered, weather-worn but magically intact. Faint and ghostly imprints of various band members appear in the inner sleeve and a repeated image of one of their eyes – most likely Gary's, if I'm not mistaken – watches the drama of the waves crashing, shrouded in the green sea spray. A ship is navigating these waters. Is it in trouble? Is anyone on board?

Jack felt the image wasn't appropriate: "I don't want to speak for anyone else but I personally thought the image of a ship was of no relevance of us as a band whatsoever," he told me. "We had a choice between that and something else, which I can't remember, and unfortunately the choice was made for the 'ship'. We had a good day of heated debates on the matter! Joe was a big fan of the 'ship' so obviously that was another major factor in the decision. I could envisage people comparing our album cover to that of Blue Peter and taking the mickey quite a bit! In a way it didn't matter that much in the end as the album didn't sell nearly as much as *Between the Senses*."

Gary also recalls the debate about this sleeve and admits that he never gave too much thought to the record's artwork initially, though now, he sees it all as much more important. He felt they were lucky to cross paths with David Moss and when they did it just all fell into place aesthetically. "We'd been down the road with design companies and seeing what happens when you create a sleeve by committee. It's the same as writing a song, you know, or cooking a stew, a broth," he laughs, "I mean he was the guy that talked about his artwork in the same sort of humble, unpretentious way, same unegotistical way as we talk about our music. He loves painting, we loved his work. It was like a kind of perfect marriage really. Jack hated the second album image and Iwan wasn't keen on it at all. I just thought it was a strong image. There's a lot going on in his painting as well if you look closely."

To me, this sleeve does complement the music and the story behind the music that eventually resulted in this record. There are lots of question marks. It's an epic journey that has yet to reach its conclusion. It's a lonely image but there's a sense of courage and conviction – that it *is* all for a reason, even when we can't glimpse the harbour lights or tell which way the wind is going to blow next. It captures the band in a place where they all pulled together, to captain their ship, but seemed to be at the mercy of things they couldn't always see, let alone understand, unsure where they were going, how they got where they were and whether land was in sight. If Radiate records or Joe Moss had a map or a compass it is unclear. They were on an exciting and powerful voyage and like any other group of young men in a similar position they set out on tour, enjoying the moment, ignoring the funny undercurrents that lapped beneath their feet, beneath the deck.

The second album promotional tour which spanned fourteen dates, kicked off in April 2004. Haven were supported by Oxfordshire band, Crackout, who were on Hut Records, therefore, label mates, in a broad sense. Radiate still hadn't expanded their roster, apart from a single or two released by eccentric Brighton band Eighties Matchbox B Line Disaster.

The tour commenced in Oxford and the two bands travelled up, down and around the UK, playing in variable-sized venues, though generally bigger than on previous tours. The London date was at Shepherd's Bush

Empire, probably the biggest and most prestigious venue they played to date.

"It was the biggest crew we ever had," remembers Jack, "I mean literally, the crew would sound-check for us. So we'd just turn up for the sound-check and play one song rather than having to sit there banging a snare drum for ten minutes. So they did all that."

In Manchester, they played Academy Two at the University, again, considered by most to be a step up from the Night and Day.

This was the only date I caught on this tour. As it was at the end, my memory is the band being, frankly, exhausted, though still somewhat exhilarated. I do remember Gary's voice being strained and them all sweating buckets, looking like they needed some pampering and recovery time. I remember little else, unfortunately.

Crackout were already aware during the tour that their label was in trouble and rumours were beginning to circulate about the stability of the the EMI giant.

"We were too busy thinking about the tour. We were excited, you know?" Gary recalls, "the kind of climax at Shepherd's Bush Empire which is like a really fucking top venue – and then we heard or someone had seen on an American website, talk about EMI getting rid of twenty per cent of its workforce. We knew EMI was the kind of umbrella to which Virgin and subsequently Hut and then our label Radiate lived under – so we thought…well, we just thought fuck it and ignored it. We thought we're on tour – and then as the tour's going on we wondered "why haven't we got any interviews?" We did have some, but like, that's really the first sign, where you're not getting any – where there's no press, no one is getting you interviews which means no-one doing a lot about your album. We noticed a sort of lack of advertising."

It was hard not to. As a fan and friend of the band in Manchester while they were on the road, I was aware that either their campaign was not being conducted very well – or – inexplicably, there wasn't really a campaign. There was next to no coverage in the music press, no radio play or radio sessions that I recall. The album appeared to have fallen into a vacuum. It was peculiar, to say the least. It wasn't that the album had come out and people weren't turned on by the music. It was that people, generally, were oblivious to the fact that a new Haven record was available. The single *Wouldn't Change a Thing* brushed the outer limits of the chart at number 57. A promotional video featuring Gary receiving a head-massage was sensual and appealing, but I'm not convinced more than a handful of people actually saw it, despite being directed by Kevin Godley and costing a substantial amount of money.

"The video which cost fifty grand never got played!" confirms Jack in frustration. "Kevin Godley's one of the biggest video producers there is. It wasn't him in particular – it was just a bit too dark – a bit too boring, and I think the song wasn't the right choice. If we were to do it again I'd do it differently. Spending fifty grand on a video – we did a few times – and it adds up. Maybe an accountant looked at it all and thought 'hang on – they've spent so much on recording, so much on this – how much are they earning?'"

Exactly what kind of budget had been ear-marked for promoting *All For A Reason* leading up to its release is unknown to me, but what was clear to everyone was that initial interest and sales were nothing like they should have been.

Around this time, Gary accompanied Joe to a label meeting in London which he describes as "a big kind of showdown".

He remembers being asked what he thought the label should do!

"I got the arse a little bit because I thought 'fucking hell, we've just made the record, we've written the songs, we've recorded it twice, and now the record company wants us to decide how to market it and tell them where they're going wrong what they should be doing!' To cut a long story short anyway, it turns out that everyone at Hut Records had been fired – all been made redundant and as a result Radiate went too." The collapse of Hut, and subsequently Radiate obviously sent shockwaves through the music industry. Looking back on that time some years later, Nat says "We had to keep reminding ourselves that it wasn't a result of us – the last thing Radiate would do was get rid of us. It signified an end of a stage in our career. I dunno how I felt at the time." When I asked him if it came as a shock he says, "We knew it was coming, because other bands, like Crackout, who we toured with who were also on a Hut subsidiary or whatever and before the beginning of the tour they got told that their record deal was no longer and we were headlining the tour and they were playing with us and I think all of us kind of like had suspicions that there was this merger or something so I think we had quite a long time to get used to the idea perhaps. Obviously with the lack of promotion with the record and the lack of publicity about the album coming out it was kind of obvious that they'd pulled the plug on the money. I think that's the first thing they did. So it was obviously just a huge shame – a real shame. From the second that they said "Ok, that's it" we just kind of looked forward to writing more songs and getting someone else into what we're doing."

Casting his mind back, Jack remembers being aware during the tour that something wasn't right, especially as Crackout had revealed their sad fate. "They already knew, so even though we didn't want to admit it to each other, we knew in the back of our minds there was something going on. And then about two weeks after that tour, Phil phoned me up and obviously now he was in New Order he was speaking to a lot of people and he said, "Have you heard that Hut's gone down?" so I was like "Has it?? That's the first I knew" so I phoned the lads – the lads phoned Joe and Joe got hold of someone in the morning and that was it – the dream was over!"

Iwan also admits to having concerns during that tour, "We knew when we were going out on tour that there were problems. When you know that your record company is going to be making cuts and you know that you're the only band on the label – who's it gonna be?!"

When I asked Iwan how he felt when the news finally was official he says it was a very tough, and not just for the obvious reasons.

"Nat had already got Bell's Palsy. It was hard and I had a lot of sort of personal problems at the time as well with my ex-girlfriend – it's a long story and I won't go into that as that's another story but it all kind of… it was hard. I think that positive things came out of it though, so that we didn't give up. I don't think we could really – I mean none of us can do anything else! We had to sit down and keep on writing and just carry on really – that's all you can do."

Gary also takes a philosophical view some years later, commenting, "It was a little bit hard to live with at the time. We thought there was a chance we'd be taken over to Virgin. We very hurriedly put together a bunch of songs which we recorded, we spent quite a bit of money doing it but it was born out of panic." I remember bumping into Joe one day that summer on Heaton Moor Road and that was the first time it was confirmed to me that the label was definitely folding, though of course I'd heard rumours. He was waiting to hear if there was a chance of the band being re-housed under the larger Virgin/EMI empire. He basically admitted if that didn't happen he was very worried.

"There was so much kind of uncertainty," Gary recalls, speaking of the songs they had hastily recorded, "that… I'm not making excuses because I'm not bitter or angry in any way but it just basically wasn't good enough and it was just one of those things. It's been good for us all, I mean, don't get me wrong – all of us would much rather have a deal at the moment but I think it kind of… it was an eye-opener. This is potentially what life is like when you're involved with a major record company. You are just a – number – because life goes on."

Suddenly that summer...

However you look at it, the demise of Radiate and the consequences for the band, was a big blow. In an insular city, like Manchester is capable of being, tongues wag quickly and misinformation regarding Haven cluttered the grapevine in no time at all. When they had travelled to RAK, the summer before, the world was full of promise and though, I don't think they are the kind of people who ever become complacent, expectation of big things was heaped upon them and it looked like their star could only rise and keep rising. Since returning from RAK, nothing had been simple.

There was talk that the band had been "dropped" by their label. Some failed to grasp that the label had ceased to exist for reasons entirely unrelated to Haven and this left the band technically "homeless." Still, the unpleasant descriptors of "dropped" or "dumped" were erroneously applied regularly within my ear-shot.

Some may say, had the second album sold in large volumes, Virgin would have quickly drawn up a new deal and stuck them on another arm of its slimmed down body. But this is like pondering if the chicken came before the egg or vice versa, as with virtually no promotion did the record ever stand a chance? Could it realistically be expected to sell in the strange circumstances in which it was released?

So, even though the band didn't have the stigma of being dropped due to poor sales or poor songs, the fact that they weren't swiftly re-housed left them a little vulnerable and with a few question marks huddled over their collective aura.

At this point, the summer of 2004, I think everyone, myself included, expected a deal to be imminent. This was a band entering their prime, on the cusp of great things and arguably already having achieved and created great and beautiful things during their life on the Radiate label. The mood around the band was a little nervous but over all optimistic.

Around this time I was knee-deep in Blue Cat business, compiling *Out Of The Blue*, a compilation album featuring artists who had roots or shoots within the venue. Naturally, Haven who had played there on so many occasions were a band I wanted to include but when the compilation idea was hatched they were still officially on Radiate. The licensing of a track proved to be far more complicated than I imagined and though Gary went out of his way to try and find a loop-hole, it seemed submitting a track would cause more legal problems than it was probably worth.

Then, at the last minute, when it finally became clear that the band were being released from their contracts, it suddenly became possible and they contributed the Eringa produced *Give More*.

Even though it was a piece of work that hadn't made it onto the album, it was a strong track which, in my mind, is faintly reminiscent of the Manic Street Preachers, pleading and pissed off in a controlled kind of way, punchy and gritty, like much of the work Eringa produces.

I was chuffed to get the track, just in time to send to the CD pressers, though, obviously saddened, for the bands sake, to learn that Virgin Records no longer cared what we did. As the CD went to press, Haven embarked on a trip to Thailand.

Coincidently, Danny shut the cafe for two weeks and left for a holiday to the same country. The place was closed to allow a local artist to create wall murals, and adorn the wooden floors with graffiti and artwork, before covering it in a thick coat of varnish. It was a delight to see the shapes and slogans manifesting, just as it was exciting for me to put together the compilation album, complete with another striking David Moss sleeve. Keeping true to the local spirit of the project, David had conjured up a scene which depicted a blue cat against the backdrop of the Stockport Viaduct, with the Mersey sweeping along at full flow. Creativity was at a high. It was summer in the moor again and Manchester now really felt like home.

Like the rest of the band, Jack clung to the hope that Virgin would find a space for them: "They were still funding us to go to Japan in the summer and in September – we did actually sign a contract, because that's what happens – a continuing contract that you've got to sign to say that you're no longer signed, so to speak. So they sent us that maybe in August and I remember saying "No, I'm not signing it – I'm not signing it – fuck off!" I remember saying to Joe what would happen if I don't sign it? He just said "fucking sign it!" so that was that – we had to sign it. Afterwards me and Nat went for a beer in town and after I went home to Jess crying my eyes out all night, because when it hits home – all that work you've done – all that hard work." I had this particular conversation with Jack three years after that summer and he followed that comment with, "And to be fair to us, I think most bands at that point would have said "it's been great, let's call it a day!" but here we are years later still trying to do it. That shows we have a bit of character at least!" It does demonstrate character but I think if anyone had told Jack at that point he could still be without a deal that far down the road he wouldn't have believed it and who would? They had songs, they had spirit, they had determination and a decently sized fan-base. What more could you need?

In August 2004, the band returned from Thailand, where they did briefly meet up with Danny who Nat describes as seeming a little out of character! "He had on all this, like, linen – all beige linen – no joke, seriously! Never seen him like that before. I was a bit spooked actually!"

They were scheduled to play at a local festival *Moorfest.* This was the festival's second year running. The Fall were head-lining and the event which billed itself as a "family-oriented" festivity took place at Heaton Moor Rugby Club. Haven took to the stage as the august sky darkened to night. They must have been in a strange head-space, no longer having the security of being a signed band. This was the first time they had played in the UK in this new, uncertain state of mind.

I remember the day clearly as we'd just got the promo copies of the *Out Of the Blue* compilation and indeed some of the acts featured on the record were taking to the stage that day.

Haven played a fired-up set which I remember watching from the side of the marquee. Joe Moss, who was swigging red wine was raving to anyone who would listen about how good they were…and they were. I hoped that Joe had a magic trick up his sleeve to get them back where they belonged. And soon.

It was now over a year since Nathan had first suffered with Bells Palsy.

In most people's eyes, myself included, he seemed to be, if not fully recovered, very close to it. Sadly, this wasn't actually the case and was he was still having to put aside time daily to exercise the muscles that were reluctant to work and to sellotape his eye shut before sleep.

"I used this machine that sends electrical stimulation, a kind of machine which basically reminds the muscles what they should be doing if they were active because, if the muscle doesn't get any messages, any signals, the muscle will basically slowly die," Nat explains, "this is just to make sure that when my nerves start working properly again that my face kind of reacts. I was doing it for two hours a day every day and it went down to an hour and now I'm on half an hour every day still," he says two years after the onset of the condition.

I asked Nat if he had ever tried acupuncture, "Yeah, I did actually start doing some acupuncture and I've been told, I actually have a friend in Cornwall who had a huge improvement after using acupuncture so I think I may have to re-visit it. I had about eight sessions with this woman. I wanna believe that it's working because so much mental stuff goes with all this as well." We talked about how the mind effects the body to which Nat says, "I completely one hundred percent believe in that so I've kind of tried a bit of everything. I mean there's a lot of alternative medicines that seem to be just arriving out of thin air and they're good for people that aren't very ill!" he breaks into laughter, "but, I grew up with homeopathy and my brother had a curing of a really serious eye disorder with homeopathy. And I like the sound of acupuncture and all that but obviously there's a load of new wave rubbish out there too. I was told by this chiropractor that reflexology could be good for my face, even a tiny little improvement would be a huge improvement."

I'm not sure why the summer of that year is so clear and the autumn and winter shrivel into an ammesic blur.

Haven played one of their legendary Christmas gigs at the Blue Cat Cafe. It was certainly nice to hear them play again, as it had been a while. I remember a huge crowd and at this point it still felt that it was only a matter of time before a label would snap them up again.

It's time the tale were told

I don't remember precisely when it occurred to me to tell this story but I do remember sounding out the idea in May 2005. It was a bustling, sticky night in the Blue Cat Cafe and I was sitting on the sofa with Gary and a friend of his, with people spilling over our feet. When I first brought up the idea, Gary spluttered on his drink. I worried momentarily that he didn't think I was up to the job but he quickly regained composure and assured me he wasn't sniggering at my proposal but found it amusing that anyone would even consider writing a book about the band. This was typical self-deprecating Gary behaviour and I told him I definitely thought it was a book worth writing and as long as they were willing to co-operate, I'd like to give it a go. Everybody generally seemed happy for me to get started and so I did.

On the first of June that year I conducted the first of many, many interviews. Gary was the first candidate. At this point, I still lived in 118 Heaton Moor Road, behind the Blue Cat Cafe. Gary came round that evening in a long black coat and a trilby type hat, as though he thought he was being interviewed for a detective novel and had to assume an appropriate character costume! The first interview was an epiphany of sorts for me because, though I had a sketchy idea of the band's history, it was a sudden steep climb to go right back to the start, with no real pre-conceptions and just let it all flow.

Ever since, I've continued to try and catch that flow, to collect all those pools and puddles of memories, to light a candle and try to tiptoe through. I feel blessed to have shared such candid chats with the band over the years but also to have witnessed sizeable chunks of the on-going story first hand, on and off.

That summer, *Moorfest* happened again. This time the event took place in the Heaton Mersey Bowl, a big grassy hollow that dives steeply down from Didsbury Road, ideal for an outdoor festival. This year the event was mainly organised by Jamie Crowley, a close friend of the band at that time. Naturally, Haven were on the bill, along with Badly Drawn

Boy and a Certain Ratio. The day was a mixture of sunshine and showers, mainly showers if I remember rightly. The band hadn't played much since the same festival a year before and had spent much of the year in their rehearsal space working on new material. Around this time, Iwan was also doing some work with Johnny Marr's Healers.

New songs, such as *Velvet Skyline* and *No One Cut So Deep* emerged that year and were performed at *Moorfest*. The new material was still somewhat fluid at this point, not entirely moulded into fixed structures. It was heartening to hear them play these new songs but I had a vague feeling that they were all starting to drift a little. I don't mean drift apart, or even drift aimlessly but that someone needed to get a stronger focus, to gently steer them onto the right path.

I certainly don't think they were disillusioned, even though they had now spent a year without a deal. Naturally, this did bring some changes, even on a purely financial level.

Iwan remarks that even when they had a ready supply of money they weren't prone to excess: "We've been there before, being skint. You only spend what you've got. We just sat down and thought well we've got to just get on with it – can't just dwell on what's happened – can't have any regrets because with the two albums we'd had such an amazing time you know?" He shrugs, adding, "like, we could go to Japan tomorrow and we could still sell out."

This comment is entirely true, and it must have been frustrating for the band to be aware that their popularity, especially in places like Japan had not diminished, but they lacked the infrastructure to take their show on the road.

At some point around this time, the band returned to rehearsing in the *Night and Day* Cafe, instead of Danny's garage. However, this time they were banished to the basement, rather than the rooms upstairs they had occupied when they were starting out.

"That became a real, surreal horrible damp place," Jack remembers, "it sort of changed from being a band going in with your head up to going in with your head down, to a bit of a downer. Obviously I still loved playing music, still loved being with the boys so if I chucked it in where would I go?" Clearly, they were still committed to the band. They turned up to rehearse and try out ideas just as they used to when they were signed.

"You can't think "oh, just pack it all in" – we'll always be a unit, whatever happens success wise – you don't know, if we'd have gotten really successful there may have been other problems," Iwan suggests wisely.

Had the band not been such closely knit friends, this hiatus in their careers would likely have been more problematic but they truly did enjoy being together and there was strength to be drawn from that gang mentality that was still alive and well.

An injection of slightly manic energy seemed to boost the band in the autumn of that year. Perhaps, the involvement of their good friend, Mickey Smith had something to do with that, as he was around on and off a lot of that time. Or perhaps there was a growing sense of there being nothing to lose so they may as well have some fun. At any rate, I remember a spirit of playfulness, partying and craziness during this period. "At one point I was living at Nat's pretty much, to-ing and fro-ing from Manchester airport on jobs and causing mayhem with Nat in between," Mickey says. "There's too many funny tales really. We always end up getting red carded."

He recalls a particularly insane night in the Elizabethan Pub on Heaton Moor Road:

"Me and Nat had been on it for a while, and people were buying us drinks to keep us quiet…when, out of the blue, we get handed a pint, Nat grins at me, and drops it – I grin back, do the same! We get bought another one, do the same thing. Then start grabbing drinks and dropping them thinking we're hilarious until we get dragged out, Iwan dragging me, and Gary dragging Nat in separate directions. Came round the next morning not knowing what had happened and it was raining so hard, so I went round to Nat's, woke him up, we put on wetsuits and started running around Heaton Moor sliding on our bellies through puddles. Then we went up to the main road and started egging on cars to hit this big puddle and soak us! People didnt know what to make of it, but in the end we had big 4wd's going as fast as they could on their way to work on a Monday morning, seeing us and hitting the puddle so hard we were getting soaked. Nat got a call later from a mate on his way to work on a building site, saying we'd made his day. Funny shit, but we're a right pair of Cornish wankers really!"

The amusing photographic evidence of these antics ended up on the band's website, as Nat and Mickey clowned around a water-logged Heaton Moor road in their wet-suits, like confused, comic amphibians, trying to reconcile two worlds.

Danny recalls some wild nights at the Blue Cat with a similar water-sport theme. "They'd been into town with Mickey and they got back here, got out all the soda water and were just fucking ski-ing up and down here," he demonstrates the length of the bar. "It was hilarious, should have videoed that – Ski Olympics at the Cat, at four in the morning!"

During 2005, Danny and I had been working with a band called Outsider. We'd recently put out an EP and the band were starting to gain a little attention. I'd booked them a tour which crossed paths with Haven beneath the dazzling lights of Blackpool that October. I think I was semi-responsible for organising these for both bands as I thought they'd work well together on the same bill but I can't remember the details. Danny and myself drove up to Blackpool that evening at break-neck speed. Danny drives everywhere at break-neck speed and told me I had to scream (with delight) when the Blackpool Tower came into view.

The venue was a bit tacky, and worse than that, water started dripping through the ceiling in the middle of Outsider's set. Fortunately for Haven, the problem was resolved by time they took to the stage.

Even though the place was half empty, I remember this set being particularly mesmerising. The new songs had really gelled and the band sounded tighter, stronger and sharper than ever. The idea was that they were using tonight as a warm-up for the gig at the *Night and Day* the following night, but they were already beyond warm. To me, they were approaching boiling point and ready to take on the world. There was a real hunger and drive that had, perhaps, been missing just a little during that last full tour they had done before the collapse of Radiate.

Following the Manchester date, the band also travelled to London, to play at the Highbury Garage. These three back-to-back dates were documented colourfully by Mickey Smith who took on the role of chauffeur/photographer and unobtrusive observer. He wrote candidly and enthusiastically about this mini-tour with the band and the diary was posted on the website. He also took some memorable photographs, which Gary has said are the images that best define them.

"He came on those dates and he was just kind of snap happy for the whole thing. He's got some brilliant shots," comments Gary, "but he's our mate and we know him. Every good photographer's got that ability to kind of turn into mist and you don't even know he's there and as a result he got some really great shots – really a true representation of us, which is nice because we never really had that before." I asked him if he meant the live shots in particular, as Mickey has taken all kinds of pictures of the band. "I mean in general, there's some great shots of us on stage but the thing is with photos like that – that's when you're on guard, your posing, you're kind of playing to your crowd, so to speak," Gary explains, "so it's more kind of background ones that he's got – like someone writing the set list or there's some great ones of us coming back in his car. Me and Nat found six cans of Stella in the boot after a big night of boozing, so we were still drunk – and then we found this bottle of ouzo under the seat – you know, an amazing find so there's some great photos of me and Nat just looning around in the back of his Nissan Micra!"

After the Highbury Garage gig, Mickey ended up coming back to Manchester with the boys to continue the party. When the party finally ended, it was time for the band to think seriously about recording some of these new songs. It seemed the third album was beginning to take shape.

On a clear day...

Mid-November, the band re-assembled in the familiar environs of Johnny Marr's Clear Studios, though this time they were in the capable hands of Jim Spencer, rather than Marr. Haven have a long history with Jim which stretches back to their early days in Manchester.

"I first met Haven with Johnny. I think he had just re-established his relationship with Joe Moss. If I remember right, the first thing I did for the band was mix a single (*Til the End*) at the Charlatans studio, Big Mushroom," Jim says. "I was struck by Gary's amazing voice and the vibe of the band as a whole. They were a very tight bunch of guys, not just musically but as friends and the chemistry as a band was really good."

Jim began his musical journey as a tape operator at Chapel Studios, ending up as "house engineer there for a couple of years, before I moved to Manchester to work with Bernard Sumner and Johnny on Electronic's second album."

The band were comfortable with Jim and their surroundings and there was an upbeat, excited mood as they re-entered the studio.

"Jim's a really great guy and we've known him a long, long time," Gary smiles fondly, "through Johnny's generosity or his kindness we've had the chance to work with Jim as well. And Jim being the great guy that he is, you know, initially he did it all for nothing on the surmise that we would get a record deal and obviously that happened. We just get on with him really well. His CV's pretty great and he's really good fun to work with, he's not uptight – nothing's a problem."

The month they spent at Clear was documented by Gary who posted an online diary of their daily experiences on the band's website. His accounts, though short and sweet hit the right balance of humour, realism and intrigue.

Here's his musings from Novemeber 18th:

Another frosty morning so i was glad to get out of the car and into the studio, get the heating cranked and fill up on tea and toast. No sign of the asbestos/area51 guys must be too cold for them as well. No-one cut so deep is really taking shape, we stayed late last night and nailed most of the guitars over a nice bottle of red and a few cold ones with our mate Big Dave Tolan, it's coming together!!! The captain, as ever is playing a blinder at the controls, helping steer the good ship Haven to new horizons.

Jim Spencer had been cast in the role as Captain, by Gary who weaved a few strange scenarios around him as well. He also created some odd x-files type visions concerning things he observed from the windows and the arrival of mysterious fog blankets that eerily enveloped Manchester persistently during that time.

Jack was another focal point of Gary's scribbling, usually to poke fun at him, affectionately, of course:

November 30 2005:

I guess it's just one of those days, but it is the only difficult day we've had so far. Everything we did felt laboured which was probably due to the fact that the track we are working on (All I Ever Knew) is the most under rehearsed. But just when we thought it couldn't get any worse it… didn't thank fuck, Jack pulled a fantastic drum track out the bag which meant he could get back to the more serious business of trawling the net. Speaking of Jack you should see the jumper he's sporting a top christmas/ Val Doonican (did i spell than right?) effort i think that might well have been the thing that hindered our progress, it even bothered the Captain…

A decision had been made by the band to utilise their website more than they had previously. It was one of the few methods left to them for connecting with their fan-base, but also a means of keeping their profile alive, so that the music industry could be aware that something was still going on. This was the main idea behind the daily digest from Clear Studios.

"When we parted company with Virgin, which we weren't really that bothered about to be honest – the only thing that bothered me was like "Where's my next meal coming from?" But I wasn't that arsed, right?" Gary said shortly after coming out of the studio at the end of that year. "There's people in far worse situations – but we thought, we've got to find a way to – we don't wanna just disappear, although in many ways we have, but on a ground level you can maintain your existence through the internet but only if you can be arsed to do it. It wasn't an easy thing to do because it doesn't come easy to me – I've never really been a big fan of the internet though I accept now that it is so important. A lot of that's come from Joe – basically saying, "well, I could sit here every day and write something for the website but unless it comes from you it's not valid, it's not gonna be worth anything in terms of the people that are on the site every day". There's not a lot of people but when you look on there in the morning, whatever I posted the night before had thirty-three views at least, comments/replies and that's really nice, you know? It's all coming from a good place – it's all good will. In the situation we're in at the moment you really thrive on that."

However, the studio diary, a little later on, landed Jack in a stressful situation when there was an unexpected knock on the door at home one night. Unbelievably, Jack had been visited by the Job Centre brigade, who had been monitoring Gary's daily journal and arrived at the door with printed out copies, claiming Jack was misleading them about his availability for work.

It stuns me that something like this can happen, when Jack clearly was penniless and doing everything in his power to get his musical career back on track. He supposes that somebody with a malicious twist had squealed to the Department for Work and Pensions.

"In the end it was fine because I'd not been earning money," Jack says, "So I got the accountant to prove that I'd not been earning. I think I'd made a £1,400 loss or something, so it was impossible for me to be earning money!"

Despite that undesirable repercussion, these few lines each day, provided a life-line for the band and the fans simultaneously. For the band, it was encouraging to see there was still an audience out there who cared about what they were doing. For the fans, it was reassurance that Haven hadn't faded away, were alive and well and working on a promising new record.

I also think, on some level, it was a good exercise for Gary himself, to gather his own thoughts and gain some clarity about what he was doing. We discussed the pressure to be interesting when representing the band and how dull the truth tends to be if you don't use a little poetic licence:

"At the end of day, if you tell the truth it's so boring, and if you tell people the truth they can hurt you with it, right? That's something that I've always had in my head. From doing interviews early on, I made the mistake a few times of sitting there being asked questions and I'm telling people straight and you realise that it makes shit reading. What did you do today? I got up, I went to the studio, worked on this guitar part for ten hours, had a chippie and went home. And the same's true of every fucking scenario. No matter how interesting your life is when you actually talk about it – it's not," Gary states. "So, yeah, I don't know, it's something that was born out of not wanting to come across as being boring. I mean I'm not directly relating this to the website and in a way it's like a kind of shield really. You see it all the time. I can think back to people that have been absolutely crucified by journalists for being honest and you think to yourself – there's two types of honesty – there's honesty for the sake of being anarchic – and there's honest and being criticised for it – d'you get me? So I decided that I'd be neither, you know? I'd be somewhere in between. It's much more fun, isn't it?"

The blurring and blending of truth and fiction is a conundrum I've wrestled with myself whilst immersed in this project. Memory can play tricks on our minds, time can distort memories. Fact and fiction merge and flicker, like a candle about to burn itself out – and we're left in the dark.

All the author can really do is tell you what she has glimpsed and gathered. Like Chinese whispers, what we hear and what was said could be two very different things. In these writings, I've deliberately chosen to leave out some recollections, some scenes, some freeze-frames that I feel should stay confined to my personal memory bank. Inevitably, the unknown and the unsaid walk side by side with any revelation. The spaces between the notes, between the words, the silences often carry loud messages we can choose to hear, or choose to ignore.

That year drew to a close with a customary Haven Christmas gig/party at the Blue Cat. I don't know that anyone felt they had a finished album in the bag, but they did at least have the bones of one, which they could flesh out in the new year.

When I asked Iwan, years later, if at that point, during that recording period, if he felt this was going where it needed to, this was the third album and it was going to come out and things could move forward, he said "Yeah, I think so. At that point, we were all raring to go and it was the same point I was doing the Healers and Johnny was still helping out a lot – he did some pre-production with us – it was all systems go again really – with songs like *Waiting for Tomorrow* – that came out of it. I thought we'd get something out of that – at least get some kind of release, but then it's the same old haven story – it didn't happen! It kind of, we thought we were good enough to do something with it."

It always felt to me it could have and should have happened. So what did happen?

Really saying something...

Things were happening, but not quickly, not directly and not in a co-ordinated manner. In January 2006, a big charity concert called *Manchester Versus Cancer* took place at the Evening News Arena, which seems to have since become an annual event. Iwan and Nathan were involved. Iwan was playing bass with Johnny Marr's Healers and Nat ended up as guitar tech to Marr and some other artists.

I watched the concert with Danny, Viv and the rest of the band, enjoying performances by the Healers and Doves. I remember New Order's set being especially powerful – but – something felt wrong. Gary and Jack both seemed rather subdued. Perhaps they were thinking WE should be on that stage, and in my mind, yes, they should have been. Nine Black Alps had been selected to represent the new generation of local talent, in the slot that could just as easily have been Haven. It felt uncomfortable seeing a guitarist as talented as Nat tending to other guitarists needs rather than playing himself. It seemed particularly odd that Haven weren't on the bill when Joe Moss was clearly involved because Marr was on the bill.

Danny told me that the night upset him "Seeing Nat as a guitar tech, I felt a bit emotional about that." Perhaps it wasn't as easy as a casual observer may think for Joe to pull some strings and get the band the big exposure an event like that would have given them. Would playing to all those people have helped pave the way for a new record deal? Nobody can answer that question for sure, but it is clear that it didn't do anything to boost band morale. Sadly, for probably the first time, this is when I felt confidence was starting to slip. I'm not saying the band were sinking into depression or giving up hope, but time was ticking away and the longer they remained in the limbo of being unsigned, the harder it became, in a way, to get signed. The stigma of being released from their Virgin contract actually increased as the limbo state became more prolonged, unfair though that stigma undoubtedly was in the first place.

There was, of course, no money coming in, apart from miniscule royalties and dole money and that in itself naturally causes a strain.

"Well, obviously there's been times when it was very tough," Jack comments on that phase, "I was on the dole for nine months and it was when me and Jess were splitting up as well – and I think that was one of the things – because I wasn't bringing in any money and I was spending a lot of time at home – so was she, so we were getting in each other's faces. I got a job in a video shop, I lasted three weeks – it was a real grim time but I never thought of jacking it all in because I thought what have I got if I jack it in?"

For the whole of their adult lives to date, being musicians was all Haven knew and all they wanted so it was almost unthinkable to consider other options. As they had created a new body of promising work there was every reason to believe they could carry on their band's story at this point. The path to doing that was uncertain but by no means impossible. I think they placed a lot of faith in Joe, hoping that he could lead them to the next stage.

I had an interesting chat with Gary one evening that January. He'd recently moved into the re-furbished flat Danny was renting out above the Blue Cat, with Iwan and their friend, Nico. We got to talking about song-writing and lyrics. Gary revealed that with the new songs, he was taking extra care with words, wanting to give them as much thought and importance as the music. This way of thinking had been at least partly inspired by a character named Jay, a friend of Joe's.

"Jay's an interesting chap. I've known him quite a long time now. Most of Joe's friends are interesting, actually. He's got an army of interesting characters who – I won't say they follow him round but they originate from the hippie days. All of them have got too much to say, y'know? But I think that's part of the generation thing," Gary explains, "I actually got that when I saw that Dylan documentary that was on recently – what I realised was – this artist, I forget who it was now, made this real point about "Oh I bumped into Ginsberg the other week" and they were like "Oh right, has he got anything to say?" I thought that was really cool. And I understood then, I understood Joe's kind of – I don't claim to know it completely but I got an insight into the way Joe's generation think or maybe thought. It was all on the words and all on having something to say – it's not like it is now, the onus now is on how you look, perhaps. We live in a society now where it's all like, everyone is freaking out because their nose is a funny shape, d'you know what I mean? Not that that's necessarily a new thing but that's the most important thing nowadays – which is – well, us thinkers know that to be rubbish. So, yeah, words and stuff, this time round on this record became really important, I think more so because, not having a deal at this present time, trying to get a deal, everything is gonna be so scrutinized, because the industry knows Haven, y'know, they're aware of us – it's like do we change the name and come back with something new or do we make sure what we're giving them is fucking great. And part of me getting my head around making sure the words and everything were great, was this evening I spent with Jay. He just pointed out the kind of theatrics that go along with singing and go along with the way you put your words together and sometimes the spaces between the words being more important. It was interesting. He kind of turned me on to a few things. He's a great guy, he's one of these guys where his only reference points are Dylan and Van Morrison, which is cool, but what reference points! Two really amazing songwriters… but yeah, that was really helpful. He'd go "What are you singing there? I can't hear what you're singing" And I'd be like, "Er this is what I'm singing" and he kind of, in a round-about-the-houses kind of way, because obviously, he's not gonna sit there and say "that line is crap" – but he made me realise that if I really thought that line was great I'd want it to be audible, you'd make it heard. So, in a roundabout way, he kind of said "that line is crap" – "that line is crap"- "you know, sort it out!" and the song greatly benefitted as a result. We were writing a song called *What we've become* at the time, which I think will make the record, it needs a bit of re-arranging at the moment. It was just a good exercise. I'm quite difficult, I take criticism really well but it has to be put in the right way, d'you know what I mean?" Gary giggles.

Listening to the six tracks I have heard from these recordings, the words do seem to spill out over the music with a new sense of conviction. I think Gary's lyrics are far more articulate, poetic and potent than he gives himself credit for generally, but with songs like the majestic *Velvet Skyline* or the uncomfortable *No One Cut So Deep*, the words reach right out and grab you, demanding your full attention. I'm not clear if these songs were ever fully mixed and considered complete. I think not. I do remember Gary once telling me that he wanted a gospel choir on *Velvet Skyline*, an awesome idea, which would have allowed it to grow wings and soar in the way it was perhaps intended. These were the songs that Joe was given to try to secure a new deal.

In February, the band played a gig at the Academy and shortly after travelled to London to play at the Highbury Garage again.

It was shortly after that London date that I interviewed Nat at length where he commented on how it felt to play these gigs:

"I mean still now it's been a hell of a long time but we know we've got really loyal fans that will come and watch us anywhere in the country and that's basically all we've got left, it's really heart-warming," he said. "You know when we played London the other week… the audience has always been the thing that we've tried to impress – like, if I'm nervous about a gig it must be because I'm nervous about the audience because I'm not nervous about playing – but this last London gig we all went out and we had a bit of a group thing together. We all had a couple of beers in the pub round the corner and came back to the gig and I didn't know – I literally didn't know whether it was gonna be empty when we walked in there because we'd done nothing for so long and we've just got this one off gig in London. I walked through the door and it was rammed. I didn't feel nervous of these people – they all looked like my friends," he laughs, "I just wanted to buy them all a drink! I was just so pleased to see all these people there still believing in what we're doing. It was very heart-warming you know? And I had no nerves with that gig whatsoever. I took a bit of an opportunity to just have a wander around and I saw everybody looking at the stage waiting for the band to come on – it was really, really lovely to see all these people."

I mentioned to Nat that I've always been struck by the devotion of their fans and suggest it's because the songs have really impacted people emotionally: "Yeah, that's right," he agrees, "because the songs are very full on – once you get into them you know they're quite… there's a lot of emotion attached to them. And if people have been caught by it or touched by it, it's gonna stay with them. And we're always developing – as a band, the songs are always developing live and we started learning to stop being so lazy and playing the same songs in the set every week. We've started looking on the website. Gary's been doing a thing on the website asking people about track-listings for gigs and stuff and we've been looking at the suggestions. We've been going back to the first album more – b-sides and the second album we tried to learn some of the songs that we'd decided we weren't gonna play. We learnt *The First Time* for the Manchester and London gig and it turned out to be all of our favourite songs in the end. We've got to give a huge amount of credit and thanks to those people that do show up to all those gigs."

I conversed with a few of these fans about what Haven meant to them during the writing of this story. Neil Arman, who's travelled around the country to see them on around forty occasions says:

"I couldn't put my finger on what made Haven so special… Some bands just get you I suppose and they 'got me' – but why didn't the world 'get it'? Maybe they were just never in the right place at the right time, they never seemed to get much luck but I don't think the quality of the songs/musicians could ever be questioned. Bloody nice chaps too."

Another devoted fan, Paul Hames mentions "The track *All For a Reason*, despite not necessarily being my favourite on CD was always my favourite live track. I just thought they absolutely nailed it each time. In retrospect, it really annoyed me that Haven were not as well recognised as they should have been.

I'm always convinced that the enforced delay between the first and second album may have cost them a little bit given the ruthlessness of the music business and the fickleness of music fans. As I said, it was completely unavoidable but think they were on a bit of a high when they had to take a bit of time out."

On that particular night in early 2006 that I interviewed Nat, Joe was in London with the tracks, visiting labels. "I really want to believe that Joe is going to make a phone call tomorrow and say listen there's a good offer – but as time goes on it gets more and more difficult," Nat said.

I agreed and though I'm sure I didn't want that phone call to the same degree that Nat did, I wished on twinkling stars as I walked home that it would happen for them. It would seem such a waste of talent for these new recordings not to come to fruition. So, we all kept our fingers crossed as Spring arrived in Heaton Moor and the buds burst into leaves on the trees.

In May 2006, the band were scheduled to travel to India to take part in what was being billed as an International Music Fiesta on MTV Network's VH1 channel. The idea was that three "Western" bands would headline each night and local Indian bands would play on the same bill.

The other non-Indian bands booked were TaxiRide from Australia and Swedish band, Empire Dogs. It may seem strange that Haven became involved in this event, but there is an explanation. *All For A Reason* was pencilled in for an American release in August of that year:

"This guy Guggan, who is gonna be putting our record out in America happens to be Indian and he's kind of pally with this guy called Gittin who is one of the main boys on VH1 in India," Gary explains, "they were talking about this thing *Rock Rules* which, in essence, is providing an opportunity for, in one evening any two Indian bands to play alongside a Western band. I got the impression it was more kind of geared for opportunities that could arise for the Indian bands, because obviously a lot of the Western bands like ourselves, and Australian bands, already have deals and get to play all over the world and the intention was to – maybe open doors for these Indian bands."

Perhaps, some may say, a peculiar trip for the boys, when they really needed some doors to open for them in the UK, yet, doors can open anywhere, and unexpectedly. As they weren't dipping into their own pockets to make this trip, it was an adventure of sorts.

Before they left for India in mid-may, they kindly agreed to play a semi-secret gig I had engineered.

The Blue Cat Cafe was coming up to a milestone anniversary. It was almost a decade since Danny Donnelly had the premises converted from a TSB bank into the quirky music bar it has become. Although, I'd only been involved in the set-up for three years I was as fond of and familiar with its floorboards as its long-term regulars. I thought the occasion should be marked. That same spring, Danny had broken his foot in a violent unprovoked scuffle in the bar. He was hobbling around on crutches and a bit down in the dumps. I figured a celebratory event was needed. Naturally, Haven were my first choice of band, and as they were all appreciative of Danny's help to them through the years they were happy to oblige. Preparations went ahead in a hushed manner as we wanted the night to be a surprise for Mr Blue Cat.

Banners and flyers were designed and sent to print, balloons were inflated and special blue and white invites exchanged hands surreptitiously all over the moor. Miraculously, for one as sharp as Danny, he didn't seem to have an inkling, despite seeing me whispering in corners most of the week ahead of the gig!

However, I guess I should have realised that not everyone likes surprises. On the 11th May, which was the day we planned the event to happen, I got a concerned call from Danny's ex-wife Maxine, telling me I must tell him or he'd freak out. I'm not quite sure why, but she said the bar was under-stocked and if a massive crowd rolled up the bar would run dry which would be embarrassing. I wish I'd gone to the cash and carry myself to prevent such a scenario but I was caught up doing other last minute arrangements and it didn't even occur to me. Reluctantly, I came clean with Danny. I told the band, with a sigh "the cat was out of the bag" and there was a slight feeling of deflation.

However, we soon got over that and once the doors opened a joyous vibe engulfed the bar and I remember this being a beautiful, spirited night. Haven were in fine form, despite not having played since the London gig a few months before. The "new" songs were sitting comfortably beside the "old" songs and the time seemed ripe for someone to bottle this musical magic and put it on a record. Why wasn't it happening? I scratched my head. After the gig, I wished them "Bon Voyage" as they were off to India in a couple of days.

Up on the roof...

I'm sitting on the roof of the Blue Cat. The sun is dazzlingly bright and the nearby trees are showering us with pollen.

Nat disappears into the kitchen to make us some tea and Iwan and Jack haven't arrived yet. Gary launches into an impassioned speech, words just seem to tumble out without the self-censorship I feel he sometimes maintains. I clearly remember this because it struck me as so heart-felt.

"This has been the weirdest fucking year of my life," he declares. "It's not what I'm about, sitting in Town Bar (nearby wine bar). Well, it is a part of what I'm about but only a small part. I'm about music. It's all about music and my life isn't about music at the moment. I need to do something about that."

I look at his hay-fevered, streaming eyes and sympathise deeply. The struggle feels too much. Yet, it should be simple. Something is wrong here and I can't quite put my finger on it but it is like he needs to re-align himself with his true path and that he is somehow being pulled off track by some invisible, undefined force. "It's all a state of mind" is all I can offer. He agrees but seems quietly distressed. We fall into a brief silence before Nat returns with tea and biscuits. Iwan arrives and I start the official interview feeling what Gary was trying to articulate is actually more important than discussing the Indian trip, yet that is why I'd called the band together, so I thought I better stick with my original line of enquiry.

Gary explains that he didn't think the whole concept of the Western bands helping Indian bands reach new audiences worked especially well: "All the Indian bands were playing covers and we were going on after these bands playing Rage against the Machine and Limp Biskit songs and God knows what else, Led Zeppelin, which was hard work, because, well, that's sort of the norm in India."

"Yeah," Nat agrees, "they do have their own songs but to bring an audience and to keep an audience they have to put a certain amount of covers in."

Apparently, *All For A Reason* had been released in India but with no promotion behind it. "You always hear this," Gary comments slightly wearily, "but they said, had they known we were coming out, they'd have put more behind it. I think now it's opened up some channels in the sense that this guy Gittin and Duggan and everyone is talking and everyone's dead positive about it all – I don't know – I don't know how much of a serious market India is really, but if we get to go out there again I'll be happy with that."

They talk about the flight, all stating they're comfortable with flying but Nat mentions Jack gets nervous on take-off. Iwan recalls their old drum tech being terrified of flying: "He'd have to drink eight or nine vodkas before he'd even get on the plane!" "Yeah and by the time he's on the plane he's ready to throw up and they want to throw him off!" laughs Nat.

They talked about how, before they left they'd been fed numerous horror stories about internal flights, food poisoning and mosquito attacks. Yet, as Iwan says calmly "All the horror stories turned out to be false."

"D'you know, that was the lasting impression I got actually," Gary considers, "I was really embarrassed for being British. We went to the Gateway to India – this is what it's known as, which is a little bit like the Arc de Triomphe but on a much smaller scale and it's got this thing saying "built to commemorate the landing of King George the 5th" and whoever his wife was at the time. I just thought that was so fucking naff, it really is – and interestingly enough it's one of the most attacked in terms of terrorism places in India – there's always bombs going off there you know?"

"Let's just say we went outside and had our photograph taken!" grins Nat. "Well, you did, yeah!" Gary retorts, "I've got a great one of you!"

Nat was the only one of the band who had been to India before this trip: "Well, I'd been to Goa before – on a holiday – pretty much a different place, you know? I think it's like if you visited England and you went to Cornwall and then you went to Manchester or London or something, it's like that – that sort of difference between places. It's really laid back in Goa. The cities are pretty frantic. Goa is nice, you've obviously got the beach and everything. Bombay is, well, you've got to have eyes in the back of your head or you'd get run over by a bloody – what are they called? Tuc tucs or something," he breaks into more giggles.

"D'you know what? According to everyone we hung out with there were very few road accidents," Gary says. "We met this guy called – Shaker, his name was. He worked for MTV and he was saying that no one in India drives over forty miles an hour – but – that sort of makes sense when you see the roads because no one's got more than forty centimetres between them and the car in front. There's no room for acceleration." "No," Nat agrees, "like at the traffic lights…" "There seems to be no rules," Gary muses. "Yeah, like everyone just goes in the same direction," Iwan laughs. "But that's the only thing they have in common!" chuckles Nat.

"It's like that big roundabout in Paris – like Wacky races!" grins Gary "that's what it's like and that constant-" he makes frustrated horn sounds. "Eveyone is on their horn the whole time!" "Their favourite bit of the car!" Nat says.

"I noticed as we were driving around, there were parts of the place where they had a road sign and it has a horn and a big cross on it where you weren't allowed to use your horn," Gary remarks with his typical dead-pan delivery. "On the back of the motors it always says "Horn Please!" Nat collapses in laughter again, then continues, "because I think if you're on a motorbike alongside a lorry you beep your horn all the way through – just to let people know your're there. So people are contstantly-" "Everyone's got the horn in India," Gary smiles at me saucily.

I've transcribed some of this exactly as it was said, to demonstrate the banter that is typical of the band. Although they are all capable of being serious when the occasion demands it, they can be entertaining and high-spirited, and much of the time they are.

"We nearly got arrested before we got to Delhi," Iwan tells me "Or Gary did!"

"What did you do?" I ask worriedly. "Er, I, inadvertently filmed the American Consulate," Gary confesses, "which apparently is an offence in India so our bus got pulled over. I didn't even know what I'd done! This guy who was looking after us said "who's got the camera?" and it had to be me, didn't it? And I had all these – I don't know how to put this without sounding impolite but I didn't have much faith in their training in handling firearms – put it that way! Most of them were brandishing rather hefty looking machine guns – it looked quite possible they could go off at any minute. I wasn't so much worried about them taking a shot at the body – more like my big toe getting shot off! Even so, it was pretty frightening!" "So they ordered you off the bus?" I ask. "Absolutely," continues Gary, "I had a video camera and I'm just like that, you know? I wasn't even filming – I was talking about the gig last night." "Some guy on a motorbike pulled up beside us," Nat smirks. "It was like something out of the A team, wasn't it? Bundled off!" exclaims Gary. "The thing was, we were all pissed off because me and him had woken up to a fucking stupid hotel room," Nat explains. "Yeah twenty-five pounds which in India is the equivalent of over here like a suite in the Waldorf or something," Gary says. "Yeah, God knows how it happened," Nat shakes his head, "but then THIS happened and we were trying to give them the tape – just saying "look take the tape!" but they weren't interested, they were saying, look, there's procedure!"

"Yeah, yeah, but the thing was – they said "I wanna see the tape!" so I'm trying to rewind it," Gary carries on, "first, I tried to eject the tape and it won't eject. Then I'm trying to re-wind the tape and it wouldn't rewind. Finally, got it working and these guys are getting agitated – and these are guys with fucking machine guns. Looking at it now, it's funny but at the time, I was, like Nat said – I was in a bad mood anyway – and the tape did finally play back but played back at twice the speed and I swear they thought I was taking the piss! At this point, I got marched to this check-point thing – sat down on a chair and this dude with this like, polished – you know those sticks like fucking sergeant majors have? I was prepared for a good lashing! Then, I managed to get it working – the thing was – no one who was with us. We didn't have anyone from the record company with us and no one from MTV – we just had this Thomas Cooke travel agent who – well, his Hindi was perfect but his English left a lot to be desired! And there lied the problem. I needed someone to translate – but I got through it. We got through it. It was fine in the end after all my passport details got taken!"

"You had to have a mug shot," Nat reminds Gary. "Yeah, mug shot from all angles," Gary confirms "they took it really seriously."

"We were all tempted to get off the bus and say "listen, what's going on here?" but we knew that the more people who got involved the longer it would go on," remembers Nat, "and we were in a real rush to get to the airport." "So was this on your way back home then?" I ask. "No, on the way to Delhi," respond Gary and Nat in strange perfect unison.

"I suppose – to back track a little," Nat rewinds his thoughts, "the reason we had a day off in Bombay, you see – or Mumbai, was because – this is another funny little story. We were due to play Bangalore. Mumbai, Bangalore and then Delhi but the Bangalore gig had been cancelled because the chief of police in Bangalore had outlawed dancing!"

Everyone falls into laughter again. "Alongside the sale of alcohol," adds Gary, "because no one was allowed to sell alcohol and dance. It was a bit like the criminal justice bill – on a much worse scale. You've seen *Footloose*, I'm sure, with Kevin Bacon? That's what was going on in Bangalore!"

"Yeah so doing a gig there is a bit tricky. They can't do it behind closed doors for some reason," Nat says. "We were saying we could play and people won't dance!" Iwan throws in. "Yeah, stand there like statues," chuckles Nat.

"But why did they even book this gig then?" I was puzzled "The day we booked it this guy had just kind of done that – in the past-" Gary begins but Nat interjects, "Everyone thought Bangalore was kind of the rock capital of India and everyone really rocks out but fucking hell they did all have to rock out in complete, er, stillness," he giggles.

There's a lengthy discussion of the audience's reaction which was generally very good but they hungered for songs they knew, as it is the norm for Indian rock bands to do a high percentage of covers.

Jack has been absent from the interview up to this point but now he clambers up the metal stairs onto the roof terrace and sits on the floor. The band discuss the food, claiming they all went vegetarian to be on the safe side, though, they also thought they were being too cautious.

"You can be too paranoid – that's what I realised at the end of it," Gary muses. "Mind you, that last hotel, get this right, we landed and wanted a hot shower and I phoned down to reception and said we've got no hot water and the guy's like I'll send you up a bucket of hot water – ok, so – then we got up the next day to leave and thought like cold shower will do – no fucking running water whatsoever!"

With temperatures of forty six degrees this was obviously unpleasant. Luckily, there was air-conditioning in some venues. The other problem was the side-effects of the malaria pills they had to take before, during and after the trip.

"They make you have the fucking wildest dreams, man!" Gary reveals. "Really do and the thing with the dreams is they're not far-fetched dreams – they're dead sort of mundane. It's almost like you haven't been to bed. You know you've been to bed because you've just opened your eyes and you're in your bed," he giggles while everyone else seems to fall into a trance. "D'you know what I mean? But other than that you would not know because it's like… that's right, isn't it?" Gary sounds like he's starting to worry that only he is suffering the strange dreams.

"Yeah, yeah," agrees Nat vaguely.

"You dream about things that are so plausible and mundane it's like being alive… being awake rather!" Gary carries on. "No, I don't get them," Iwan states matter-of-factly.

"Every night I get them – I keep waking up feeling depressed or whatever because something's happened – then I realise no, that was a dream," Gary explains.

"Do you take them in the evening though or the morning?" enquires Jack. "I just take them whenever I remember – not remembered for a couple of days," Gary admits.

"Try taking them in the morning," suggests Jack helpfully, "if I take 'em at something like half ten at night then I get really bad dreams."

"Oh right. Horrible, isn't it?" Gary says seeming relieved that he's not totally alone with these horrors. "Things coming towards me in the room and stuff," Jack shudders. He's also concerned that the sinister pills can cause hair loss and Iwan adds that they can also cause blindness.

We talk for about another twenty minutes about the trip, about a character they met who looked like Freddie Mercury, about the fashion, the clubs and the massive void between the rich and poor.

Danny comes down from his flat which is on the floor above Gary and Iwan's, thrusting CD's into everyone's hands. Nico, who also lives in the abode turns up and we wind up the interview. It's a sunny evening and we all troop down the metal staircase and go for some drinks.

City of Angels

Another overseas trip was on the horizon for the month after.

All For A Reason was belatedly due for release in America. Gary and Nat were assigned the task of going over there and investigating the set up as they were hearing conflicting stories from Joe via their American Manager, Jay. Emails were floating about that didn't make a great deal of sense and it seemed a good idea to actually go over there and talk to the people involved in the release.

Between the Senses was their only American release at this time. "Virgin didn't exist in America anymore," Gary explained, "so we were kind of homeless in terms of a label."

"We went as a pair of detectives to suss out what the fuck was going on because everything that we heard smelt of bullshit," Nat says, "as well as having some quality time together."

The pair joked about the idea of spending "quality time" together, but that genuinely was part of the plan. It seemed to really benefit them, as on return from L.A, I found them much more fired up and focused than just after the India trip, though maybe the malaria pills were partly to blame! They now seemed keen to get on with things as well as developing an increased awareness of what they valued and why they were even making music in the first place. There had obviously been a lot of discussion and decision during the trip.

"You know me and him – we've always been close and we always will be but from time to time you sort of shift a little bit, don't you?" Gary remarked. "It was nice just spending time together. So we were on this plane, I don't know how long the journey should've taken but we were delayed. We left the hanger at New York and we sat on the run way for four hours – we were really starting to get wound up so by time we arrived in LA we'd been up for twenty-four hours and the guy we were staying with pulled out this bag of crystal meth, right?"

"And we were up for another forty-eight hours!" guffaws Nat.

The boys made no secret of the illegal substances involved in this trip. For some reason, they seemed to downplay the use of drugs when we talked about the previous American journey, yet I can't imagine this trip was any more debauched than the first one. Or maybe it was…

"It all got fucking weird," Gary admits. "It was great hooking up with friends because a really good friend of ours – a guy called Rick came to the airport and it was weird because Jay who we were staying with had not had any contact with Rick for maybe two years and we'd not seen Jay for maybe five or six and we saw Rick maybe three years ago so it was great because the four of us always partied together when we were out there – we just fell back into it."

The pair had every chance to get cosily re-connected with each other as their sleeping arrangements, obviously to keep the budget low, meant they had to share a bed. They joked about enjoying cuddling up to each other but in reality they must have both ended up sleep-deprived as if one rolled over the other got woken up.

"Fourteen days in the same fucking bed and it ended up – sometimes you just feel a bit rough and want to get your head down – so it was like you go out tonight and we kind of took it in shifts," Nat explained.

"Nah, you loved it," Gary joked. "He's phoned me up every night since we got home!"

Overall, I'm sure it a good experience for Gary and Nat to have time away together with a useful purpose attached to it like this but I couldn't help thinking Iwan and Jack must feel a bit left out. I asked them if it felt strange without them.

"Not really because we weren't there to play any gigs" Gary replied. "We were there to talk really and we've kind of resigned ourselves to the fact that nine times out of ten – if it's a business meeting with a record company involving all of us then four of us would go, but nine times out of ten if it's an interview they want to speak to the singer and the guitar player – it's just one of those things…"

"I think when me and him first heard about it maybe for a split second we would have thought 'oh shit, what's Jack and Iwan going to think about us going to America and they're not'," Nat continued, "but that's followed immediately by -"

"As soon as we were on the plane it was 'fuck them!'" Gary says with a mock sneer. "Nah, they understood the situation and to be honest, when there's four people talking – it's the reason Joe didn't go as well to be fair. The agenda was to go and meet Guggan. For me and Nat to go and speak to Guggan and get him fired up about us. We're talking about him getting fired up about our band and you can only do that by keeping things concise, it's like how we're talking now, you can't talk to four people and get anything decent out of it. You can't do it. Because apart from the obvious contradictions that are bound to occur – talking over each other – it happens."

So, what did Gary and Nat get up to in Los Angeles?

They mentioned that the Los Angeles they touched down in was not the same city they remembered from the last time they were there.

Perhaps, the city itself was much the same but the circles they had moved in last time had shrunk dramatically. People's mind-sets seemed to have become strangely conservative.

"The whole time you're there, in the back of your mind you're saying to yourself 'This is LA, everything's just too fucking' – you know how, like, someone has a glass of wine every night before they go to bed? In Los Angeles that means you've got a drink problem," Gary explains. "They love building this shit up. Which is ironic given that they've spawned the most supposedly rock n roll bands in terms of booze and drug consumption and excess that there's been. The whole fucking city seems obsessed with AA meetings and Narcotics Anonymous meetings, y'know? It's weird."

"Our circle of friends have diminished," Nat comments. "They don't want to know us!" "Well, not us" Gary clarifies, "the people we're staying with."

"The people that we associate ourselves with," Nat corrects himself "because the second you go to an AA meeting or a narcotics meeting they say stop hanging out with people like us!"

"It's weird really – because we arrived, and I would've been devastated if Rick hadn't have been at the airport because he came to stay with us when we did the *Move Festival* and then we did *T in the Park* and *Witness Festival* all in one weekend. He came along for the ride and we had a great time and so I was really pleased to see him," Gary explains. Rick is in a band called The Tender Box who I remember stopping by at the Blue Cat once when they visited Manchester. "I was gonna say, we do have a lot of friends in LA – well we did have a lot of friends," Gary stresses, "but for one reason or another all of them, bar Jay and Rick, seem to have cleaned up their act. I mean not to say that you or I have got a problem," he addresses Nat, who agrees, pointing out that he and Gary had toned down their drinking a bit over the years, but only in the way most people do as they grow up and realise they're not immortal.

"It's one extreme or the other in LA," Gary states.

"I don't drink, I don't do this, I don't do that," Nat sighs.

"Our circle was like, massive – because Jay is nuts, right and Jay has always been nuts there's no change there. Rick's always been Rick but we've always like – you can't rely on Jay to take you out because we'd be like "we're leaving in five minutes!" and he'd be pulling his hard drive apart or something – fucking weirdo – and then an hour later you're still waiting. So we've learnt over the years – you don't rely on Jay to take you out!" laughs Gary. Jay was their American manager "in the loosest sense," Gary clarifies, "more like, our American drug dealer.

In terms of weird experiences – I had a few. It's fourth of July right? And bearing in mind, when we arrived there Jay who's told us "we're going to fucking party our asses off when you get here" So I'm thinking 'Great! there's gonna be loads of beer and a bit of charlie' and then when we arrived there, he's got that vial of crystal meth."

"Yeah, and that was it!" Nat laughs.

"Yeah, anyway, fourth of July comes and I'm sick – I'm sick of sitting up for forty-eight hours on this horrible speed that everyone seems to be sniffing out there," Gary continues, "there's this Mexican kid that we met, this guy called Haviez who was a friend of a friend who also kind of jammed with us when we were there. He's got the weirdest voice – I was gonna try and do it but I'm not going to." Nat and myself demand that he impersonates Haviez. "You know *Wallace and Gromit*? You know the big cheesy grin?" Gary paints the picture and Nat and I have already collapsed in hysterics before he's even begun. "'OK. You wanna get some cocaine? – it' cool'" Gary develops a strange chirpy Mexican accent to imitate Haviez, "I'll take you to the studio get some cocaine. It's cool, man!' That's what he sounds like! And he's doing this Wallace and Gromit thing in between. So, I'm like 'Great!' Bearing in mind, we're now touching on three o clock in the afternoon. I've been trying to get Jay out of the house since midday so three hours later he's still fucking demolishing and re-building his hard drive. So, Haviez says he'll take me to this guy and – we'll hang out. So he took me to the studio and you've got this guy, he's about five foot nothing. He looks like Steve-O from *Jackass* and happens to be a drummer and also happens to be Marilyn Manson's drug dealer. Now we walk into his room, out of this blazing LA sunshine straight into this pitch black fucking recording studio, right? And this guy is bouncing around the room right, really high and going on about this fight he's just had in this place called *Popeye's* which is like, I think, a pizza / and beer joint and this guy has got a real Napoleon complex and says these two black beards – these are his words – had been bullying him so he ordered them out in the alley way and has this brawl with them and to add insult to injury he gets back to his house to his pregnant girlfriend who starts screaming at him "where've you been?" so he gives her the big like "fuck you" and goes to the studio. He's there with some real dweeby EMO type guy and this is the best bit right? There's this stripper, who goes by the name of Cindy who's very fond of being spat on, right? Due to the fact that she's got spit on her belt that she's wearing – it's the only way I can describe it so every time she keeps standing up and bending over, he keeps spitting on her! I'm going to Haviez "get me the fuck out of here!" you know? I didn't even want this coke anymore I just wanted to go home!

And he says to this Cindy after spitting on her "Give us those scissors" and she gets this set of scissors out of her bag which he goes and throws across the other side of the room. She stands up and calls him a bitch and goes and collects them and I shit you not, right? Stands in front of me, pulls the scissors out and gives herself four – scars – what d'you call it – cuts herself four times about four inches long – very neat – real attention to detail I must add! And then says "Where's the tequila salt when you need it?!By this point I'm freaking out – and the rest is history…"

Things degenerated further with Cindy ordering Gary to call her various expletive-laden names resulting in Gary feeling very embarrassed. Marilyn Manson's dealer insists he must, so fearing for his life, Gary does what he's told and the cocaine deal finally gets done. "I get the fuck out of there and never go back! It was so weird, and then back out in the blazing sunshine. It was like a scene from I don't know what film!" he shudders at the memory.

While Gary was stuck in this sado-masochistic Hunter S Thomposn style scenario, Nat's memories of Independence day are more pleasant: "Jay said I'll drive you up to Mulholland Drive and it's a really famous little spot where you can see the whole of LA and you can see downtown Beverley Hills and you can see the coast," he enthuses. "There's fire-works going off everywhere because it's the fourth of July. We were sat there – we were really high – it was fucking brilliant. That was the best moment of the whole fucking thing."

"You can see right into the Hollywood Bowl," Gary explains, "that's what people do, if they haven't got tickets – like, to see the Stones in Hollywood Bowl – go up to Mulholland and see it all."

"It was like sitting at Alderley Edge looking over Manchester – which is not quite as good but still…" Nat laughs. We all pause and muse over what's just been said and I wonder if Gary might have embellished his story a little – though there's also the chance he played it down in order not to shock me. "Was that all real, what you just said?" I find myself asking. "Yeah, I promise you it all happened," Gary says sincerely, "This Haviez guy is great though. We wrote a song with him. He was great because we were, maybe, a bit bummed out – we hooked up with Haviez for maybe the last five days we were there – there was all this arguing by emails going on across the Atlantic – transatlantic rowing."

"And it was all to do with us but we weren't involved in the arguments," adds Nat.

"Yeah it was grinding us down and we were watching this guy – Jay – and it's got to be said, he was a shadow of the guy we knew and it was really upsetting in a way to see him get so bogged down," Gary continues, "his whole life seems to be about proving points now, which is a shame because the guy has – he's got problems but I still love him to death and I'd always be there for him but Haviez was like this ray of Mexican sunshine, you know what I mean? I met him actually – you were in bed that night," he nods to Nat, "I went to this club with Rick and he was this weird kid – looks like a club kid but he's into electronic music and he's got his own band – pretty cool, actually, I'm pissed and all that and I say 'you should come round, man, and we'll jam' because he also knows Jay and then two days later Haviez comes round very sheepishly with a bass guitar and sticks it in the corner like you're not meant to see it – but you are!" Gary grins while Nat cracks up with laughter again, "but he's not going to mention it's there unless you say-" "What's that?!" giggles Nat. "Yeah and anyway to cut a long story short" Gary says, "the bass comes out and (in funny mexican accent) "Yeah, man, it's my bass guitar, man!" and we start and then he comes along with an organ you know? He's a real cool kid!"

"Yeah, to be honest I was going out there to get ourselves playing together and get the creative thing sparked up again," Nat comments, "and Haviez or whatever he was called, was acutally driving us a long – keeping us going. We're actually in debt to him."

"He took us to various places a few times – he was cool because, not that we ever really wanna be around normal people," Gary states, "and he was definitely not normal, but he had one foot in normality which is quite good when you live in LA… as opposed to Jay, who was fucking out to lunch, man!"

I asked them if they unearthed what they needed to regarding the release of *All For A Reason.*

"Basically, the long and short of it was," Gary explains, "everything we were involved in with this label, this independent who's got distribution through Fontana which is then through Universal – his company, his label, obviously with our say so, approached Virgin, UK and got all of our videos and the right to release *All for a Reason* and everything that goes along with it. And until we went to LA it was all going through Jay. And Jay as we found out when we got there, is not really up to it because – well, he's got a lot of shit he's got to work through before I could trust him as a part of our team. So, it was important for us to get out there to assess what was really going on and get face to face with Guggan who was the guy who set up that India trip we went on. The guy – he's a young guy but he's got a lot of good stuff on his label – he's gonna be releasing the whole Ride back catalogue. The guy is hungry. He's a little bit naive but I think that comes from – his pedigree relates to Indian records – Indian music business – whatever you want to call it but he has released records before in America and it was interesting because this guy never met us – never spoken to us so it was good to kind of establish that really – establish an independent line of contact between us and him and unfortunately bypass Jay. Sometimes you've got to, you have to be that way and at the end of the day, it's our music, it's our lives, it's our thing and I don't believe you can rely on someone like Jay at the moment in his present state which is a shame, but what can you do?"

Gary's comments here demonstrate the general change I was detecting from the band around this time. They seemed to have developed a more daring drive to take things back into their own hands, not to rely on figureheads, on people from the past, even on their own reputation from the past but as the conversation went on I could see that they had all done a lot of soul searching and thankfully, they had re-evaluated their position and attitude in what I considered positive terms.

Aside from investigating the business of their album release, the partying, seeing some bands, they also wrote some music. My understanding is that though they clearly wanted to re-kindle their connection on a personal level, that naturally spilled over into the creative sphere and they spent some time trying out new musical ideas. I got the impression 2006 had been quite a fallow time for them in terms of song-writing, despite the positive results of the time spent with Jim Spencer at Clear, the tail-end of the year before. "We haven't written a good song since Christmas," Gary commented when he and Nat came round to discuss the L.A trip with me that August evening. Whether going to L.A revived their creative spark is unclear, but it did seem to allow them a new state of mind which is just as important.

They mentioned that they'd had an offer from a independent label in Bristol and though they were considering it, they weren't overly enamoured with the label's current rosta.

"Our idea is we wanna put a single out. In an ideal world we'll pop it in the Top 40, that's the best case scenario," Gary suggests. "Worst case scenario, we raise our profile again and we kind of exist officially again. Then we're gonna spend between now and the single release which obviously as yet is not finalised/talked about or even set in stone. Between the four of us, decide, right this is the ten to twelve songs whatever that will make the album up so the plan is get a single out by which time we've got our shit together completely. We know what the album is, what the songs are, they're done to the best of our ability," he pauses, "done to the best of our ability – that sounds like complete shit …" he considers what he's just said.

"The world will get super-excited about them," Nat throws in optimistically.

"Get it cast, finished, arranged songs because at the moment, none of us can agree – I don't think any of us believe we've got our album yet. We've got a lot of songs – we've got a ridiculous amount of songs and none of us, hand on heart can say these ten songs or these twelve songs genuinely make the album. Sounds dead simple, doesn't it?" he giggles.

It does and in a way it is, or was… but "Yeah, it's kind of been the plan for a while, hasn't it?" Nat says. "Well, not really no," Gary tells him. "Ok, maybe not," Nat re-thinks, "because we thought we'd write the seven songs and this is going to get us a record deal and we had a bit of a reality check the other day. We had seven songs and a lot of them are over four and a half minutes long," Gary continues "But that's not to say we're gonna start going 'right, we're gonna write a three minute pop song' but we're gonna get back to what it should be about – which is, forget about getting a deal, forgetting about what our manager's doing. Getting the four of us together and making great music."

"It felt wrong for a long time," Nat admits.

"We had all these songs and Joe was saying 'You need more songs, you need more songs!'. And we were associating the band with money, right? Which straight away is… because we're all skint – there's no secret in that, we're all looking at the band being the way out of this financial problem we're in. Whereas, in actual fact, that should be the last thing on your mind. It happened last time, the minute we relaxed, well, not relaxed but thought "fuck the money"… we've been skint before, we can handle it. We put our heads down and we came up with some of the best songs we've ever written you know?" Gary declares with passionate conviction. "I certainly believe that will be the case this time, you know? Well, we are, no doubt about it, gonna have to get some sort of part time job, you know? Jack's already done that. I've been thinking about it for some time as has Nat, as has Iwan. But that is by no means a kind of waving the white flag defeatist stance. What it means is, we're gonna take the money out of the equation."

"Take the financial strain away from Haven," Nat agrees.

"Because also, we've been very lucky. We've had the last four years having as much money as we wanted, we had a lot of money," Gary states and Nat agrees.

"And alright we've got nothing to show for it – a lot of equipment I guess," Gary considers. "My leather jacket's pretty cool," Nat grins and we all laugh.

"But that's the problem – it's get back to basics – a real wake- up call," Gary insists, "and the power thing and it's easy to pretend that everything is great and it isn't- I'm too proud for my own good, that's my worst trait – I dunno …" he trails off.

"So what are you living on now?" I venture to ask.

"Brass buttons," Gary replies immediately and Nat giggles.

"Doesn't anything filter through from royalties?" I ask.

"Little bits – all that's by the by," Gary says, "obviously there's Her Majesty's Unemployment Benefit," he grins devilishly. "But it doesn't matter. It really doesn't matter because I'm kind of – I feel like I'm turning the corner now because the money thing is not-"

"It's more the realisation that we had," Nat speaks up. "Or Gary had or I don't know when it happened – what Gary's just said there it's kind of – it takes the heat off – it's gonna take time…"

"In three months time if we haven't got a record deal does that mean the band's finished?" Gary asks "And the only reason that anyone would be saying that is because there's a lack of money – so let's fucking take that out of the picture. At the end of the day – if the only reason you're in a band is to make money you're not gonna want to be in a band anymore."

"We were never in it for that," Nat says "And it so nearly became that because we'd been broke so long – it was like the only way we can resolve this is…"

"Iggy Pop to this day still lives in a two-bedroomed house in Malibu – a two-bedroomed wooden house in Malibu – this guy, I don't know how old he is but has only just now started earning proper money where he could buy a mansion," Gary comments, "but he has spend his whole life in debt to the record company, selling all his equipment so he could go and buy some drugs. I'm not comparing us to Iggy and the Stooges but I'm saying you've got to suffer for your art!"

Incidentally, this conversation happened before Iggy Pop strayed into the murky world of advertising insurance.

"I'm only joking," Gary smirks, "for the record" when Nat looks a little unconvinced as to whether you do have to suffer for your art or not.

"So how are you going to keep your profile alive?" I ask them. "Put a single out," Nat replies simply. "We haven't got one – so it doesn't matter…" Gary says.

"It does – don't you think?" I ponder in confusion. "No, it doesn't right? Cos we've been away for so long it really doesn't matter," Gary argues. "When we release the single that will – hopefully if the record company is worth its salt that will fall into place but it's gone beyond the time factor – it's gone beyond the time of being important. It's been over two years since we released a record so it really is not an issue. The only other issue is the financial issue which hopefully now we've resolved ourselves – the only issue now is making great fucking music."

"And enjoying it!" Nat emphasises.

"Exactly! And we will. We will. We're not waking up every morning freaking out about rent, freaking out about debts bills,"
Gary agrees.

"If you're not enjoying the music," Nat says philosophically "How can we expect people to dig it, if we're not?"

"Yeah, the gigs are always great," Gary says thankfully.

"Yeah, that's one thing that you touched on there," Nat says. "We can't expect to do the odd gig here and there and for it to be sold out and so far, touch wood, it has been. Fucking credit to those people that have been showing up."

"That's also keeping the thing alive," Gary says, "and the internet thing."

"It's really heart-warming, you know," Nat comments. "We've done fuck all for so long and we go to the Garage in London or the Academy in town and there's a roomful of people and I want to go give them all a kiss you know? But I know they're all there to see something that is really fucking good, at the same time."

"The plan hasn't changed. Everything is still moving as it was, except for the fact that we feel – like we've got to do the job properly," Gary says decisively. "We've got to be able to say to Joe "THIS is an album, these are the twelve songs here – there are x number of potential singles on it – not that we're going to be writing singles for all of it but he needs that to do his job. We can't be giving him these five minute tracks and expecting some guy who's looking for the next Franz Ferdinand to sit and listen to it. Obviously our name matters – we can sell records in Japan – we can sell out gigs in England. We've got a record coming out in America. I mean we do matter on however small a scale, it does exist, it is real. It's not being talked up. We've got to kind of be a bit business like about it. We'll always write the songs that we write but there are certain parameters that we've got to bear in mind. We've got plenty of like weird, arty five minute songs but what we need now is the killer punch. We've got that in the form of *No one cut so deep* and *Velvet Skyline* but I think these days – sorry I know I'm going on – but when we got signed initially it was on the back of *Say Something*. Back then, record companies were signing bands on what was basically a promise – a promise of what's to come – *Say Something* – classic three and a half minute pop song – classic! We got a record deal on the strength of that song alone – not on the strength of *Let it Live,* not on the strength of *Beautiful Thing* – on the strength of that song and that we might write another one. We're in a position now where we've had a couple of records out – been in the studio – everyone is aware of us. We've got a fan-base, however small. But we now need to show these people that are only interested in figures and columns and numbers, that we can still do it – that we can still cut it. *Velvet Skyline* has got single screaming out of the top of its voice but it is over four and a half minutes long so we're going into mix that and turn that into what that should be. Equally *No One Cut So Deep* comes in at four mins sixteen seconds, which equally needs to be taken down and the thing is this is the realisation that we're coming to naturally, not because anyone's said "That's too long, that's too long!" We know the game. And the irony is we're still writing like a band who's got a record deal, d'you see what I mean?"

"Yes, which is a good thing," I conclude.

"Which is a good thing, it is and we'll always do that," Gary says, "but we've got to be realistic and we've got to go now OK – this is an industry – you can be creative on six or eight of the tracks on the album but four of them you've got to grab someone by the throat and go…" he makes a crunching, strangling sound. "Know what I mean?"

I couldn't believe how much sense Gary was talking that night. Not to suggest that he doesn't regularly talk sense because he does, but this was all so logical, so simple, but comprising on none of the important matters. It seemed that if they stuck with this mind-set they couldn't fail. And the important nugget of truth that seemed to have been grasped was that, whatever happened, it wasn't about failing. It was about being true to themselves as artists without shooting themselves in the foot.

To me, it made perfect sense to focus on the music not as a passport to a decent pay-cheque but as a pleasurable, creatively satisfying experience. My only concern was the quality of part-time jobs that might be available to them and how soul-destroying they might potentially be, but I didn't want to dampen the positivity by going down that road that night. The conviction and direction that were being demonstrated impressed me. We chatted some more, drank some more wine and it felt like things, finally, were ready to fall into place.

Round and round the block...

It was that time of year again, when, with breath-taking beauty, the crimson, gold and dirty yellow leaves cruise from the trees to carpet the pavements of Heaton Moor. Despite the constructive conversations that had happened during the summer, the autumn seemed to herald another lengthy lull. Sometimes lulls are necessary though, as we can't charge through life all guns blazing, day in and day out.

Perhaps the lull just signalled the band had their heads down, working on perfecting the album.

I have a memory of Gary turning up one evening with his arm in a sling and his hand in plaster around this time. He was cagey about what had happened and just said the accident occurred "in a drunken stupor". I thought it best not to interfere but I felt uneasy. Eerily, the same accident befell Nathan a few years later, though, in typical Nat style, his misadventure occurred when playing on a bouncy castle.

During that autumn, Jack was working extensively with the newly reformed Marion. This is unsurprising in many ways, considering his enduring friendship with Phil Cunningham, an original member of the band. Marion are a band with an especially loyal and passionate fan-base and Manchester generally rejoiced at the news that the band had re-grouped. For Jack, it was fun to be working with Phil again and exciting to be involved in the dramatic return of the enigmatic Jamie Harding. There were four gigs between September and December but nothing clashed with Jack's Haven schedule.

So this was a welcome release for Jack, a chance to get back in the groove and enjoy being part of it. He also felt that playing in the two bands improved his technique: "Doing the Marion thing has really made me work harder as a drummer but also do new stuff. It's healthy going out doing new stuff, it's good for me."

When I asked him if he found it easy to switch between the two bands he replied "Yeah I do, but since I've been doing the Marion thing and now I've got back to Haven I notice I've been playing a little bit different with Haven, but in a good way. They've all said that as well, that I'm a better drummer since I've been doing the Marion thing."

I'm not sure, at this point, if there were any discussions about the long-term implications of being in two bands. By all accounts, Jack was still a full and committed member of Haven.

As the leaves withered and November arrived, the lull was broken and a bustle of activity occurred in the Haven diary. The band played another London date in late November at Madame Jo Jo's in London's Soho and had another date booked at the Academy for December, as well as two Christmas gigs at the Blue Cat. It's difficult to discover what was happening with the tracks. Even Iwan himself admits that he's unclear if there was any interest expressed in them to Joe.

"I'm not sure if Joe showed it to anyone or anything," he confesses. "I'm not sure if he got a good response from it. I think it was more to do with the fact that we'd released something, we'd been dropped and then started off again – it was just the wrong time to do that really – but I still don't know who he showed it to – but – at any rate nothing kind of happened."

To me, the stand out track from the new songs was *All I Ever Knew* which I thought was the most instantly catchy and the possible come-back single they needed.

"Mickey used that quite a lot for his surfing videos," Iwan mentions. "Yeah, that got mixed and *Velvet Skyline* got mixed and they're the only two. We had to start paying for that ourselves. It started to be awkward because obviously Jim's really good but he needed a certain amount of payment."

Naturally, Jim did need payment and at this point it seems finances were an issue, unfortunately. However, there is also a suggestion that the songs were still not ready, still not what was needed to convince the right label to come on board.

When I asked Joe about the situation he said "There was no third album because there were no songs that were good enough for release." I tried to encourage him to elaborate, to try to clarify what the problem was from his perspective. He commented that "Some of the songs were OK, but not good enough to form a future."

Jim Spencer himself believed the tracks had potential: "As I recall, the tunes were really good," he told me. "The intention was to demo them up, but I can't really recall too much about the session to be honest. I do remember a couple of the tunes, like *Velvet Skyline* for example were potential classics."

When I asked him why he thinks a release didn't come about quickly he said "It's always really difficult for a band to sign with a new label after being dropped. There is a stigma attached to it that in Haven's case was really quite unfair, as it wasn't their fault what happened with Radiate.

I recently listened to some of the demos we did. The tracks were good, but I don't think they were ready to mix and release."

Although I agree there were stigma issues and timing issues in terms of how the industry was changing and being less willing to take risks, I also feel that the outlook was not all bleak, by any means. With the right attitude and right guidance, a plan could surely be hatched and carried out, even if that meant putting the album out themselves and functioning on a grass-roots level.

I often found the band to either be on a high or a low rather than somewhere in between, but at the end of the day, they weren't business men and thankfully don't aspire to be. That was never what it was all about. They were spontaneous, creative people who seemed to be having their minds clouded with too many opinions, other people's doubts and agendas that perhaps weren't helpful. It all seemed to lead to an overall inertia, punctuated by sudden bursts of enthusiasm and activity.

That year, Iwan certainly seemed to have come to the conclusion that they needed to reclaim their own power. "It's awkward but you've just got to get on with it really," he said "The new songs, a lot of them have got more angst. There's a certain ballsiness to it now. We just kind of think we'll write what we want and just get on with it. You realise when you go to London and can sell out the Garage and you look on the website and see all these comments about the albums. You can't think "oh, just pack it all in" – we'll always be a unit, whatever happens success wise – you don't know, if we'd have got really successful there may have been other problems. So, as long as you're happy together then – that's the main thing really.

The next record company we get, we'll do things differently. I think a lot of the time, like any new band, particularly from our point of view, we come up to Manchester from Cornwall and we don't know how the record industry works. We just think our record's being put in shops and having interviews set up and videos and stuff like that. We'll try not to spend like sixty grand on a video!" he laughs. "When you've got an advance you don't know what's coming in and out – we didn't know – we didn't have a clue. They don't tell you – they just go "it's alright, it's alright." At the end of the day, this time around we've learned so much. It's not just that side of things it's being around Johnny and Joe – you just pick up on it. You've got to be the boss. Especially today, bands might not even need record companies soon. Things have changed so much now, everyone can do stuff off the net – you don't necessarily need someone saying "oh you've got to do this, you've got to do that". It's just a learning curve, you know, all the new people you meet – people who you trust – like, we should've been called the Trust Band or something cos we trusted everyone!"

"So are you more wary now?" I ask him.

"Yeah, we suss people out a bit more now," Iwan says wisely. "You're the band, you're the product – that's what you have to realise – so you should call the shots, really. Because none of these guys can write the songs – they're all failed this and that – failed photographers – failed everything and they just got a lucky break in a record company."

Iwan made perfect sense with this approach and I had my fingers crossed that they could somehow by-pass all nay-sayers and cut out their path again.

I seem to have complete amnesia about the Academy gig but long-time Haven fan, Paul Hames handily wrote a review of that night. He reports that a new song *To The Bone* was aired for the first time at this gig. "It Turned out to be an awesome track, proving Haven's hunger to continue improving and writing beautiful, soulful tracks," Paul reveals. "There was an unexpected intermission as Gary was approached by some bloke at the bottom of the stage. Gary revealed that the bloke was trying to give him some money – it was hard to see whether the Haven front-man obliged." At this same gig, Paul observed that "Gary was approached by a Japanese couple who handed him a gift of poetry about Haven which they had made themselves." It's a testament to the band's enduring popularity in Japan that this kind of devotion continued, despite the lack of a new release or even a trip to Japan since the end of their Radiate contract.

To The Bone is a flinchingly, acute acoustic number, drenched with dread, which feels to be about recoil and walking away from a destructive situation. I wondered how many more equally powerful songs had been crafted. I seem to recall Jack telling me there were at least twenty….somewhere….

In keeping with tradition, the band played two sold out Christmas dates at the Blue Cat. David Moss and Roger Saville attended, capturing some of the set on film. As always, these gigs were warm, fuzzy and feel good occasions.

Nat tells an amusing story following possibly this gig, or certainly one of these gigs which for many people, myself included, are hard to differentiate in hindsight:

"I remember after the gig, there was one Japanese guy and two girls and I was pissed and invited them back to my house. I shouldn't have done it…but I did!" he clasps his head, shuddering and laughing at the memory at the same time. "I invited them back to my house and that's the only thing I did wrong!" Bear in mind, at his point, Nat lived very close to the Blue Cat Cafe, on Peel Moat road and so it was a stone's throw away to walk the fans back there. "The girl was nervous because she was sat in my house," Nat continues, "I had this bottle of Jack Daniels and put it on the table and she was going glug, glug, glug and I was like "Fucking hell!" and just having a couple of shots. She was doubling what I was drinking and I can handle it way better than she could. Anyway, she toddled off to the spare room then I went to bed and got woken up in the middle of the night by the Japanese guy going "Ahh! Vomito! Vomito!" I was like, what does vomito mean? And then discovered she'd been spraying sick all over the spare room, so there I was trying to suck it all up with a hoover!!"

Nothing changes on New Year's Day...

I met with Jack, one chilly January evening 2007, in what was then the Bakery Bar, at the epicentre of Heaton Moor. As the tape rolled and we talked, it became clear that Jack was in the midst of, if not an annus horriblis, then at least a month of misery. Jack had been saying that the band had stressed to each other, and Joe, that something had to happen this year. This *had* to be the year. It simply couldn't drag on like it was. I agreed that something had to give.

"I've had a shocking new year. Really bad," Jack revealed. "I think I told you I was seeing a girl for a few months and then on New Year's Day she phoned me and said it's over. Totally out of the blue! She's only young, she's twenty – so she's saying things like she doesn't want anything serious. So, I've had that to deal with. And then Che, from Marion falling down the stairs and breaking his neck."

Che Hargreaves, the bass player in the band had the misfortune of falling downstairs and breaking the vertebrae in his neck. Thankfully, he is now fully recovered but this must have been a shock for Jack at the time. Jamie Harding had also done a disappearing act. "We can't get hold of Jamie. No one's heard from him for about a month," Jack said worriedly. "No one can get hold of him. His phone is off. His girlfriend's phone is off."

Thankfully, Jamie did re-surface but at that moment, Jack had no clue where or how he was.

To add insult to injury, another strange episode occurred when Jack went out with a friend of his called Seb. "We went to St Thomas's Chop House – six o clock in the evening this was – straight from work," Jack tells me "This guy just walked past and lamped Seb for no reason! Nearly knocked him out… spent three hours in Bootle Street Police Station. I think it's been one of the worst months on record. It's weird how it all comes at once!"

Despite his recent difficulties there was nothing self-pitying in the way Jack described recent events, though I think he feared some other horror may be looming around the corner. He mentioned that there had been a ray of light relief in the shape of an envelope that turned up on his door-step. At first glance, it being an official Department of Work and Pensions envelope he was apprehensive but thankfully it turned out to be a much needed tax rebate.

At this point, Jack was working in Urban Outfitters, a fashionable clothing shop in central Manchester for four days a week. Working as something other than a musician is something none of the band were keen to do but as weeks turned into months and at this stage, years, and there was still no album deal glimmering on the horizon, getting a 'proper' job with a reliable pay-cheque or struggling to survive on jobseekers allowance was a serious choice that had to be made.

Each of the band seemed to wince at the thought of a non-musical career and it seemed wrong to have to take on any other role. Jack had given it some thought:

"I used to want to be a hairdresser – I even spoke to the guy who cuts my hair, Bruce. If it all went tits up music wise, I think I might probably learn a trade. Maybe become a plumber or something. Apparently it's easier to find a brain surgeon in London than a plumber. There's always that – if I don't get to play drums for forever I could always become a plumber!" he grins but you can tell it would be a desperate last resort. "I don't really tend to think about it because it's a horrible thought and I want to play drums. That's the thing with working in a shop – it's easy to forget that you're in a band. I work four days in that shop, working again tomorrow – feels like I'm not in a band. Feel like I'm a sales man in a clothes shop, because at the moment there's nothing happening with Haven or Marion – nothing to look forward to."

I found it really sad to hear Jack mention that occasionally local musicians he knew dropped in to browse and he wanted to hide. He didn't want to be seen in the role of salesperson instead of who he really was. I found it heart-breaking and maddening that somehow the necessary wasn't being done in Haven HQ. Nobody was especially to blame but at the same time, no one seemed to be taking the beast by the horns, and *making* something happen.

"Something needs to happen quickly here," I found myself saying, sensing that if it didn't the band would all fall into dead-end jobs to pay the bills and the energy for making music would diminish along with the dream. The Victorian style street lights flickered ominously on Shaw road as we sat, staring out.

"Yeah, of course it does," Jack agreed, "to be honest we all sat here about six months ago saying something needs to happen with us or we may have to think about what else can we do – because we haven't really thought about what's going to happen if it doesn't happen. It's really horrible thinking about it – but it will come to that point if we don't make a move in the next six months or someone will make a move if you know what I mean? Or something will happen – because it has to – it's either going to happen or it's just gonna fizzle out really and it would be horrible if it did."

I whole-heartedly agreed, suggesting that putting a record out themselves would be preferable to just throwing up their hands in defeat. Jack agreed and said they were starting to talk about this. At the same time, he mentioned there was the possibility of a deal which Joe was waiting to hear back from.

"We've just got to carry on – see what happens this year," he concluded. "Obviously though, we can't go on like this forever. We can't be sat here now in five, six years time having this same conversation. Gary's thirty this year. He's an old bastard, isn't he? You know, we need to be getting something going!"

Jack clearly had no difficulty adapting to the demands of both Haven and Marion. The difficulty for him was sitting around twiddling his thumbs, not that anyone actually was twiddling their thumbs but to those on the outside there was very little visibly happening with Haven. In fact, around this time, the band as a whole became a little less cohesive, not because anyone wanted to abandon ship, or had given up hope, but creative souls need to immerse themselves in something meaningful to keep the spark alive.

For some time, Iwan had been playing bass on and off with The Healers, though now that Marr was heavily involved in Modest Mouse, The Healers had been put on the back-burner. Iwan also had developed a side project called Gilded Lily.

"That's something I seem to do in Cornwall. It's like we all just get together – there's five of us, including Mickey and Matt from McCluskey. That spawned out of a load of stuff that I'd written and then I got Mickey involved in it and that took years really," Iwan explains, "and there was different people involved, I think Hewitt was in it at one point – it was just for enjoyment really and getting friends together. We did a few gigs. We ended up doing a gig a year or something. I remember Mickey saying we should get a tour shirt and list out one gig every year because that's what it's like!" he laughs. "We've only recorded two songs." At various points, Nat and Jack lent a hand in Gilded Lily too, but it remained, at all times, a chance for friends to play music together and have some light relief rather than a project with serious ambitions.

Mickey comments on his involvement and the spirit of Gilded Lily: "Iwan wanted to turn some demos he'd written into songs and I helped him do that. It was a great thing for me to get stuck into, because it was dark music and it involved no commitment from anyone. Most of the work we did was over email, sending ideas back and forth, and then for random gigs, which were epic fun, there was no pressure with the Lily, just a chance to play and get stuck into some spooky music, and I loved it."

It was during this year that Iwan became involved with another local band called The Cardinals.

"Yeah, that kind of came about through Nick (Mallins)," explains Iwan. "With Haven, we weren't that busy really. Nick had four or five gigs – he dropped me a CD – I didn't like it really at first but it sort of grew on me a bit and I did a gig initially to help him out. Then we hung out a bit and I ended up doing those gigs and that was going to be it. But there ended up being more gigs and stuff and it was – just to keep busy really. It ended up we wrote some songs together but I don't think we really thought we were going to be in a band together."

Despite Iwan's intentions of just helping out, before he knew it, he was appearing regularly with The Cardinals and it was hard not to consider him one of the band. However, whilst Haven were still trying to find a way forward there seemed little harm in moonlighting with other bands. Still, however you looked at it, energies were starting to scatter.

Fragments, fractures and fusions

Clearly, as they needed to find jobs to help pay the bills, it made sense as musicians to look at possibilities that still kept their toes dipped in their field. Gary started to build a name for himself as a DJ, doing a regular slot at the Bakery Bar on Sunday evenings as well as occasional parties and events. This was a pleasant recreational activity for him as well as bringing in a little cash.

Nathan became a self-employed guitar tutor and very quickly found that sharing his gift created more demand than he could fulfil. He had a permanent waiting list of aspiring guitarists queuing to learn from him. Iwan and Jack also became music teachers, though both simultaneously worked in retail to help make ends meet.

Around this time, Gary and Nat explored some new musical territory with a side-project called Red Sails. This was a collaborative effort with Joe's son, Ivan Moss and 'Real Dave' from the band *The Real Dolls.*

For Gary, the project was a snatch of liberation, a chance to cast aside his guitar duties for the first time.

"Working with Dave and Ivan is quite refreshing really," he comments. "They don't have songs but they have drum beats and little hints of melody instrumentation-wise, like in chord progression and key-board lines and it's all cobbled together and I went in and started la-la-laing over it and finding my feet with it. It's good. It's nice for me because I kind of got a bit bored with the guitar – had a bit of a creative low if you wanna call it that, and with Red Sails, I was just enjoying singing and not have to think about anything else really – just turning up, sitting down there for a few hours, smoking a few fags and singing some vocal melody ideas."

Nat contributed some guitar to the project. The pair enjoyed working in a different way with Red Sails, in between the song-crafting and rehearsals that continued with Haven, who still met on a regular basis and the intention remained to find a new label.

The Red Sails affair was a little different to Iwan and Jack's participation in The Cardinals and Marion in the sense that it was completely a studio project. Even their 'my space' page which hosted a few tracks had an anonymous and transient feel to it. If you were familiar with Gary's vocals, then obviously you couldn't fail to recognise them, but unless you were clued up, Red Sails was faceless. In keeping with the name, they were a collective of musicians seemingly sailing on a breeze, experimenting, drifting dreamily into unspecified waters. Iwan and Jack, on the other hand, were committed to live gigs with bands that had reasonably high profiles, at least on a local level.

Naturally, though inappropriately, tongues began to wag.

It was Gary, particularly, at this point, who appeared a little uncomfortable with the concept of being involved with more than one band. When speaking about enjoying the sessions with Red Sails he seemed to feel almost guilty about it.

"I feel a sense of betrayal sometimes, I hate that," he told me, "if things aren't going particularly well, you start putting your attention into something else and it sort of looks wrong. I think it looks bad anyway."

I felt he was being too hard on himself, yet I understand why he felt this way. In some ways, he was the Captain of the good ship Haven and perhaps felt responsible for keeping it afloat.

When I discussed group dynamics with Nat, he concurred that "Gary is a driving force. I think without him, we wouldn't have that fierce single-minded sort of thing. He provides that. We were playing – the three of us, minus Jack – minus Gary as well for ages, right in the early days before Gary. When Gary arrived suddenly we had a direction and that's not just to do with his ability to sing. It had a lot to do with his personality."

I asked Nat if he thought Gary was the leader, "Yeah, I do feel like that. I think it's because he's not just the singer but the lyricist. Unless he's behind a decision more than likely it won't carry much weight. If he is, it will. That's more of a reflection of his position more than his character. I thought I was the leader when we started. In the first few years I thought the leader says "let's play music!" and I carried that for a few years," Nat laughs.

"Do you think you might be the musical leader then?" I ask him. "No, I don't think so, but I feel like I've got the same drive as Gary in a certain sense but I'm probably a lot more understanding. I do a lot of standing up for people in this band! A lot for Gary as well, and for all of them but throughout the whole thing me and him are the ones that have shared a hotel room and Jack and Iwan are together so that alone makes it sort of closer," Nat comments. "Gary and Iwan are kind of famously similar enough to get at each other and sometimes they do get at each other – but I feel like I'm the one like, I probably know what a D7th is and the rest of them probably don't so that might give me some kind of musical advantage or whatever, but no, not really, no. I feel like Gary walked into a very tight band, a very self-assured kind of unit but he soon became... kind of became, I won't say the leader, but the guy that was kind of steering it."

The recurring ship analogy has become peculiarly anchored to this band. Perhaps the second album's sleeve was more symbolic of the troubles at sea that loomed ahead than anyone could have foreseen at the time. Around the early part of 2007, Gary did admit that he was finding some people's incessant questioning regarding the future of Haven, or their current state, somewhat irritating. Despite being a big city, Manchester has a tightly knit musical community and when people saw Jack onstage with Marion, or Iwan playing with The Cardinals, some put two and two together and made five.

"Iwan's always been doing other things. Iwan's pretty much a member of The Cardinals now I think," Gary suddenly revealed one evening "Is he?" I spluttered. "I don't know, but that's kind of what he's saying in a roundabout way – that's what he's doing. Not saying he's not committed to our thing but the problem is everyone's panicking at the moment. It's not quite rats jumping the sinking ship yet but there's an element of that. It's coming from outside. That's what really fucking winds me up," Gary continued. "I remember years ago – similar situation – had my old man going, what's happening, Iwans's dad banging everyone's ear and Nat's dad. Everyone was asking and questioning because we'd been in Manchester a year and half and hadn't been on Top Of The Pops yet! It was only when we listened to them people that it bothered us, because we were quite happy and content and we knew what we were working towards. We knew what we had to do and obviously it happened, it worked. And in a way that's the situation we're in now, because you've got – don't get me wrong, they all mean well, but you've got the likes of Danny and naturally friends, girlfriends – we know more people now to question it. So every time you walk down the street someone says "How's the band doing?" and what you going to say? "Oh terrible actually – don't look like we'll get a record deal and everyone's thinking about doing different things!" The point is – if you get left alone you can just get on with it."

I could sympathise. Heaton Moor is the kind of place where everyone knows everybody's business, or worse, everybody *thinks* they do. It can't have been easy for Haven, who, even at the height of their fame never threw their egos around. They are all down to earth, friendly people, so they wouldn't find it easy to just remain completely aloof. When things suddenly weren't going so well, what they possibly needed was a bit of space and respect rather than interrogation.

"It's just the fact there is nothing to say, that's what makes it difficult," Gary sighs. "It doesn't help matters when people like David Sue are writing things like 'ex-haven drummer' Jack Mitchell in Marion reviews and Iwan's on stage with the Cardinals and Johnny Marr and Nat's helping Katie Ware out on guitar… it's never been called into question their commitment." "I know," I say, "just the public perception." "Exactly," Gary says in frustration. "It fucking pisses you off, puts you on the verge of snapping sometimes because people go "oh what's Iwans band called?" I mean what d'you mean Iwan's band, *this* is Iwan's band! It's not anyone's fault – though some people do enjoy it – enjoy the Spanish inquisition. Some people fucking love it – there's people round here that have been waiting for this for a while, you know, petty!"

Jack encountered similar problems when he went out to gigs in Manchester, which it seems he tended to do more than the rest of the band.

"I try to get out as often as I can. I think we need to do that," he told me during this period. "Even now when I go out and people say "What's going on with Haven? Are you still going?" I get that all the time. I did say to the lads they need to go into town a bit more – show our faces. Just get out there. I mean I work in town and go out in town – pain getting home for me but I still do it."

I think Jack is suggesting that they needed to project more of a unified front, a business as usual approach, to dispel the rumours that the band were somehow not a band anymore. But then again, why did they need to prove anything to anyone?

I asked Mickey Smith, who'd obviously been around the band for a long time and shared some of the highs and the lows how he felt about this particular stage in the story.

"I guess it's a difficult thing for anyone to get your heads round fast enough to push forward," Mickey offered, "especially young lads. They lived the opportunities they had to the full though, you could never say they did it by halves! I guess you could think maybe they were naive in some of the decision making at the time, but when you're not in that position yourself, at that point in time, until you know what's goin' on, who's to say or judge? You listen to peoples advice instead of your instincts for a second, and before you know it you don't know where you are I s'pose. For me, the stuff they wrote for the third album was some of their best musically, I loved it."

It's impossible to say, whether things would have been any different if the guys had run away to a remote shack in the highlands, switched off all their phones and somehow finished the tracks minus opinions of approval or disapproval from anyone other than their own.

If the band were having a lot of questions thrown at them, then I imagine that Joe Moss must have had a lot of people looking to him for answers.

I asked Joe how open the band were to his advice and he said that sometimes they could be "too open".

"Do you mean by that they were perhaps a little too easily influenced by the opinions of others?" I asked. "Sometimes they could be," Joe replied.

My feeling is that none of the band would disagree with this and there is a sense that it was becoming more and more difficult to be objective, about the tracks, about the direction they should take, almost about who they were in terms of a musical identity. I'm not saying anyone had lost the plot or was to blame but when you unravel the various strands of this story, part of the problem seems to come back to an uncertainty about who to listen to.

It feels as though their collective confidence was becoming undermined by the day-to-day cloudiness of the situation

This was entirely natural, though by no means inevitable. The longer the limbo lasted the less clear the lens became.

I saw the band around fairly regularly at this point and though we always kept our chins up, I knew it must be really hard. Did it have to be this way?

Jack admits to feeling really fed up around this time, largely due to the lack of activity but also because he wasn't keen on the day job.

"I went to play with another band – a favour for a friend – because I still felt a bit down and everything and this guy gave me a CD," he says, "and because Haven weren't doing much and I wasn't playing, all I was doing was working in that shop and on a downer so I gave this guy a ring – in a band called Glass. He'd been asking me for years to do some drums and stuff and I did it – not because I thought it would go anywhere or anything – just purely to be playing and doing something. I mean it's not because we didn't *want* to do anything!" Fittingly, when listening to the tape of this interview with Jack, I can't fail to notice Radiohead's *No surprises* is solemnly playing in the background, a sadly resigned refrain that illustrates the general mood. "There was nothing going on behind the scenes with management either. Late 2006 some guys came down from Sanctuary records but I think everyone in the whole music business were going through troubles – people getting sacked and losing money and nothing really came out of that. We played in the Dry Bar as part of In the City – it wasn't the best gig or the best venue – but I think they came down to that and they said they liked it but nothing came of it," Jack continues. "Then Phil from New Order came to me and got me involved in *Bad Lieutenant* – so I ended up playing on four or five of their tracks. As it stood, I was gonna be the live drummer as well – so I was already taking time away from the Haven stuff." He repeatedly points out it wasn't because he wanted to but because there was nothing happening.

"Even now, we could easily go to Japan for a week – get paid for – through the gigs," he adds. But it seemed that there was no one to either initiate or organise this. "We were just four musicians," concludes Jack, "it wasn't our role to sit down and say let's gig or let's do that – that was a managers role – or someone else's role. Joe wasn't the kind of guy who was gonna jump out of anywhere and go 'Right, we're gonna do this today, lads!'"

Jack comments that in meetings recently Joe had admitted to feeling a bit responsible for things not working out. Yet, blame could not be squarely placed on anybody's door. In hindsight, very recently Joe has said "I think they did really well to achieve what they did, it isn't easy to get the kind of deal they had. We were unlucky that EMI closed the label down, but if the songs they wrote after we lost the deal had been better songs, they could have secured another label.

I was always sad that it didn't work out for Tom, the original drummer, he didn't want to be up here though. He's a fisherman in Cornwall now, with his own boat, it takes a special kind of courage to do that. Tom is quite a special person. I still value my relationship with them and I am hoping they can sustain a career in music, I'll always be available to them for any help or advice I can give."

Unfortunately, no one could wave a magic wand, and there was no point lamenting the demise of Radiate or pining for the past.

It was a question of making the most of what they had now. They had so much to offer.

Day in, day out...

There's a curious parallel between Nat and Gary on so many levels. Superficially, they are so different but the stuff that bonds these two is deep and mysterious. It always struck me as significant that they both had quite serious health scares during their years in Haven and both with conditions that are little understood and that originate in the neurological field.

I remember quite clearly one day phoning Gary, for a purpose that escapes me. He answered in a hushed tone and I knew something was up. He explained he was sitting at the doctor's surgery. Feeling concerned, I asked if he was alright. He said "I will be when I get these pills." I didn't want to ask too many questions as this sounded like something of a sensitive nature so we said we'd speak later and he promised he would tell me what was wrong on Sunday if I came to his DJ session. I put down the phone and scratched my head. What could it be? And why did I feel I knew this was coming or I should already know the answer? I had no idea.

Gary soon revealed he had some form of epilepsy, as he sat playing records in the Bakery that weekend and I hovered amongst the wires and cables at our feet. He was vague, a little shy and perhaps still coming to terms with it himself.

"Will it always be there or will it could it get better?" I blurted out childishly but instinctively. "It will always be there," he said softly. I knew it was a condition that these days could be well-managed with the right treatment but I found it hard not to worry about Gary as he never had been someone, in my eyes, that was very good at looking after himself but maybe now, with this condition, he would learn to. There was no reason in the world why this diagnosis should hinder him, yet I saw him as so vulnerable at that point, and wished I could do something to brighten his day.

A little while after that I did have a chance to do just that, or at least an opportunity presented itself to possibly improve things.

Gary dropped round one April evening to update me on the band situation for the book. We hadn't had a proper talk for a while so I had invited him over to talk over what had been happening since Christmas.

It didn't take him long to summarise that not a great deal had occurred and that nothing much was in the pipeline. There had been a recent trip that February to Japan for himself and Nat. These had been a handful of acoustic sets, all completely sold out to rapturous response.

"Japan was great – but again, Japan is only gonna work if we get something going here," Gary states logically. "If we get a record made that's full of singalong *Say Somethings* and *Beautiful Things* and *Let it Lives* everything would be fucking rosy, but it's not really where we are – what we want to do. That record was a good record but it's – such a long time ago." "Like another life," I nod. "Yeah," Gary agrees. "They want to – we sent them some recordings and they said – a woman who had an involvement in our last two records over there – went to the gig, and she loved it – wants to do something. She said she can help get a third party deal together but it's all – that will only work if we get a record together, i.e a finished product, which, at the moment we haven't got, largely because of a lack of money. If someone came along at the moment and said here's five grand we could go and finish the record and do a really good job of it. The point is, we're skint, it's very hard. It's easy to go this is why, that is why, it's his fault or whatever but at the moment everything just feels very fragmented, bit of a drag really because you get up in the morning, in your head it hasn't changed, but everything around you does, and you can't really ignore that. It's one of those things you've got to try and grin and bear it really – it sounds all doom and gloom," he says flatly and we both just kind of laugh to try and lighten the mood.

He does make a good point about how the public and press have a perception of Haven based largely on the success and popularity of *Say Something*. We spoke on this in relation to the difficulty Joe was having presenting labels with their current songs.

"It's funny really, because I didn't really think of it like this, I didn't realise how much of a pop band we were viewed as. I suppose it totally makes sense when you listen to something like *Say Something* – it's like the ultimate – almost ultimate, guitar sort of pop song, you know? So when you're trying to develop and change it's really hard thinking – if we write another *Say Something*, then things might be different which is weird. Like it's probably our least favourite song, we never rehearse it and it's meant to be our biggest song. It's the song that got us a record deal. It's dead weird that, because it's not what we're about – well it is, in terms of the industry, in terms of everybody else that's what we're about. It's really hard when you're giving your manager who got you a deal on the strength of that song, songs like *All I Ever Knew* and *Velvet Skyline* and then him being able to go out and knock on doors and say this is the new stuff. I think in a way everyone goes "oh, alright..." expecting something along the lines of *Say Something*. I suppose, it's just the way it is."

I can completely see Gary's point, yet, at the same time, when you consider *Say Something* was a record from six years earlier, it seems unfair not to expect the band to change, to mature, to diversify. Yet, with the music business being on its knees as it was this point, not many A & R men were going to stick their necks on the line and consider that though *Say Something* was their biggest hit to date, this was a band with a whole range of other potential hits, even if geared at a different audience.

Joe's job wasn't easy but part of me found it impossible to believe that someone somewhere couldn't recognise the appeal of this band.

We talked a little about the fate of *All For A Reason* in America. Despite Gary and Nat's trip to Los Angeles the summer before, the record had yet to be released though Gary said a date was now pencilled in for May.

"But again, it's like everything in this game, until it happens then it hasn't," he says with that dead-pan delivery that semi-conceals a loveable sense of humour, "but I don't hold a lot of hope. I mean it's happening. We went out there and we met up with the guy but this guy's got no money, he's got no pedigree. I mean we were involved with it because of Jay but he's gone off the radar a bit – drug problems and a few other things. It might work, it might not. Somehow I can't see us selling half a million albums or anything like that. I'm a bit at my wits end with the whole thing because I feel," he pauses and says softly, "I don't really know what to do."

Other than re-filling his glass I didn't know what to do either but my brain was ticking rapidly. This couldn't and shouldn't be allowed to go on.

"Other than get up every morning and try to write," he continued bravely, "and pay your bills at the same time. That's the other thing. When you're approaching thirty years old and you haven't got a pot to piss in – or anything to call your own, you start saying – should I – should I – I don't know, go and get a proper job or whatever – it does your head in really. Unfortunately it is what it is at the moment. We're all sort of as involved as we can be. We get together most days and we're still writing really good songs. Wrote a great one the other night, it sounds brilliant and the one we're working on at the moment we're meeting up later to finish it off. It's like starting again. Songs like *Velvet Skyline* and *All I Ever Knew*, *Love is a Ghost*, that make up the ten tracks – that are meant to make up the third album, some of them are like over a year and a half old – and you think, blimey – it's just not gonna unfold for us, we need someone to do something more."

We talked, sipped wine and then I took the plunge and brought up the possibility of working with Danny and bringing out the album through his Blue Cat enterprise. This may seem a little cheeky of me but Danny and I had discussed working with the boys before. Sensibly, Haven were hoping for a bigger label to step up at that point, and Danny and I had our hands full with another band, Outsider. As Outsider were no longer with us and Danny had recently been considering various new projects, this seemed a good time to seize the moment. Although I didn't know for sure if Danny had the finances necessary for the kind of campaign needed here, surely we could at least talk about it.

Gary agreed it was worth a shot and suddenly we both perked up and there seemed a buzz of energy in the air. Gary told me he'd go and speak to the rest of the band and I told him I'd go and sound out Danny. There was nothing to lose. We hugged and exited.

A walk in the park

It was an unseasonably warm Easter. Danny suggested a meeting with the band in Heaton Moor Park. We sat down on the grass as though we were having a picnic and a discussion ensued on what kind of arrangement was both desired and possible. Gary and Danny did most of the talking. Danny's main concern seemed to be the band didn't have a manager, as such. Although they still had ties with Joe, and he was there for them in an advice capacity, they didn't really have anybody to fight their corner for them, to chart their journey, to keep them motivated and focused. Personally, I didn't feel that another person coming on board was necessarily the answer. The motivation was there. I could feel it racing through their veins and see it in their eyes, even if they did occasionally waiver a bit. This was natural due to the prolonged waiting period they had endured. I knew them all well enough to know they could successfully be re-launched. I had no doubts. I even saw myself as being able to play the role of motivating manager, if necessary.

We didn't make any definite decisions that day. Everything was still up for negotiation. Danny wanted them to go away and find a new manager. We agreed to reconvene in a week or so to talk again.

The next time we met was in the Blue Cat Cafe on a Sunday afternoon. Straight away, when I walked in I sensed tension. We all sat down and Danny produced some sheets of paper with a proposed budget for the album/single campaign on it. I was completely gob-smacked because none of this had been discussed with me. On a professional level, I felt I had to keep my mouth shut but I was furious that this had been engineered without consulting me. Not only that, but the figures were wildly speculative and exaggerated.

As myself, and the band scanned the figures, Danny told us that the campaign was way too costly and he couldn't make that kind of financial investment. We all felt completely crest-fallen. Though all is forgiven now, I have to admit to feeling cross with Danny at this point, not because he wouldn't or couldn't make the investment, but for raising their hopes and then having them dashed. I had to bite my tongue until the band had left.

It seemed such a shame as I felt convinced the plan could have worked but unfortunately we never had a chance to even try.

So, that was the end of that. No deal. No break-through. Despite looking promising, it was back to square one.

Still, on some level, following this anti-climax, a tentative renewal of purpose occurred. Most noticeably, this could be seen in a string of live performances that were arranged. The band played at Sankey's nightclub in May, and then booked several gigs at The Blue Cat. What was striking for me when observing them play during this time was how keenly they had perfected their live set. They had always been a strong live band, and some have said, their live sound surpasses the recorded. Although I wouldn't rate one above the other, I do agree that their live sound is very different to the studio sound, and very powerful.

Their friend, Mickey Smith, who had seen them live on countless occasions, described the experience of watching a Haven gig and how hard-hitting it could be:

"Musically they were on another level to me. I don't think people really realised the calibre of musicians they were at the time. They looked like just another indie band, but they are each so talented, with the right support they could have done anything they set their sights on. They worked so hard at what they did live, but it never seemed to come across with the same vibe in the recordings. Live it was something else, not many people can sing like Gary, wearing their heart on their sleeve live and make it sound so good. They used to nail it every time, like I say with the right support things would have been so different. But I always felt they needed to play heavier shit, go back to their roots more. Even though all the quiet and slower stuff was so beautiful, that's where they were most exciting to me, the intense heavier stuff they touched on, that's where the music shined. Nat doing crazy shit with his guitar, Iwan playing mad bass-line melodies underneath it all, and Gary's voice cutting straight through you like a knife, you couldn't help be moved by that live, it was mega."

The maddening thing was that most of these live performances habitually happened off the beaten track, rarely in a venue where A & R were likely to gravitate towards.

As the year slid softly into autumn, unfortunately there was still nothing of particular significance brewing for the band.

By now, even Gary had taken a proper job which involved mentoring people through the new deal for musicians. It seemed poignant that, though I'm sure he had a lot to offer in terms of advice and experience, that somehow he couldn't call in assistance with his own musical career.

Several years earlier I asked him what he thought he would have done if he wasn't a singer in a band.

"I dunno, really… I couldn't see myself working in an office because I can't kiss arse enough to get anywhere, you know?," he smirked. "I'd be late a lot and I'd be sacked. I mean I tried my hand at working in kitchens when I was a lot younger and that was ,OK but I get bored very easily so I think if I wasn't doing this I'd probably have done ten maybe twelve different jobs by now. The nice thing about being in a band is there's always something new – always something new to be aiming for – there's always a new song around the corner or a new instrument to learn or something like that, you know? And the travelling as well, keeps it interesting. I'd have to do something that was constantly evolving… maybe a gardener!"

So, either Gary learned to kiss arse or he transformed into someone who could hold down an office job, as that is what happened. I like the gardener idea, though, with its seasonal variations and the beautiful things that can be nurtured and created. Perhaps, it may have been gentler on his soul than having to turn up nine to five in an office.

Iwan jokingly replied to this same question that he'd end up as a down and out on the street corner asking for spare change. I don't think he was entirely serious but I think he was implying that rock and roll was the only life for him. I think collectively the band felt this way. Had the third album manifested when it should have, I don't think any of them would have dreamed of taking a normal, conventional job. Still, romantic as it is to hold out for your dreams, living in poverty and suffering for your art, a means of keeping a roof over their heads was essential. Still, the musical muse kept calling and from what I'm told, new songs were still being written and the shared desire to continue Haven remained, even if rehearsals were becoming less frequent.

I remember an overwhelming feeling of 'endings' at the annual Haven Christmas gig in December 2007. Everything seemed strange, tense, hasty and hurt. I was supposed to be relieved of my usual door duties for this gig so that I could actually let my hair down and enjoy the show for a change, but due to various cock-ups with arrangements, that didn't happen. As ever, the band performed with passion and the audience drowned in a sea of festive cheer and mulled wine. Even though I did get in the spirit and escaped from fighting off the gate-crashers eventually, I felt curiously removed from events as though I was watching from the sky rather than participating. Something felt decidedly strained. Despite the tinsel and laughter which was by no means absent, the atmosphere was vaguely hollow. I remember looking at the empty stage at one point, late into the night when many guests had left and thinking that they would never take to that Blue Cat stage again – or any stage at that. And they didn't for a long, long time.

Shape of things to come...

The new year did usher in some definite changes. Things had hung in mid-air for longer than anyone expected. Nature abhors a vacuum and a sea of new shapes came swirling in quite rapidly as 2008 found its feet.

The Cardinals had disbanded. From the seeds of various discontinuing or non-active bands, a new group crystallised known as The Mutineers.

At the tail end of the previous year, there had been rehearsals. At first it was very low-key and involved Iwan, Jack and Nicholas Mallins who had been the singer in the Cardinals meeting up at Iwan's house and kicking ideas around.

According to both Jack and Iwan, they felt they could co-exist within this new band alongside Haven, and it wasn't a question of turning their backs on their original group. There had been no talk about calling it a day and indeed, Nat was spending all his spare time cooped up in Danny's garage, which was still their rehearsal space at this time, mixing the tracks for the semi-mythical third album.

Regarding the birth of the Mutineer's Iwan says:

"It was just to try to write something different. Nick's a really good songwriter – he's constantly doing it and I really enjoyed just working on something new – we didn't even think… it just happened really."

Around the same time as Iwan and Jack were embarking on this new voyage, Gary was recruited for Peter Hook's Freebass project. The project involved three of Manchester's most famous bassists, Hook, Mani and also, Andy Rourke at this point, though Rourke's presence always seemed remote.

It was a collaboration that had been in the works for several years and for some reason they had never settled on a singer, instead employing various individuals, both established, such as Tim Burgess and Pete Wylie, as well as trying out some unknown vocalists. It would appear that they were getting closer to actually recording a record properly in 2008 and decided they needed a permanent vocalist who would be a proper member of the band rather than a transient voice. Whether Freebass were ever seriously intended to be a "proper" band is a good question because at all times, the various members had substantial commitments to other projects. My understanding was, certainly at this point, that it was a serious collaboration, but not a fully fledged band.

Gary had mentioned his possible involvement before and even though I was pleased for him, something about the Freebass operation made me slightly wary. The concept of these Mancunian music giants ganging together for something other than a tentative side-project, or hobby seemed unlikely. However, for Gary, in his current position, it's easy to see how it looked like an opportunity too good to let slip by. If nothing else, I hoped it could be his launch-pad, the wake-up call to the world concerning the unsung talent of Gary Briggs's singing.

Meanwhile, the Mutineers were finding their feet. "We realised we weren't a band without a guitarist, so we got a guitarist," Jack says. This was Michael 'Mikey' Reed, a very talented guitarist who was still a member of another local band, Bauer, at the time.

Reed brought a vibrant, jingle jangle sound to the group which worked pleasingly well with the others.

Within a few months, they began to play live. The first time I saw them was at The Ruby Lounge in early April 2008. They had a spring in their step and a cheekiness that was immediately appealing. It felt initially odd to see Iwan and Jack on stage, playing their traditional instruments but having a different cast on vocals and guitar. Even weirder, to observe Nat standing close by and if it felt odd for me, how much odder must it have felt for him?

Back in Heaton Moor, Gary had switched to DJ-ing at a night billed as *Russian Roulette* at the Blue Cat. This was following the end of his residency at the Bakery Bar which had recently morphed into another Kro Bar. I've got a vivid memory of one of these nights, when he was officially appointed singer in Freebass because he was clearly over-joyed and I hadn't seen him so giddy for quite a long time. He was climbing all over the Blue Cat furniture like a big kid, enthusing about the ill-defined sound of Freebass. For quite some time, Freebass were a mish-mash concept which were sonically difficult for me to imagine.

The news that he had landed the role of vocalist had spilt all over the internet and Gary was clearly thrilled.

Interestingly, when Nat spoke about Gary's temperament he said "His moods go all over the shop – this is his bad thing – he's all over the fucking place in terms of – he can be completely over-excited and giddy as fuck to just like, non-responsive! He can be really hard work – it means that when he gets behind something it becomes really powerful – I suppose that's one of his big positives. So that's a positive with a negative thrown in but we can't function without his drive, sometimes he has the least drive – I think that sums it up. It's really complicated but when he wants it to happen and he's kind of got it in him he'll pull us through it whereas the rest of the time we're kind of stabbing him going "Come on, mate!' It's double-edged sword that one."

In contrast, Nat describes himself as "quite even tempered and I'm in the same mood every day, so I'm reliable in that sense."

This is not to suggest that Gary is extreme in a bi-polar kind of way, but it's sometimes striking how he can leap from colourful animation to slouching silence and sobriety. Nat, on the other hand, is generally the same person every day.

His characteristic steadiness was demonstrated during this strange, uncertain year where, at least superficially, Nat was the only one properly and actively involved in the band. Diligently, he went to work on the songs they had together created, listening, re-listening, bending, shaping, mixing and moulding – attempting to get them into a state where they could be released. That was the goal. It was a process and a discipline that he had assigned himself.

"I think probably my last memory of being committed one hundred percent to Haven is being stuck in the studio on my own, mixing and compiling and I was going round and round in circles because I didn't really have the equipment to do it but I had the energy – I had the belief that I could do it," he says looking back on this period some two years later. Each time I'd run into Nat and ask how things were going I always got the same reply. This was his chief occupation, aside from his numerous guitar lessons, of course. "It was a bit like groundhog day," he laughs, "I did have the support from the boys but it was me doing all the groundwork."

I don't think any of the others would disagree with this: "To be fair to Nat, bless him, he worked his balls off in the garage," Jack admits, "he was there every night and every day and he was mixing stuff and sending us mixes and then he was teaching at night, so he'd literally be working so hard."

Casting his mind back, Iwan suggests they should have just put the record out there, regardless of its level of perfection:

"I think, looking back at it we should have just got it out really and perhaps we would have carried on. It was tough on Nat I know, because he was basically living in the garage, yeah, really tough and I knew that but it was always like it wasn't finished yet, it wasn't done – but I think we should have just put it out – I mean we didn't have any money. We couldn't afford to get it mixed or recorded somewhere better – we weren't able to do that. I think it just kind of sat there and as it sat there, for longer and longer, it was just hard to listen to it really."

When I asked Nat why he had assumed the role of keeper and nurturer of the tracks he jokes, "I think it was because I was living nearest to the garage and I had the garage keys and we only had one set!" Although he says this in jest, it's curiously reminiscent of bygone days in their shared flat when they endured all kinds of inconveniences and dramas because they only had one key. Proximity to the garage was a factor, though a minor one, as though the others no longer lived as close as they used to, it was still in easy reach of all of them.

"I think it was my nature really," Nat continues, "I think, quietly, maybe I liked that little bit of control and I hope it doesn't come across like that, hope it comes across as I'm willing to go the extra yard but I think it might be that I like a little bit of control over things."

I asked him if he meant control in the sense of how the music was produced, how the end result actually sounded?

"Yes, I'm willing to spend three days listening to the same thing over and over again and getting it wrong to get it right – I don't know if the others are," Nathan states. "And when you don't know what the hell you're doing it takes you six months or a year!"

When I questioned Nat on whether he thought the record would see the light of day and if that was concretely the plan, he replied,"Absolutely, yeah, don't think we were going to get a serious record label to put it out, well, not a major label anyway, we were looking at ways to put it out ourselves and that's something I'm not too good at you know? I'm not good at instigating things. I'm good at joining in with things. I'm a good 'joiner-inner'. So I was never gonna be looking out for the next internet coup. I would happily bury my head in the studio to get it sounding good."

I was relieved to hear that the ambition to find a platform for the music to be heard was still there but there was something else keeping Nat tied to those tracks at the time, which really came down to a feeling that if someone didn't take care of them then the band would dissolve and the whole world of Haven would be washed away:

"It was all I had, it was all I ever worked for and I was desperately trying to keep it alive. New music was grinding to a halt. We weren't really writing very much. What we had was what we'd recorded and I saw that, getting that fixed up and ready to go as the kind of fix to keep everyone together."

Perhaps it also felt like admitting defeat, to walk away with the job incomplete. My impression is that Nat gave those tracks everything he had at the time but somehow that didn't seem to be enough. The weeks kept whizzing by. The Mutineers were beginning to draw an audience and develop a fan-base of their own.

Haven hadn't played a gig since last Christmas at the Blue Cat.

Still, no one had said it was over and indeed a message Gary posted on the band's message board in June of that year implied quite the opposite:

Hi Everyone

I know things have been very quiet on the site. I thought I should give you the lowdown on what's been happening and what's about to. I've been working on a-lot of different projects feeling my way and experimenting. The Redsails has kind of run its course. I dont think much more is happening there. I am however very much involved with FreeBass still early days but sounding good so far. You will all be pleased to hear that Nat and myself have been putting the finishing touches to the last two years worth of HAVEN material. It WILL be available to download from this site as well as our myspace site. We have two shows coming up that are confirmed one being the Surfstock festival and a Night and Day show that we are all really pleased about. So hopefully we will see you at one or both and who knows we may just be able to pull a modest tour out of the bag we'll see once we've put the music out there. Stay happy and keep the faith. Gary

I would absolutely believe that this was the plan at the time Gary wrote this. Yet, the tracks didn't appear on their website.

During that year, Nat told me, "Haven only existed in the sense that I was in the studio mixing haven songs – to be fair, with minimum input from everyone else. I don't think we were rehearsing. We might have had the odd rehearsal. It was a fallow period. If I ever had a year in my life where I did nothing it was that one. It was probably quite a shit year."

Gary's announcement feels more like an intention to wrap things up in many ways, even though he speaks of potential tours. Perhaps a lid did need to be put on things. How much longer could the tracks be mixed for?

There were two issues here. One, the collective chemistry of the band had lost its fizz. Secondly, there was no one feeling inclined to re-ignite it or lead the way back to creativity again. Sparks can die and be reborn in an instant but someone or something has to light the fuse. Where there's a will there is usually a way. There was a certain amount of will, there was a shadowy path with foggy signposts that could point to the way but it was going to take more than that to rebirth the band. There needed to be a blazing path, a shining desire that would infuse the entire group and fan the flames of their music. They needed to set their hearts on fire again or it just wasn't going to work.

Nat is quick to point out that the spark between him and the others on an individual basis remained intact, but the problem was that as a group, as Haven, something had waned and no matter how they tried, things just weren't feeling exciting anymore.

"I think, no matter how much you love your band mates – after – just try and think… me and Iwan got it together sixteen or seventeen years ago – it doesn't matter how much good friends you are, the chemistry had died a bit, I think we'd all agree with that. Mine and Iwan's chemistry never died, mine and Gary's never, mine and Jack's never. As a group, as Haven – with that tag on it, we started boring ourselves with how we'd write songs and no matter what we did they'd always come out the same," he laughs. "Same one, isn't it guys?"

Jamie Harding, of Marion had re-surfaced and performed some low-key solo gigs that July. Further full band dates were planned for October and November which Jack was looking forward to. Nat had been drafted in to play guitar but late that summer he broke his hand, clowning around on a bouncy castle in Cornwall which made it impossible. Sadly, the Marion dates never materialised anyway, as Jamie came down with pneumonia and was hospitalised.

The gig that Haven had planned for the Night and Day on October 15th did happen though, and Nat's bones had happily mended for the occasion.

A rainy night in Oldham Street

Rain was dribbling all over the Northern Quarter. I'd brought my friend Alison along to catch her first Haven gig and together with Viv, we squashed into a packed tight Night and Day, where I promptly managed to spill a whiskey and coke all over myself. I can't honestly say, I stood there that night thinking "This is the end" but I did stand there, thinking "Something's up!"

The night was billed as *Urban Detox,* a charity event for Mental Health Day.

I don't remember much about the set-list other than it was similar to the last few Blue Cat dates, which meant a complete mixture of old, recently new and somewhere in between. Night and Day gigs were normally high-spirited affairs but I'd be lying if I said the guys looked like they were especially enjoying the show that night. They were professional and nothing was exactly wrong but nothing was exactly right either. To be blunt, there was a feeling that they were simply going through the motions. Because their songs are so strong, their musicianship is faultless and Gary sings like an angel, they are always a joy to watch but there was definitely a laboured feeling that night. I put it down to there being a ten month gap since they last played, and just being out of the loop. However, had I never caught the band before I have no doubt I would have been highly impressed. But when you know the magnitude of their capabilities and how their music literally pelts you with a continuous rush of rock and roll pleasure darts, this was not a highlight.

Speaking to Nat about this gig some time after the event, he told me tensions were running high that night. Yet, Gary remembers the gig as being "cool, it gave us a sense of purpose because we hadn't done anything in a while."

After the show, I was hanging out with Viv and Alison and Jack's Mum, Janice, who told me it was rumoured that the band were splitting up. I hadn't heard this from any of the band and I thought if it was official they would surely let me know. I was dimly aware that Gary and Nat were working on something that apparently didn't involve Jack and Iwan but that didn't signal the end of Haven necessarily, as Jack and Iwan had been Mutineers for the best part of a year now. I hoped it wasn't true that this was the final curtain but at the same time, the current set-up felt unsustainable.

Beginning where you end...

At quite a few junctures in this story, the details have been sketchy and confused, lost in the layers of yesterdays or mildly distorted through a myriad of angles and eyes. However, the actual 'ending' of Haven appears to be particularly fuzzy.

From what I can piece together, at the time of the gig that became their final performance, I believe that none of them intended that to be the case. Simultaneously, I also believe that none of them were envisioning a definite future together. What appears to have happened is that Haven had almost slid into hibernation until this Night and Day gig occurred. This gig actually happening forced the band to get back on a stage together and that alone must have caused them to ask themselves, and each other, a few questions.

Looking back on the gig, Gary comments, "As it happened, it became our last gig. And I'm pleased we filled the place out. There was a nice reaction but I think at that point it started to feel like work. I mean, you can't force anyone to do anything."

Perhaps there is a certain kind of dignity in your last gig not being declared as such. There is no forced sentimentality or nostalgia. Jack remembers that night as being a little weird.

It seems that Gary and Nat had already started rehearsing in the garage without Iwan and Jack, working on their new project around the time of the gig. "I can't remember if it was before the Night and Day gig," Jack mentions, "Gary phoned up Iwan and said that he and Nat had started a new band. My first reaction was I was really chuffed because me and Iwan had been saying what a waste if those two don't do anything and to see Nat just in the garage doing stuff, mixing those Haven tracks – it was heartbreaking for us."

In many ways, Nat is pivotal in the dissolution of Haven because he was the glue holding the band together. He had the keys to the garage and he had pumped so much energy into the unreleased tracks. When one day Nat stopped mixing those tracks, he symbolically took those keys and locked Haven away – at least temporarily.

Nat finds it impossible to say when or how he reached the point when he put those headphones down and gave up.

"I don't think I can really pinpoint it. I went for a break to Cornwall. I went for a couple of weeks. I was doing quite a lot of humming and hawing as whether I would leave Manchester," he told me.

"Really? And go back there?" I asked slightly shocked, though I don't know why, as I had always instinctively felt Nat would return to Cornwall on a long-term basis one day.

"Yeah, I always knew that Manchester was a temporary stop and I sort of still have that feeling now," he continued when we spoke in the Spring of 2010. "Haven was the reason I was in Manchester so it was sort of like ideal as my kind of get out clause. Haven – had… it had a brilliant life and maybe it was coming to the end quite naturally. Maybe it was my chance to go home and live the easy life… picking berries!" he collapses in laughter and I join him, knowing he is being serious and humorous at the same time, as he is so gifted at being.

"But then me and Gary became involved in our new project and that kind of gave me a slap around the face and got me back in the real world and what it is to be a musician and it really gave me a focus again and a sense of purpose so perhaps the months I spent mixing might have been working in vain but during that time I had a goal and it kept me sane and kept me happy," he says.

"Like a sense of discipline," I nod.

"Yeah, and I need it. That gets me to wake up in the morning and know what I have to do. I hate to float. I like knowing what I'm good at doing and doing it. What happened with our thing, Matt Ryan, who's been a mate of ours ever since we got here, he actually gave us a bit of a rattling saying "What are you doing? What's happening?" and we sort of told him the situation. That was the first time that it had even entered my head."

"When you were still haven… technically?" I check.

"Yeah, technically," Nat confirms. "We weren't in a room together but we were still Haven because no one had uttered a word otherwise. Jack and Iwan were playing with their band obviously. Matt sort of suggested that me and Gary make a band that was heavy and really bollocking. I can't remember his exact words something like a cross between Metallica and Jane's Addiction and my ears kind of pricked up.

He went to India, he said "I'm going to India for two months and when I come back I want to know that you're in a band" – that's how our new thing started."

Matt Ryan had been a close friend of the band since their arrival in Manchester. He is well known around Manchester as a Yoga teacher and devotee but historically he was involved in running club nights at venues such as The Hacienda and South. For whatever reason, Matt's words seemed to hit both Nat and Gary hard.

According to Nat, by time he came back from Cornwall:

"Gary had two blokes lined up and we were gonna try out a few things. First song we played was *Superlungs* – a cover of a Donovan tune, Terry Reid covered it – it's a beautiful tune. And then we started writing some stuff."

No matter how hard I try to stitch the pieces of the story together here, it feels unsteady and contradictory. There's either something missing or the facts are so shrouded in myth that no amount of pondering is going to clarify matters. Assuming that Nat didn't escape to Cornwall until after the Night and Day gig, it doesn't quite add up that the new band could have been rehearsing in the garage around the time of that 'final' gig. Things become even more confusing when I read the powerful and cryptic piece of prose penned by Gary that surfaced on the new band's blog early the following year. For here, though he's writing in a strange third person style, almost like he's having, or had, an out of the body experience, he suggests he has been separated from Nat who sounds as though he is in Ireland, with Mickey, rather than Cornwall:

With 'we got to get out of this place' ringing in his ears he set off for the quiet of Ireland. The lure of the ocean and an old friendship too strong to ignore. Some distance was needed and needed badly. He soon slipped back into the feeling of just being, but the promise of greatness was always there like a past addiction gnawing away at his subconscious, little reminders too small to notice at first but the more time Nat and Mickey spent talking and laughing they could no longer pretend it wasn't there as it started to shine a light over them both.

Gary then writes about himself, being hospitalised due to epilepsy and experiencing a range of unusual mental states, being both enlightened and drowsy, delirious and focused:

It's frightening how quickly you feel like your life has changed, it can feel like in one instance, the rules you've followed forever are no longer part of the game. We tell ourselves this but if we look back far enough, the warning signs were clear and present alerting us to the danger we chose to ignore. As he lay in the hospital corridor eyes stinging from the fluorescent strip light and nose irritated from the odour of disinfected floors and walls he knew something had to give. The seizures somehow gave Gary a clarity he never possessed before, he decided to start organising his thoughts and put pen to paper and maybe even track down a guitar player.

The number was unfamiliar and had called twice? If he wasn't so drowsy from his stay in the hospital he would have called back, or maybe not, the paranoia that surrounds unknown numbers, the curse of the age of mobile phones. If it's important they will call back thought Gary. His mind wandered into a dream-like state full of dark and white light, an impossible alliance bound by the same cause, each needing the other yet battling for existence. Some where in the blurred, splintered edges of his conscious a siren called him from his sleep and reality crashed in like a drunk at a funeral.

He answered the phone, a familiar voice stirred emotions that had been buried so deep they burst like euphoric bubbles rising to the surface of a deep still water. The conversation moved at a lightning pace with more acknowledged and spoken between the lines than down the phones receivers. It became clear that the separation had brought their creativity together. All that stood in the way was the Irish Sea and two plane tickets. So there they stood the three of them, united in their belief and hunger, charged and ready to explode.

It's a very moving account of the birth of the new band but one that he didn't choose to relay to me when I spoke to him about how things happened in the summer of 2009. At that point, I hadn't read this account. He gave the impression the new band simply manifested – no effort or anguish required. The various pieces shuffled into place with no deliberate orchestration. In many ways I feel that is true but the account given above describes the unusual energy that emanates from the new project, as though individually they had been travelling through a long, dark night of the soul and in coming back together the darkness burst dramatically into sunlight. Seeing the new band play live is like the splintering light of dawn, dizzying and uncertain but also filled with relief – that big, deep in your belly relief you feel when you suddenly know it's going to be alright – whatever happens…

In early November 2008, about three weeks after the Night and Day gig, one evening in the Blue Cat, Danny asked me if I knew that the band had split up. I said "Er, yes" even though I didn't officially know that – only intuitively, and somehow, I didn't sense it was as clear-cut as that either. I decided I wanted to know what was going on. I was engaged in writing this book after all, so I called Gary and straight-forwardly enquired "I've heard Haven have split up. Have you?" He seemed to have to think about it, I could almost feel him scratching his head through the phone line and then he said something like "Yeah, I suppose we have" as though he hadn't totally reached that conclusion but that it was a conclusion that could reasonably be drawn. I remember expressing some sadness about it but he was upbeat and started enthusing about the new band that he and Nat were involved in. Gary seemed to have no regrets and if he did, he wasn't voicing them. I'm not sure that the new direction felt quite as clean and positive for the other three, even though as a band, they had done next to nothing for the entire year.

Although I have heard numerous whispers that there was a lot of tension between Iwan and Gary during the build up to the split, I honestly don't think this was anything other than an accumulation of normal, little things that can cause friction in any group of people who have shared a lot of time and energy.

"I don't think it was ever really to do with me," Nat comments, "I don't know if it's because I'm good at sitting on the fence. Well, I AM good at sitting on the fence! You can sit out of trouble, can't you? – by just agreeing with everyone. I was generally that person. It comes back to Gary and Iwan both being quite strong-minded. They would always have a clash or two here and there. Jack was more in my camp really – wishy-washy."

Iwan or Gary have never spoken directly about falling out with each other to my ears, but others have hinted at it and Gary does admit that Iwan is "the most like me in his kind of stubbornness." However, I don't think Haven stopped working together because of any kind of internal dispute and that Iwan and Gary probably never had any more than the occasional healthy outburst. Basically, the band ground to a halt because the creative energy between them was stagnating. They no longer felt inspired to work as Haven and they didn't see a way forward. As Gary stated: "Everything seems to run its course. Everything's got a shelf life in some way. You've always got to believe in something to get something off the ground. We had plenty of belief but in all the other things it was kind of difficult with no money, and difficult for everyone to keep ploughing on. Everyone had their own individual frustrations. That's just the way it went, to be honest."

Danny Donnelly suggests that Iwan may have felt over-looked a little musically: "Iwan took a back-seat because of the stronger influence of Gary and Nat," Danny observed. "Up to when they split he took a back seat. But now he's 'King of the Castle' and quite rightly so as he's an experienced guy and he knows what he's doing."

Danny may be right, but I don't especially share his view here. If Iwan wanted more of the limelight he most probably wouldn't have chosen to become bass-player in the Mutineers but would have thrust himself more obviously into the foreground. I don't sense that Iwan was dissatisfied with his position in Haven but I do feel he was very frustrated with the lack of progress following their departure from Virgin. He is a very driven person, very active and perhaps not as content to have semi-idle time as the others. According to Nat, Iwan is "the rock, in a way – he's the enthusiast."

In the days when the band were still very much together I asked Nat if they ever had rows?

"Erm, yeah! Yeah, we do yeah," he grins. "Where someone storms out and slams the door and all that kind of thing?" I ask. "Yeah, we've had loads of them and everyone will agree that they're generally between Iwan and Gary just because, it must just be to do with the nature of their temperaments. The way they see things is like black and white and suddenly it kicks off and they have to do their thing. I don't have that in me to slam doors. Maybe because that's the same as confronting things, it's showing your emotions, isn't it? We've not had any of that for a long time though."

Jack, on the other hand, feels the band were not inclined to argue: "I think as far as bands go I don't think we argue at all. We argue about the key things – the album, the artwork – the only time we argue is when we're really pissed or something and it's never about the band – and it's never that serious. We might not speak for a day or two – that's the worst possible case. Because no, as a band, we don't. We're four mates really. We could easily have gone out the night Radiate went bust and got pissed and gone it's his fault, it's their fault – had a big barney – but we didn't. We were all upset but we didn't go out and argue about it."

Jamie Colgan who has spent a great deal of time around the band speaks candidly about the internal dynamics involved:

"When I first met them, Gary and Nat were the two people I bonded with but Gary's got a stronger personality and Nat's a bit more placid. Everybody likes Nat. I don't know one person that doesn't. Gary maybe will get more people disliking him because, like me, he's got more of an opinion. Occasionally me and Gary would clash, never had an argument as such but he's strong-willed. Jack's the one everyone laughed at… laughed with, not laughed at. Iwan and Gary have got stronger personalities, a stronger sense of what they want to do so that's where the friction occurred generally. I didn't see any serious arguments but then, I wasn't there all the time."

My general impression and from the time I've spent with the band over the years, is they really all are the best of friends and it's hard to imagine any serious disagreements. Perhaps *because* of the depth of their friendships, the dismantling of the band did cause some upset. How could it not? For their entire adult lives to date they had been locked together in that collective identity. The bond between Iwan and Nat extended even further back into childhood.

Straying of these roads...

One inky black evening that November, I strolled into the Blue Cat. Danny was sitting in one of the 'pews' with Gary and Nat. For some reason I hadn't seen either of them for a while and I sensed something pretty big had been going on. Gary was speaking solemnly about hospital and the problems he had been having with epilepsy, which seemed to have taken a turn for the worse. Luckily things seemed to now have stabilised and he sat patiently nodding, while Danny reminded him of the importance of healthy and regular eating. I remember this evening because the boys were enthusing about the new band, but they weren't giving much away.

Teasingly, Gary said the new band had a killer name. He wouldn't tell me what it was and I strained to telepathically decipher it.

"Is it one word?" I asked. "Yes," Gary revealed mysteriously. "It's called 'Gary'" giggled Nat. We all started giggling. They wouldn't reveal the name or much about it but it was clear it had got their creativity tingling and flowing again.

I went home that evening pondering what this one word name could be. Nomenclature has always been quite important to me so I was intrigued because I believed the name would reveal something about their musical essence but I couldn't guess – nor could I imagine what they sounded like. Time would tell.

As mentioned before, the new band had already begun to rehearse in the garage but there was something that needed to be dealt with before they could really start raising the roof and letting it happen.

Jack's drums were still housed there, in that same space they had all shared on and off for so long. Some of Iwan's equipment also remained. If I understand correctly, Jack and Iwan were still contributing to the cost of the rehearsal space up to this point and as well as shelling out for the Mutineer's rehearsal space.

"We obviously never had a conversation and said we're splitting up – even now I'm sort of thinking, have we split up, really? Maybe, I just assume that there will be a day when we can play together and in that sense we've not split up," Nat told me in the early part of 2010. "The day when it became a reality that Haven was no longer a priority is when it no longer became *my* priority. Jack and Iwan were in a band and I didn't have any bad feelings about that. Even the word split doesn't sound right – that usually suggests there's been a fall out. Jack and Iwan were occupied and were getting their creative juices going and I wasn't. Gary wasn't. And the day that me and Gary got together with another drummer and bass-player was probably the day when it became official which I think hurt Iwan quite a lot and it was not done in a way to hurt him but I think it did because he suddenly realised that Haven might have seen the end."

What Nat seems to be implying is that his involvement in the new band overtook and ultimately replaced his involvement in Haven rather than a decision ever being made to dis-band.

He makes it clear that he never had any issues with other band members being in more bands than one "Fuck it! Musicians throughout history have played music with other people – it's what we do – it's quite an incestuous thing. And since joining Strays I've done gigs with other bands."

"I think Iwan took it a little more personally than me because he'd grown up with them in Cornwall but because we were already in a band it was only right and only natural for them to start," Jack comments, "that was when Gary phoned Iwan, as at this point we were still paying the rent on the rehearsal space even though we weren't using it – still giving Danny money! So one day Gary said 'Listen there's no point you guys paying for the room and we've got a new band together and these new guys are going to come and rehearse'. So I guess that was the official end when me and Iwan got our stuff out. It was a horrible day, really horrible – It was late 2008 – before Christmas."

Jack was upset. He recognised it was the end of an era though at no point did he feel it was the end of everything. Still, removing their gear spelt it out in black and white and it was a type of closure, even if no one had officially declared that Haven were history.

"Iwan took it more emotionally than me because he'd known them for longer but I was emotional too. At the same time I was really happy they were doing stuff," Jack reiterates, "that was the end. Before that, we all went into Town Bar and it was like a splitting up night. We all got drunk and we had that conversation that you never want to have about who's gonna get what gear – who's gonna keep what etc as we had a lot of gear. We said we'll take our own stuff obviously, I'll take the drums and Iwan takes the bass and maybe after that see what's left – that was just after the gig. Iwan got his stuff soon afterwards like he just wanted to get it done whereas I kind of left it to the point where Gary and Nat were saying "Come and get your fucking drums out!" Every time they went in there my drum kit was there!"

Iwan remembers walking in and seeing the new drummer's kit assembled in their old space, "It's like, you know, if you leave your girlfriend and a new bloke comes in dumping his stuff round the place?" he says, "It's exactly the same – so we split some stuff up – it was pretty hard really – then it felt like it was sort of over. That was a bit of a weird time really. I remember Nat unlocked the door and I came in and grabbed all the stuff. It was pretty horrible and then they moved on with their thing and we moved on with our thing."

Nat recalls this clear out time with equal discomfort: "There was a couple of horrible days, that was a little bit of a shitty period. We did a couple of rehearsals with the other boys in there using Jack's kit and that's not – I think me and Gary got told off about that. In the bigger picture, none of us are upset about it now but I think at the time it was a bit sore.

I remember Iwan coming through – we sort of divided up the gear. All I've got to show for Haven is a Les Paul and a leather jacket and a load of fucking scars so we were like divying out all of our electrical equipment – you can have a drum machine – you can have a guitar case – you can have a guitar amp. That was officially a fucking grim day, it really was. I helped Iwan into the back of the van with a few things and he said "Can I take the keyboard?" and I said "Go on" – horrible!" Nat winces.

But it had to be done. Gary seems very matter of fact about this period, commenting "It came to its conclusion and that was that. Naturally there was a lot of equipment that was bought with band money. With any kind of partnership or arrangement, whatever you want to call it, there's always loose ends that need to be dealt with. Being in a band, once you get involved in the music industry, however much you want to deny it, it becomes as much a business as it does a creative alliance."

However difficult this transitional phase was, it was surely necessary as a decision and direction was arguably long overdue.

The heavy velvet 'Haven' curtain tumbled to the stage floor as 2008 came to a close. New scenery was rapidly being assembled on the stage out of view.

Between the dark and the dawn...

For some reason, before I'd been exposed to the new band I couldn't form a visual or auditory impression of them and didn't try to. With Gary and Nat as the nucleus, I knew I would like the music, beyond that, I had no fixed expectations.

I can't remember at what point I heard that Mickey Smith was in the new band. When I *did* hear this, the penny dropped, the wave broke on the shore, the light switch was suddenly located and now everyone could see. Of course! Mickey was the vital ingredient that, when added to the mix, turned the project from something special into something extra special, something truly exceptional.

It wasn't so much that he was the missing piece of the jigsaw, as in many ways he had been there all along, dancing on the edges of the story. It felt more as though Gary and Nat had dared to step up to those edges, had taken a plunge and met him there. Cliffs, heights and depths are no strangers to Mickey and the soulful journeying he has done. These cliffs conjure up the dizzy delight, the beauty and the danger the new band immediately encapsulated.

Strays. I think I first heard the name when somebody posted it on the neglected Haven message board early in 2009. It was another "of course!" moment for me. If Haven is about shelter and homecoming then Strays are about homelessness and pushing yourself out of your comfort zone. Strays are loitering on the street. Haven is off the street. You could say, they were polar opposites and probably that isn't so strange, as what would be the point of re-creating a band identical to the one just put away?

It struck me as interesting that the name of Iwan and Jack's band, The Mutineers, also has an unruly inference, as though all four felt a need to overturn the cosy world of Haven. They had either jumped or been thrown overboard to start all over again, though in different landscapes and with different impulses.

Subconsciously, I sense Nat had Mickey in mind all along to be a part of Strays, though it seemed to take Matt Ryan suggesting they needed a second guitarist to grant him permission to bring his friend to the forefront. Nat and Mickey had been making music for a long time, particularly in the last couple of years when Nat was officially still in Haven, even if Haven had ground to a halt.

"Folk music," Nat defined it, "twisted bluesy folk music on an acoustic and he really stretched me as a guitarist a lot – really, really stretched me and he still does today."

"Me and Nat have always played guitar together, we are really similar guitarists in tastes and style," Mickey mentions. "We've been writing weird guitar tunes together for years, he even came out to Ireland and we recorded some once. We always said we'd be some old cunts playing pubs together one day, 'the spare oom' brothers was what we'd call ourselves. That's the room I used to stay in at Nats, 'spare oom'!"

"A few names got thrown around – in the back of my mind… you wanna be with your mates," Nat smiles. "I kept it under my hat for a while and then eventually I just said, "let's get Mickey over" – he lived in Ireland – – totally inconvenient – totally doesn't work!"

Convenience was not an issue and Mickey was invited over.

"Nat phoned up out the blue and said we're putting together a band, it's going to be the kind of shit we like, do you want to try out for it?" Mickey recalls. "I jumped at it, I'm not the kind of person that needs to think twice when it comes to grabbing opportunities to do the things I love, and to play in a band writing with Gary and Nat, well there was no way in hell I wasn't going to give it one hundred percent and see what happened."

By time Mickey flew to Manchester, Strays had already been rehearsing on and off in the garage with drummer Charlie (Chas) Morrison and bassist, Stuart Lawler.

"We didn't look hard for people," Gary says, "we just seemed to fall together. We had a couple of rehearsals, get togethers, it just felt like fun. There's no blue print, no agenda – no plan for world domination. We just wanna get together, have a laugh, make some music. That's just the way it's been really. It's quite boring. There's no interesting rock and roll stories. It's just literally one of those things that just happened."

This may well be the case but the end result was far from boring and somehow Gary's casual comments don't quite match the dramatic and revolutionary styled pronouncements he placed on their web-spaces:

A middle way is a death sentence for those who get caught up in the net of deceit. There is no way back just a way through. Unexpected freedom is a well-kept secret so don't let it out of the bag. Open your eyes turn the music up and enjoy some truth for always in your life – the future is no-ones, that was a mistake. Accept nothing less. Taking the Rock with the Roll, Strays will open your heart and mind. No time for past or future – Strays are the now consideration for new beat generation. Strays are the guilty for the blame culture, we accept your accusations. Strays for prescience, Strays for the ever falling.

My perception is that the creative passion channelled into this new band was coming from a very pure and natural place. It's like they'd laughingly lit a match and set fire to the "How to make it in the Music Business" rule book before hurling it irreverently out the window. There simply *were* no rules anymore. At various points in the Haven story the band seemed to grapple with the dilemma of needing to be successful so as to be able to earn a living, so that they could get on with making the music they wanted to. Trying to follow that through seemed to stifle their energies and trap their souls. Because things had worked like a dream in their early career in Manchester, it was easy to believe that in order to re-establish themselves they needed to be re-signed and re-follow that same designated route that most bands follow which should theoretically lead to commercial success.

Bravely and honestly, Strays seemed happy to chuck all the tried and tested formulas out the window along with the smouldering rule book and look at the world with fresh eyes, with no preconceptions. I think this is what Gary means when he says they have no agenda. Strays were placing themselves very much in the now, wisely living for the moment – for what else can you really live for?

"At first I think it was something Gary and Nat needed to do for themselves, for the soul," Mickey explains. "Play music they could believe in, and give their heart and soul to, regardless of trying to 'make it'. This was something for their innards, and that's exactly how it's always felt. Joyful and natural and fuckin' exciting! No bullshit anywhere in sight. Just a bunch of brothers playing the music they want to play as best they can. Like Haven was way back in the day."

Nathan arrived back from his trip to Cornwall and Gary had lined up Stuart and Charlie as rhythm section. Nat didn't know either of them and wasn't even sure where he was going with this, but he was excited by Matt Ryan's ideas and suddenly an alternative path to Haven was a real possibility.

"I didn't have a huge first impression at the first rehearsal to be honest," Nat recalls. "I think everyone was quite shy. I knew straight away that the drummer was going to be up for it – he was frigging good. He approached songs quite naturally and heavy and I quite liked that. And the bass player has just grown from day one – just grown into – a great bass player. He's solid as a rock now. He was nervous to begin with. He was worried that he wasn't as capable as everyone else but he's ok now. He's exactly the kind of guy you want in the band."

Matt Ryan's thinking was that Gary was a brilliant singer but not a great guitarist, and this is where the door swung open for Mickey.

"All credit to Matt, really," Nat says. "Gary can't really play guitar – he's shit on the guitar but he's good at singing. Mickey came over and we got fucking like dickheads before our first rehearsal – coked up and drinking loads of jager bombs in Town Bar and then we went into rehearsals with our heads down, couldn't look up. Gary was like "alright, Mick?" and Mickey was like that – gurning his tits off and both of us played like dog shit but we were good enough for everyone to know it was right – I fucking knew it!"

Mickey has similar intoxicated memories of the rehearsal:

"I was actually really nervous trying out for the band, so much so that I got really fuckin' leathered before the rehearsal. I managed to pull it off though and got the job, fuck knows how!"

Matt Ryan's fortieth birthday was happening in February next year. "He asked us to play for his birthday," Gary says. "He was kind of driving it really." He may well have been but something bigger than any of us seemed to be driving it as well I discovered, when Strays took to the stage for the first time for Matt's birthday.

February 21 2009

It was drizzling and shiny on Oxford Road that evening. Matt Ryan's birthday celebration was taking place at the Deaf Institute, a recently renovated venue that has the feel of an old Victorian Music Hall but with silver disco balls bobbing from the ceilings.

Johnny Marr's son, Nile, who I'd met a few times in the Blue Cat, was opening the show that night. He did a remarkable job for one so young, to fight his way through those lovely songs, to a crowd who were cheerfully noisy and distracted.

It was with odd anticipation that I waited for Strays to take to the stage. I still didn't know what to expect and felt just a little jittery as the next chapter in the life of these fine musicians, these dear friends, was about to unfurl before my eyes.

Once they appeared and the beat kicked in, my senses all woke up at once and I couldn't quite believe what was happening. It felt like a door had been blasted open and anyone who chose to could now step through. When I experienced the mood of the band the name made even more sense. They *were* Strays – unkempt, unorthodox but most strongly of all, untethered.

Where Haven had often seemed to effortlessly glide and conjure up pretty images, Strays seemed to strain and push with undeniable urgency. Sweetness had been replaced by grittiness – dreaminess replaced by sharp reality.

I suddenly found Johnny Marr standing beside me, clearly digging what he was hearing. "They're so good!"I barked in his ear. "Yeah, it's happening," he grinned.

For seven or eight songs this intensity that felt impossible to maintain was sustained. I could sense invisible rock and roll paper aeroplanes, playful rockets tearing back and forth across the stage. The performance was incendiary, and increasingly so.

A most startling thing for me was seeing Gary minus a guitar, so exposed, so vulnerable – yet, as a result, clearly liberated.

Nat and Mickey assumed twin posts on either side of the stage, mirroring each other with an extraordinary symmetry. All five members of the band appeared passionately wrapped up in their individual journey, yet they were all intrinsically on the same road. It was glorious – they lit up that stage like a roaring flame. A brave new chapter had been launched in the Deaf Institute that night.

Wherever this was going, I wanted to go too!

I love rock and roll

Nat said later that he felt they may have "revealed themselves too soon" on this particular occasion, though in the same breath he said "it didn't matter." It didn't. The new band was clearly a massive departure from the old band, yet I feel it's also true to say that Strays couldn't or wouldn't be what they are if the Haven story hadn't happened quite the way it did. All our experiences, even the hardest knocks we take, have the power to shape us, break us or allow ourselves to shine brighter than ever before, when we just throw it all into the alchemical fire of the soul and keep on going.

Looking back at the pre-Strays story, Mickey observes, "They played their music, gave it its time, lived that dream, and it ended. Thousands never get near that close. They moved on. They'll always have more tales and memories than the average bear, that's for sure. I'm just glad none of them lost faith or turned their backs on their music, and they kept pushing forwards. In a way those experiences have made them better musicians, I don't think they'd ever listen to anyone's advice now if it clashed with what they felt, real and straight from the heart, like. Those experiences have given Gary more aggression and conviction in his writing, and Nat the chance to write the guitar parts he's always needed to with Strays. It's good, man! It's positive. It all works out in the end."

The next time the band played was at South nightclub. Not long after they played in the familiar environs of the Night and Day. After seeing them a few times, my feeling about how powerful and exciting they were hadn't diminished at all. If anything, they were getting better each time they played. I still didn't know the songs very well as there was nothing recorded other than a track they had uploaded on MySpace called "Love like a loaded gun" – an excruciating, scintillating tour de force that had an energy reminiscent of *Queens of The Stone Age* – a song of scorched suffocation, even annihilation *"It's getting harder to breathe, harder to breathe, harder to breathe"* followed by apparent nonchalant abandon *"It doesn't matter to me, matter to me, matter to me."*

"Two mean motherfuckers on the guitar and you've got a real band," Nat says when we discussed Strays' sound. "What we had with Haven always is a wall of chords plus a melody – that's how I used to write songs – chord, wall and there's a melody," he laughs. "There's a wall of c's and a minors and now with two guitar players, we can just do anything, bounce on each other, take the high spot. Johnny Marr came to that first gig and he sent a text to Gary saying "new band rocks! What is there not to like about two guys going nuts on telecasters!" The other thing that Gary did at the beginning of Strays, he said "I'm just going to do the singing" and he stopped writing the wall of chords – the chord wall. He's gonna kill me for saying that. I don't mean that – he just said, "you do the music, I'll do the vocals." He's got a massive influence on the music though because he'll be the one that goes "Yes, no, no, no, no, no, no, no YES!" So you're all working your tits off on something and he's got the power to go 'NOOO!" And he'll say, "that's great, but you can find someone else to sing on it." So he's still very much got his position within the writing process and writes all the words and melodies – so, friggin' hell, that's enough. We hit him with all of the music. I write music, Mickey writes music and me and Mickey write music together – they're the three things, Chas is really critical and clever with music so he's good at putting things in and Stuart comes to the table with a couple of tunes that have turned into songs – so there's a good mix. I'm kicking Gary up the ass at the moment saying 'Come on Gary, I want to hear one of your tunes, bring us one of your tunes and we'll turn it into a song'".

"It's all really different, isn't it? It's so much heavier than Haven – it's hard to believe, in a way, you're the same people," I find myself musing. "Yeah, Gary's really not going for the melancholic beauty anymore, he's going for something completely different – much more, like ready salted meat and potatoes!" Nat giggles. "And it's good, you know, banging it out and he's still got the ability when he needs it to do what he can do – I mean we all know what he can do – he's a fucking phenomenal singer – I wouldn't have hung out with him this long if he wasn't!"

We both laugh. "There's so much energy, though," I continue, "I didn't think anything could top Haven really but this is, not so much topped it, just offering something completely different."

"Yeah, Haven was a big lovely cuddle round you and it was a total heart warmer – whereas this …" Nat stops and thinks.

"It's an explosion, it blows your head off!" I tell him.

"Yeah exactly, I also don't think it tops Haven, being honest," Nat says, "I think Haven was fucking brilliant – but this for me, is doing it for me now."

"The weird thing, in a way," I venture, "it feels like Haven's music was written by quite mature, older people and this – this feels more adolescent, almost, but in a really good way."

"Yeah, this is like idiot rock and roll! Yeah, I think the same," Nat agrees, "after Haven, I started writing that acoustic bluesy folk with Mickey and I thought that was where it was going – thought I had my finger on the pulse and I've got about twenty five tracks – music of me and Mick – and it's beautiful and it's really clever and it's well recorded and then when Matt said this thing about Metallica and Jane's Addiction I sort of thought, whilst I'm young, youngish… I may as well have one more crack. I love rock and roll. Good, good fun!"

Indeed. If Strays are on the menu, it's a case of put another dime in the juke-box, baby…and another and another.

June 2009

I met with Gary in the garage to talk about the band.

I'd stopped working at the Blue Cat Cafe that January and I hadn't seen much of him or that immediate vicinity for a while so it felt a little strange to be sitting there that evening. I felt out of touch with the whole thing, even unsure where I was going with this writing, yet I knew I had to persevere, to keep weaving together this story even if it kept taking turns I couldn't understand, or led me up dark answerless alleyways. While it did this it also gave me jumps of great joy. This was important. This journey was, sometimes, awesome. I would keep weaving words.

There was something different about Gary. I couldn't put my finger on it, exactly. Perhaps he was tired, perhaps he was bored but the spark in his eyes was absent and he seemed a little on edge.

Still, we talked and tossed ideas around. One of the interesting things he said related to the name of the band and how that tied in with his own feelings of being, not so much lost, but not quite belonging no matter where he went.

"I suppose, in a way, it echoes the feeling I certainly had with the last band that you were a little bit disconnected from what was going on," Gary said, "I certainly felt like a bit of an outsider in Cornwall, not being from there. It's quite a patriotic – patriotic is the wrong word but if you're from Cornwall, the Cornish are quite a proud bunch of people. Equally, up here, if you're from Manchester you wear it like a badge of honour. I'm sort of between the two. It summed up the vibe and also everyone who's involved has always been creative, always involved in other things and so it seemed kind of appropriate."

There certainly is a kind of exclusivity among people from certain places, almost like the tribes of old and in Manchester that is quite pronounced. Even after living here for eight years myself, although I feel accepted, because you haven't grown up here you are immediately labelled as different. There's a certain price you pay for embracing a cosmopolitan outlook and lifestyle and I would say it's one worth paying, if you can cope with often feeling on the outside. I don't think Gary is complaining about this and in his case, I feel his sense of uprootedness likely stems from his early childhood experiences. There's a certain freedom that comes from being a stray but equally there's things you may long for, that others take for granted. With Gary, I'm never sure how much he's wanted to belong. Some part of him clearly does and even being "chosen" to front Freebass was a massive mark of approval and initiation into the Manchester Musical Mafia. However, I would argue, he *didn't* belong there and that episode didn't do him any favours. I will expand on this later.

That evening in the garage, I asked Gary if Strays were going to put out a record. "Like, I said, we haven't got an agenda," he repeated. "We've started recording, we've been recording in here. We've got about eight or nine songs that are taking shape. We've played a handful of gigs that have all been sold out. At South they were turning people away…So, in terms of getting the job done it's been good but there isn't a plan. I just want to have a laugh. I just want to enjoy making music again. I just want to have fun making music, that's my only agenda."

Even though he was saying these things, something wasn't quite adding up for me. I wanted to believe him but he seemed so low. "How is your health?" I asked.

"My health is fine," he replied. "It wasn't though, was it?" I asked quietly. "I haven't had a seizure for six months," he said. "The medicine seems to be working so everything's alright. The doctors seem quite happy with how things are. I'm not worried about it. I'm looking after myself. I'm getting plenty of rest, making sure I'm in bed early and all that sort of stuff so yeah, absolutely fine. I've had moments where I was worried and everything but the NHS is, or can be, a wonderful thing. They've been great. I've just had to reign it in, like we all do when you get a bit older," he started getting up and pacing around. "You're not exactly old," I remind him, "Well, no, but I'm not twenty one anymore," he continues. "I'm feeling good. I'm feeling fit and healthy. Can't complain. We all have our moments, but I feel fine. The medicine they have these days is great. It keeps things under control as long as you look after yourself which I am doing. I feel good, feel good."

I half expected him to burst into the James Brown song to prove the point. Perhaps my perception was clouded but I wasn't convinced things were as hunky dory as he was making out but I guess he had his reasons for keeping inside whatever he was keeping inside. We wrapped things up soon after, though he kept saying "we must reconvene, we must reconvene" as he shut up the garage.

Out on Shaw Road the dampness from the earlier rain had magically evaporated and the sun was creeping back into the picture. We chatted as we cut through Derby Range up to Heaton Moor Rd and as we did, I had that odd feeling of nothing having changed though everything had changed simultaneously. I readily admit after this talk with Gary I was feeling a bit lost, as though I couldn't quite catch or integrate the various strands of the story that were blowing past in the wind like dandelion flowers. Perhaps the truth is that the story had become more ephemeral than I had previously envisioned it. A solid plot was absent and any sense of narrative I tried to construct seemed to trail off into a haze. At this point I felt I could draw no conclusions because there weren't any.

Harking back to Haven

When Strays had played their official debut gig at South, David Sue of Manchester Evening News/City Life, conducted an interview with Gary and billed the night "Gig of the Week". Following on from this, however, the media seemed to turn a blind eye to the band. It was almost like they couldn't get a proper handle on them so decided to ignore them. Gary had said in this MEN interview that he couldn't "guarantee to Haven fans that they'll even like this new band."

David Sue appeared to want to proclaim some kind of second coming but that was never the feel of Strays. They weren't trying to re-invent themselves. They weren't trying to be anything in particular other than to do justice to their own artistic integrity, to enjoy themselves and to surrender happily to the swell of blazing energy that was demanding at outlet through them. In the summer of 2009, following a gig at the Night and Day, they headed to Glasgow for an appearance at King Tut's, the first time Gary or Nat had played there since the height of their Haven days. At no point was the name Haven highlighted or shoved in people's faces as a reference point. Strays really did seem to be starting from a clean slate and the past wasn't travelling with them.

Of course, all this time, things were happening simultaneously in camp Mutineers. The band had been playing regularly around Manchester but also had some key support slots with bands such as Bad Lieutenant, the Twilight Sad and even Pete Doherty. I caught them at the Night and Day towards the latter end of 2009. Sadly, it was a poorly attended gig but they performed a lively and infectious set. I remember having to tear myself away for the last bus because I was particularly skint. Mutineers were a very good band but I couldn't pretend I found the music as exciting as Haven or Strays. It pains me to say that because of my respect and fondness for Jack and Iwan, but musically, it just didn't set my soul on fire.

However, what they did seem to have, was a plan. They had a booking agent and management team and some sort of agenda. They also had developed a formidable internet presence and their social networking skills seemed to have pulled people from far and wide to wake up to their music. Strays, on the other hand were still operating without an agenda. For whatever reason, whether it was due to this lack of formal strategy or not, something within the group seemed to keep the exhilaration alive and well.

I remember a particularly potent Strays performance, again at the Deaf Institute which I believe was in November 2009. I was sitting up in the balcony area so I had a bird's eye view of what was happening on that stage. A whirlwind of intoxication, they tore through those songs with a kind of demented delight, true fuel for the soul. Where was the rest of the world? Why wasn't this being beamed from the main stage at every major festival in the world? They had that ability to reach the masses, I was sure about that but then again, they had no agenda, so did they want to? Did it matter? I wasn't sure but I could see no reason why they should have to do mundane day jobs when they had THIS flowing through their veins? But did they want to make that transition? It was something for them to figure out but I hoped things would conspire in their favour. I hoped they could take this however and wherever they wanted.

When I caught up with Jack for a chat towards the end of the year, we talked a lot more about Haven than the Mutineers and I sensed that Jack would deep down rather still be in Haven than where he was. I'm not for a moment suggesting he wasn't happy being a Mutineer but a big piece of his heart seemed to lie with Nat and Gary, and he seemed to feel that Haven had come to a premature end in many ways. We discussed again the why of the way things happened or didn't happen. No blame was attached to anyone but there were some regrets.

"It's a massive shame – no one's more frustrated or upset about it than I am," Jack declared. "People, friends, family, people I've never met before say "What happened, you should have been massive – you should have been as big as Coldplay" and you sort of say to yourself "yeah we should have" but you can't really dwell on it."

We spoke about the haziness of the "ending" again to which Jack said: "Well you know, we've not – even now really – we've still not – said it. And in conversation between me and Nat the other week – I don't see Nat as often as I did obviously, but every time we get together we always have a great night and we were sitting in Nat's place and we were like "Let's do a gig! Let's do a gig!" – but yeah, no one's officially said Haven have split up."

Iwan echoed similar sentiments when I spoke with him early in 2010: "The thing is it's always still there and I hope at some point it will be heard and we'll be able to do some gigs and stuff," he said regarding the unreleased tracks. "We never said that it was over – I think Gary and Nat wanted to do something different. I was kind of doing stuff before and I was doing the Healers and doing all sorts of bits really and I think sometimes you forget what you've got and you do all this stuff and you forget – you lose track of it really and I was doing all this stuff with Johnny and the MEN thing and stuff like that and I really enjoyed it but when you look back on it – your first thing – your real band – is what matters – we should have put a bit more time into it."

Iwan felt that it was good for all of them to work with different people at various points. Perhaps it was necessary for them all both personally and professionally to try different things. I reported that Jack and Nat had both mentioned the possibility of working together again as Haven, but Gary seemed to have drawn a line under it.

"Yeah I think he had the idea once it's over then you don't wanna listen to it," Iwan said, "but the last time I saw him we sat around listening to all the stuff and it all sounded really good. I've sat and listened to the second album – the first recordings that we did and I was just in tears all the way through it – and I couldn't stop it – it just happened, to the whole album and I've not listened to it in years and then it was quite hard really."

"Yeah, I guess, there's just so many memories and so many feelings. So, you didn't really split up – but you did!" I laugh. Iwan laughs too. "We just all did different things," he shrugs, "I don't know if we would come back to it or when we'd come back to it – I can't see that it would be that much longer, really but I don't know, it depends what everyone else feels."

"Would you like to re-group?" I ask.

"Yeah I would," Iwan admits and we both ponder the possibility for a moment.

"You never made a statement to say you were splitting up," I mention. "I always felt your fans deserved an explanation about what happened."

"Yeah, you're right – perhaps didn't treat them as well as we should really – they knew about the different bands but they didn't know what was going on," Iwan says.

They may not have had armies of fans during those wilderness years but they did have a core of very loyal followers, not just in Britain but in Japan, Thailand and various other countries around the world. People had been asking questions on the band's message board, some quite heartfelt posts seeking news of a release for those tracks or an explanation as to where the guys were at.

This was a point I raised with Gary also. "That's the sort of thing U2 would do," he scoffed. On closer examination though, he seemed to feel that no one would actually care enough to warrant an explanation which I found rather sad and didn't think was true.

"It never crossed my mind," Gary said, "I didn't feel it was my responsibility. It was one of those things. Nobody wants to be the one to say it. I don't know actually… I just kind of accepted it. Do you think we should have said something then?"

"Well, yes," I said explaining to him that in the world of fan culture which I was familiar with since my Manic Street Preachers fanzine days, fans like to be communicated with and if their favourite band split, it perhaps offers them some form of closure. "It never really crossed our mind," Gary said, "I never considered us successful. I certainly never thought we'd made it. I didn't feel any different the day I signed a record deal then I did the day before. I didn't feel any social responsibility or responsibility towards anyone else. I would struggle…" he breaks off to catch his thoughts coherently, "I didn't think anyone would be interested anyway so if you actually analyse it I felt we were *almost* on the cusp of something. We sold, if you compare it to today, we sold shitloads more records than bands do currently. I felt we were always on the periphery, always on the edge, always outsiders. We weren't a cutting edge band but we weren't a total pop outfit. I don't think we really knew our place. It promotes a kind of insular attitude in that all you're thinking about are the people that are in the room at the time."

Jack echoes Gary in that he said, when I asked him the same question: "I think we thought at that point no one gives a shit," though he adds on reflection. "Could have said thanks for your support over the years – yeah we should have." "Yes, because nothing at all was said, it was a bit like you just evaporated," I comment. "Yeah, we did," Jack agrees, "but then we never said we were splitting up either so..." "Just wanted to leave the door ajar?" I suggest, "Yeah I'd like to think that maybe – we're all still mates, it could still happen," Jack says.

I guess in many ways the band had been in a kind of suspended animation for a long time and there wasn't a clear cut ending point. In that sense I can see in hindsight why it didn't occur to Gary, as general spokesperson to even contemplate telling the world the band were no more. Does something have to be declared over to be over, and was it over anyway?

It feels as though, the band had moved into new personal territories that made sense for them and they didn't expect anyone else to want to or need to make sense of it. Nobody had pulled firmly shut the door to Haven, yet it feels that Gary and Nat had walked through another door with less looking over their shoulders than Iwan or Jack – not to suggest that Iwan or Jack were constantly looking over their shoulders as that's not what I'm implying, but they have both specifically expressed a desire to reunite.

Nat's viewpoint is neither dismissive or nostalgic. For quite some time while Strays were finding their feet and Haven had ceased to be an active band, he refrained from talking to me about the situation in any kind of detail saying that it was all too raw and emotional. This I could completely understand. In time, however, Nat seemed to develop a balanced and healthy view to the recent events, acknowledging the great significance of his former band but jumping headfirst into his new band with gusto.

When Nat did finally feel ready to talk, the initial pain involved in parting with Iwan and Jack as band-members had subsided and he had also come to terms with the fate of the unreleased tracks.

"Does it bother you that the tracks you spent so long working with, were never released?" I asked him.

"No," Nat states. "It really, really did – but any sort of sadness or regret or anything I had has been washed away by my belief in the new music, which is great. I think we've all taken quite a big step back now. I've not put it on for over twelve months – I've not wanted to go down that alley way and that's why I'm getting the odd text now because obviously enough time has gone by where I could have a listen out of curiosity. And I think during that time there was quite a lot of healing going on.

It's not ideal no, because we recorded on shitty equipment. I don't think the mood in camp was as good as it could have been during a lot of it. I'd want to go into Abbey Road and do it all again. As it happens I've never been happy with anything I've ever recorded so… I know that there was good material there and that the songs stand up and that the recording as well so it could have quite happily been released. I can't even remember what the song titles were!"

I ask him about Matt Ryan's continued involvement and what might be next in the world of Strays: "Matt said from the beginning that he only wanted to take it so far – he just wanted to start something good – I suppose we're in the market for someone – the industry's on its head isn't it? We don't really know. We're sort of scratching our head about how we do this and what we do next but my new band's now become my remit for living again. Last night I stayed in and recorded a song – that's kind of what I do – I sit at home and I take them into the room – three or four ideas get booted out and one of them turns into a song and it gives me a feeling of pride when I get one right. I wanna impress the boys – that's as much gratification as I need – sounds stupid – no one's gonna ever hear it. I think if you ask, as a musician, I'm doing it because I've got aspirations but when it comes to it, the process of doing it and making the music, and recording the music and refining the songs is rewarding in itself. Even though it's frustrating and it doesn't bring you any money or anything – that is the process that we're involved with and the process that we love. It might be that when you're on your death bed you go "that's why I did it – I didn't give a shit about the rest of it" the process of doing it is what matters."

"Yes, the actual act of creation and what goes with it," I agree.

"Yeah, yeah, yeah," enthuses Nat, "it makes me feel good. Obviously we do hope for the next phase where things get a bit bigger – I'd love to be out there touring again."

"And there's no reason why you shouldn't be," I tell him. "This band is better than anything I've seen for a long time." "Yeah," Nat agrees, "it's happening – I know it is!"

Climbing into a new decade...

I could say that this should have been the year that Strays and/or Mutineers broke on a national level, if not international level. Then again, is there any such thing as should have been? Strays had closed the previous year with another exceptional performance at the Ruby Lounge. The set was tighter, more reigned in and sent shivers down the collective spines of many that night. The venue seemed particularly dark and was freezing due to strange gusts of December wind sweeping down the stairs from the street – so maybe some of the effects were not induced by the music!

On the very same night, Mutineers were playing their Christmas gig at the Underground, in Ashton, which obviously I didn't catch as I was shivering at the Ruby Lounge.

Mutineers also had a trip to Penzance pencilled in late January and according to Jack and Iwan, were beginning to seriously work on getting an album together. They were working closely with their management team and following a gig at Shepherd's Bush in March, they seemed to retire to the studio to focus on the task at hand.

Things were a little stranger in the world of Strays because other activities, broadly labelled under the banner of Peter Hook projects, began to nose their way in. Early in the year, Nat told me that he had to learn almost the entire New Order and Joy Division back catalogue as he had been recruited by Hook to play with him at the grand opening on his new Factory night-club in February 2010.

Hook and his business partners had recently taken over the building that used to house the old Factory Offices on the corner of Charles Street and converted it into a swish nightclub designed by Ben Kelly to be purposefully reminiscent of the Hacienda.

Hook had decided to perform tracks spanning from all eras of his career to date and put together a band he christened *The Light* to facilitate this. At the time, I believed and I'm sure Nat believed, this was a one-off but I remember meeting with Nat after the event and him worriedly mentioning that 'Hooky' was considering the idea of taking this project further and that he may need young Nathan's services again – and again. No real alarm bells sounded at this point but I secretly hoped Hook would change his mind and set Nat free to concentrate on his own band which, at least to me, seemed a lot more exciting.

Don't get me wrong. I completely love the music of both Joy Division and New Order and indeed these bands held quite some sway over me, at least partially influencing my idea to ever come up North and work within the rich musical back-drop that I have.

I wasn't present for the opening night and I couldn't even decide if I wanted to be. I was interested and supportive because of Nat's involvement. It turns out Gary was also called upon to perform a couple of Freebass numbers. From the sounds of it the club was successfully launched along with the re-launch of Mr Hook's back catalogue with himself largely on vocal duties.

The Light re-assembled in May to perform the entire *Unknown Pleasure*'s album at the Factory to mark the thirty year anniversary of Ian Curtis's death. Nat played guitar and Hook's son, Jack played bass with his father taking lead vocals, calling occasionally on Rowetta to guest on certain tracks. I didn't feel entirely comfortable with the idea. It may have felt different if all the other living members of Joy Division had also been involved and if the performance really was a one-off event to celebrate Curtis. Instead, it seemed to wet Hook's appetite for more of the same, and sensing there was indeed a market for this kind of nostalgia, The Light were booked to play at various European festivals throughout the summer.

At the very same time that the Light was revving up and raring to go, the long overdue Freebass project was also finally trying to rear its uncertain head and establish a presence.

The album entitled *It's a beautiful life* was scheduled for release in September. A string of fairly low-key dates were put together in June to pave the way.

In the temple...

Before the Freebass project took off, Strays assembled in their rehearsal space/studio, nicknamed 'The Temple' in Stockport to record their album.

Mickey wrote vividly about the experience on the band's blog:

"We dove underground these last few months, locking ourselves away in the temple honing material for our first record, and only surfacing for the odd full blast gig here and there. The last ten days saw us lay down eight tracks for the record. It was a mighty experience, fifteen hour days blurring into a whirlwind of intensity, but it brought the best out of us, and all the last years hard work has paid off with a genuinely special sounding record. We went for full live takes on individual parts, no drop ins or overdubs on dodgy sections allowed. If you fucked it up you were sent straight back to the starting line to play a full take again, each time summoning as much intensity as you could muster whilst hanging on the edge of chaos and the brink of a disastrous return to the starting line. This paid off with some raw, skitzy, electrifying individual performances that we could never have captured if we'd played by the rules of produced perfection."

I was excited to read about the spontaneous, verging on brutal way they had immersed themselves in this recording. For a band with such an intense live sound, it was probably the only fitting way to do their music justice in the recording process. Strangely and sadly, the record which Mickey speaks of has yet to see the light of day at the time of writing (April 2011) but hopefully that will soon change.

I sometimes wondered how Mickey seemed to cope with living on the other side of the Irish sea, photo-shooting surfers and being a Stray at the same time. It's sometimes hard enough for bands to juggle things even when they live in the same neighbourhood. Luckily Mickey had the kind of attitude that made this arrangement completely workable:

"I just do as much as I can and try and prioritise the things I love," he told me. "Inevitably there's clashes but you can usually call which thing is the right thing to choose at each time. Taking on the band is a big commitment from me as I have to fly into the country every time we rehearse or have a gig, but it's worth every mission and every ball ache for a few minutes playing the music I believe in and that comes naturally to me. To have a chance to do that doesn't come round twice."

I asked him if he ever considered moving to Manchester, even though I guessed his surfing life dictated that he needed to be near water. "I love Manchester, I'm pretty adaptable and I can live anywhere really as long as I can leave regularly, that's about it for me, I'm not one for staying put long," he responded.

"It is really something being a part of Strays, writing songs and ideas with Nat and seeing Gary and the boys bring them to life, or just bringing an idea into the room and seeing it evolve into a song, the like of which I've always wanted to write, it's special man, I love it, come what may it's been the best musical experiences of my life so far."

The band returned to play the Night and Day straight after these demanding 'Temple' sessions but by some mixed up madness I arrived too late to catch the show. Things went quiet immediately after this, as Freebass rehearsals for the coming live dates were lined-up, as well as festival appearances for Nat with Peter Hook's *The Light*.

I thought I was mistaken...

I don't want to get too bogged down in the reasons why the much hyped Freebass didn't flourish and the only reason the topic is being raised is the obvious impact it had on Gary, and to a lesser extent, Nathan.

I am a huge fan of The Smiths, as I've already mentioned, likewise New Order. The Stone Roses and Primal Scream are mighty fine bands. However, taking the bass players from those acts and expecting some magic musical fusion to occur is misguided, to say the least.

Bringing together three legends of the Manchester music scene, Hooky, Mani and Andy Rourke (who was never a real presence in the project, but functioned almost like the third invisible point of this mythical rock and roll triangle) was bound to get people's attention. When you look a little closer, however, it's a bit like trying to build a house with three plasterers and no electrician – or no plumber. I would not for a moment deny the individual talents of these three bass players, but a supergroup is not super unless their combined creative force exceeds their individual offerings or at least equals them. Also, as with most supergroups, individual egos need to dissolve to let the music speak for itself.

I felt sorry for Gary, the self-confessed outsider, walking onto the stage with two of these three giants when I went to see the band play at The Factory on June 2nd 2010. I watched him struggle to find his stride, to find his own groove within whatever was going on. He kept his eyes closed for a great deal of the performance and when he did look out at the crowd he seemed oddly detached and ill at ease, frankly, just plain ill. He wasn't overshadowed physically by the others, though Hook's stubborn stance seemed to monopolise the little space that was available on the oddly cramped factory stage. Gary looked like he couldn't breathe, like he had not been granted permission to be himself by the heavyweights. Mani kept mainly to the back of the stage and pulled faces at the crowd in his typical court jester style, but even he seemed uncomfortable, as though he was having to work very hard just to make it through the set.

Nat has never been one to bask in the limelight. It's not what he's about and never will be. He simply got on with the show, head down, functioning more like a session musician then a member of the band. The question as to whether he actually WAS a member of the band is a valid one as he was never involved in promotional pictures or even credited on the album sleeve, despite the fact he contributed guitar parts and played on it. With the exception of Peter Hook, all the band looked like they couldn't wait to get off the stage that night. I don't know if it was like this at the other dates. They had played London's 100 Club the night before. This night, at any rate, was not the happy 'homecoming' gig you might expect. The mood in the crowd was mixed. Some were too pissed to be able to even know which band they were watching. Others stood, arms folded waiting to be impressed. A few were jumping about enjoying some kind of buzz, but I think many, myself included, were somewhat perplexed, unsure what on earth to make of the whole strange spectacle.

To my arguably biased ears, Gary's vocals were the best thing about Freebass by a long shot. However, this opinion doesn't seem to have been shared by the inherited Freebass audience, by which I mean largely New Order fans who seemed to dominate those who had an interest. Though there were some positive nods from various corners, from the handful of reviews I read and the postings on New Order related forums, I was shocked to read that some claimed to dislike Gary's voice or harshly dismiss him as a credible lead singer.

The truth of the matter is that I strongly feel these very same people would have been equally critical of almost anyone who dared grab that mike and be the voice of Freebass. However, the person might have stood a chance if they were a born and bred Mancunian, from another legendary local band, somebody like Liam Gallagher or even Shaun Ryder.

Perhaps Gary just wasn't wearing the "right" badge. He wasn't a complete unknown, of course, but the Haven baggage with all its question marks and ambiguities quite possibly hindered as much as it helped to make him an "acceptable" front man for this slightly clumsy collective.

Not only that, but his beautiful voice didn't entirely gel with the Freebass sound which was a confused sound to begin with. Anyone who has heard Gary sing will know his range and style can be diverse, and this is even more apparent when you compare Strays and Haven. Perhaps, he was almost too sensitive sounding, too subtle, too complex for a project as 'in your face' as Freebass seemed to be intended.

I am hoping, in hindsight, that Gary went through this experience to teach him something about his own strengths and that being a front man is something he was born to do, but he needs to front the *right* band. My feeling is, the right band were right under his nose all along. Chemistry is key. Trust is key. Commitment and enjoyment are vital. Freebass had lots of key-players but no key.

Bad mouthing, bargain bins and bewilderment...

Following the short Freebass tour there was a brief interlude before the album was released in a physical format. It had been available to download around the time of the gigs. During this time, Freebass also travelled to Japan to appear at SummerSonic festival. For whatever reason, there was clearly a lack of promotion for the record. Even the mini tour seemed to be orchestrated on a shoe-string budget with Mani driving the band around in a van and Gary and Nat basically working as roadies after each show. I'm aware that the record was released on Hook's own 'in house' label but it surely would have been worthwhile to have spent a little more on publicity and promotion after going to the bother of releasing the record at all. Even the band's 'official' website had a slightly amateur, can't-be-arsed feel to it.

So, perhaps it was no great surprise when September arrived and Mani stunned the world with his outbursts on Twitter. Mani's pronouncements appeared to come out of nowhere, yet it seems clear frustration must have been bubbling under for some time.

The feud was short-lived and has been well documented in the press so I don't want to dwell on it, but in essence Mani hurled some harsh-sounding criticism at Hooky via his Twitter account. The timing was shortly before the release of the record and before the band were due to put in an appearance at "The British Music Experience" both for a gig and a bass master-class.

The Twitter postings ranged from comments such as "Three things visible from space, Great Wall of China, Peter Hook's wallet stuffed with Ian Curtis' blood money, Man City's empty trophy cabinet!" to gems such as "I've actually got an ongoing career, so I don't feel the need to exploit my past glories. I exist in the here and the now." He even condemned the actual Freebass album which he himself had spent so much time on claiming it was where it belonged "in the fucking bargain bin before it's even released".

Personally, I did have some sympathy with some of Mani's statements, even if they were a bit over the top. I did find it extraordinary that Peter Hook seemed more interested in The Light who didn't have an album to promote than Freebass, who did. The incessant nostalgia sickness that has been sweeping Manchester for some time and is not confined to Hook by any means, but he does seem to be one of the main champions of it. If we constantly celebrate the past we neglect the present, strangling the creative force of young musicians trying to find their way right now. Even Hook's Factory Club which he suggested would be a place intent on nurturing new music has done very little to live up to that ethos to date. A recent glance at the listings could fool you into thinking we were still in the eighties as old factory linked bands clearly dominate.

Within a short space of time the band had made a statement claiming they were splitting: "Recent events have made Freebass entirely unviable as a band, and with this in mind, it has been decided that the project should be shelved, rather than placed on hiatus while members pursue their other interests."

Meanwhile Mani retracted his statements, apologising to Hook and claiming that he had behaved out of character: "I wish to apologise unreservedly to Peter Hook and his family regarding comments made on a social networking site which was totally out of character for me. It was a venomous, spiteful reaction to a lot of things that are going on in my life right now and I chose to vent my frustrations and anger at one of my true friends in this filthy business, and ventured into territory which was none of my concern. The Freebass thing has tipped me over the edge and became the focus of my bilious rants. Twenty-two years of being tripped up, face down in the mud and being kicked in the face with an iron boot will do that to the most stable of men. I hope I haven't blown a great friendship forever. Sorry Pete."

He then attempted to fish the Freebass album out of the bargain bin he had previously relegated it to:

"In a funny way my outburst might make people want to check the record out. I'm proud of what we achieved really. It's not often bass players get to step out of the shadows and create something from scratch, and between us we've managed it. A bumpy ride but we got there…give it a listen.

I hope I'm not turning into a bitter and twisted old rocker, that's not what I'm about as anybody who knows the real me will be happy to confirm."

When Nat and I discussed Freebass around six months after they had imploded, he said: "From my point of view, I was drafted in quite late, when, according to some parties involved, it was already done. Some others said "It's not done until Nat plays on it." So, I got hired to do some guitars. I think I only had four hours in the studio or something. The tracks were all kind of set in stone the way they were and I was just given a track to play over the top. I wish I had been either been involved from an earlier stage or had more time or been able get a little more involved, to get a little more satisfaction out of it but the record at that point… there were some tunes on it I could connect with and there was some stuff that I was a bit lost with. The record was written pretty much remotely and there's a few jams mashed into the computer and turned into songs and in my book, that's not how you do it, but that's how it happened. It could have been "now let's go and record the record now we've got the musicians – let's get in a room and play". I don't think there was ever a band. A record arrived and there was a lot of stress and anxiety at the time it was being made and by time it was done everyone's fuses were a little bit short and we ended up becoming the shortest lived band ever! Well, we did eight gigs and then it just fucking exploded. I'm very proud to have been involved with the various musicians. Everyone in their own right is phenomenal."

Understandably, Nat remains diplomatic about the collapse of the project though he does state that he feels Mani's actions were "out of character. I think he is a little ashamed of the whole thing and that Hooky was very big about it. I don't think it's something that anyone wants to dwell on."

The truth behind any of these public accusations and statements is unlikely to ever be fully known or explained and it's not something I'm drawn to investigate. It did, however, impact on Gary and Nat in quite different ways. For Nat, it meant being whisked away on an extensive tour with Peter Hook's *The Light*, performing *Unknown Pleasures* to largely enthusiastic reactions around the globe. Gary just appeared to keep his mouth shut and his head down. Clearly he was caught in the crossfire and he remained dignified throughout the strange proceedings.

Mani returned to his Primal Scream duties. The Freebass album was released and promptly swept under the carpet and that was the end of that.

Although for Nathan, the opportunity to travel and earn some cash as a working musician with The Light was obviously welcome, the collapse of Freebass and departure of his right-hand man on a extensive global tour arguably left Gary a little high and dry – or at least left without clear direction.

Like many gifted songwriters, Gary appears to battle with his inner demons. I've sensed him to be almost battling with himself at times. A line from a Strays song supports this notion "Is who you are what you deny?" Fighting your very self seems a peculiar idea at first glance, yet, I believe it's not an uncommon phenomenon.

I don't believe Gary belongs strictly to the whiskey-soaked confessional school of song-writing, as I feel his scope and stance is broad and unconfined. He can write an intimate love song as expertly as the sharp socio-political commentary to be found in *Enough Rope*. Still, he does inhabit a place that requires him to delve down deep and translate what's there into lines that speak to people on an emotional level, lines that he knows will be judged.

I sometimes have wondered if Gary felt he needed to almost torture himself, in order to be an authentic singer-songwriter, as though without the pain, he felt he wouldn't have anything to say. There may be an element of truth in that suggestion, but it's also a misconception. We don't have to be miserable to be meaningful, relevant artists but of *course* pain can be a catalyst for great works where tremendous release can be found for both performer and listener. On the other hand, this same pain can also cause creative blocks, cause us to shut down, crush our spirits, or lead us to simply withdraw.

So much in life takes its toll on us in ways we don't always expect. For myself, I've learned through narrating this story a great deal about how fragile but also how resilient the human spirit can be. All of Haven went through many challenges and changes in the decade this book spans and I'm aware that some of that is outside the realm of the actual story of the band which is where my focus is. There are suggestions that hover between the lines, some that even poke out obtrusively and though my intention is never to be evasive, it's also not go places that aren't my business. The story is still alive and fluid but soon I will have to bow out, for the rest is yet to be lived and as 2010 slid to a close I decided it was time for me to to draw the line.

Whatever happened to our rock and roll?

Towards the end of that year, Mutineers released their debut album *Friends, Lovers, Rivals* via iTunes but strangely enough played no live dates to support its launch. I played the album several times. The majority of the tracks were highly listenable and they had a piercing purity to their sound, a clear and unashamed rallying call that proclaimed they had arrived and were making no apologies. The musicianship was faultless, the lyrics were interesting, the tunes were pleasing, but it somehow, at least for me, seemed to lack that vital punch. However, it was no small achievement to have put their work out there, to have at least created a body of work that people could listen to.

I couldn't understand why they weren't touring it because these songs needed to be brought alive. When I finally caught up with Iwan early in 2011 he explained:

"We had some label interest from guy called Paul Harris who worked at Sony and that all seemed to be going really well. Then it just crumbled – like a lot of stuff at the moment. Supervision have been taken over. HMV have come in to buy the mother group out. A lot of acts were just dropped. With the label, he wasn't allowed to sign any more guitar bands or something stupid like that. We did a couple of gigs in London – we wrote some new stuff and everything and then we decided basically we should just get the album out really. Duffy put it all out on iTunes. It's good it exists really. There was a few reviews of the single and album. I don't really know how many of the album we sold because with iTunes it's weird because a lot of people just buy songs – so the album probably suffered a bit from that. But it's good that it's there. There's some good songs on it. We've not had a bad review so it's all quite positive really."

I'm pleased that Mutineers managed to at least make their tracks available and in a universally acknowledged difficult climate for new acts to break through, they did well to establish some kind of presence, however small.

According to Iwan, once the album had been released they more or less wound things down due to the fact that sustaining the band was becoming increasingly difficult. Lead singer, Nick, had started a new job which took him away from Manchester for the bulk of the week.

"It was hard to keep going so we decided to move on and do something else instead," Iwan comments. "I don't know. It's all up in the air really. It's done and it's out. I dunno if everyone just wanted a bit of a rest, really. We'd done quite a lot. It was all going in the right direction – I think it probably got to the point where it's hard to just throw everything into your band where you've got to weigh up other things in your life. We were having to throw money at it to get on with stuff and it was hard to keep it rolling. We did put quite a bit of money into it as well. It cost us a lot of money to keep it going and we couldn't just keep doing that so we just thought there's no point us carrying on and fighting for this huge deal that's never gonna be there. It was better to just get it done and try to move on to something else maybe."

At the time of writing, the Mutineers are scheduled to play at the Friends of Mine Festival in May, their only live performance since the album release. Iwan had also begun collaborating with his friends Duncan and Kyle, under the name of 'Stonewall Jackson'. It's very early days for this project and for now it's simply about having fun and trying out some ideas. For Iwan, it was a chance to experiment with playing lead guitar for a change.

Jack recounted a similar tale of how the Mutineer's had wound things down when we had a chat in the Spring of 2011.

"It's a bit of a strange one. We got the album recorded and then for whatever reason, the management thought we weren't going to be able to get a deal so we all just decided to say, well, are we all going to slog it around for the next year doing loads of shit gigs or are we just going to call it a day? I personally felt I'd just rather call it a day. We'd been doing it for nearly three years and we were doing these gigs which were alright but it was a bit quiet. It's a bit crap when you're doing gigs and there's no one there. And then I was thinking, well, I'm thirty this year in April and I need to get a job, get myself money, and started driving lessons – wanna get my life going, basically. If you think of all the years I've spent in bands not earning any money." My impression is that Jack and Iwan both decided they didn't want to put any more energy into the Mutineers and sensibly walked away to consider other options rather than keep things ticking over in a half-hearted way.

Recently, Jack had been approached by a local band called Ten Bears who wanted to recruit him as their drummer but though they had some decent songs, when he weighed it up, to get involved felt like yet another jaunt into the world of vague, flickering promises and dead-end leads. He'd had enough of being skint.

Jack had been working with an IT company in Chorlton for over a year now and so had finally crawled out of debt and was keen to make more of a life for himself. With that milestone birthday coming up, this is totally understandable and in some ways echoes sentiments that Nat expressed around the same time, that it was now time to do something for himself and that making music was being assigned a back seat for the probably the first time in their lives.

In Strays camp, things had become quiet also. Aside from a gig in St Ives in August, which was a charity event in memory of local ,surfing hero Tom Greenaway they didn't really come above ground apart from a brief appearance in London at the Garage just before Christmas.

The eight songs that they had recorded with the intention of creating an album have yet to surface. "The mixing process got delayed because our payment to the guy who recorded it got delayed," Nat explains with no sense of urgency about the matter. "And he's still not been paid properly," he laughs. "I've mixed it now with my limited knowledge and limited equipment. It sounds… nearly like a record. It sounds like a good demo. It's at a point where I'm saying I can't do much more with it."

When I quizzed him about what they planned to do with these songs a strange vagueness descended, which I think perplexed Nat as much as it did me:

"We're going to do our very best for it to reach its natural conclusion. Hopefully something will occur. I think if someone said to me, in an ideal world what would you like to happen I wouldn't know what the answer was! Do you know what I mean? Seriously…"

"You wouldn't want to get signed to a major label?" I suggest.

"Well, no, I certainly wouldn't turn my nose up at that. I would want that probably, I think. But what do I really want to be doing?" Nat ponders.

I think Nat's ambiguity is not as odd as it may sound when you take into account that before this conversation he told me he was soon to become a father. This kind of sudden news can spin anyone's life into a whole new dimension. He had also recently embarked on a new romantic relationship as well and was planning to leave Heaton Moor and return to his native Cornwall. Bearing all this in mind, it's unsurprising that his thoughts about the band were subject to review.,

"Things have changed" he states. "My life's just changed so I've certainly got a few different things to consider and my priorities are probably going to shift a little bit. Still, if I turned my back on Strays now I would regret it. I know I would – it's what I love."

The night before this conversation I'd watched Strays perform at an almost deserted Moho Live. It wasn't an official gig and its sole purpose had been a trial to see how things worked without Mickey. Although Mickey remains committed to the band, Nat mentions that "We're finding it hard to tag him down. He seems to be going from strength to strength with his video stuff. He's getting recognised outside the surfing industry now and is being asked to do music videos, films, all kinds of things and he really deserves it to be honest."

This increased recognition for Mickey stems partly from an unusual, inspirational short film he created called *Dark Side of the Lens.* In this piece, Mickey, in his natural and unassuming manner invites the viewer inside his largely sub-aqua life. It's a film of sea, spray and soul – a testament to the strength and beauty of the human spirit amplified by breath-taking natural landscapes. The experience of watching it is truly visionary, and somehow prompts you to want to cast off all that doesn't matter, all oppression, all the rules – to just intoxicate yourself with the joy and freedom that only comes from being true to who you really are, from unshackling your soul.

This is the same kind of energy that smashed through the speakers at the first string of Strays gigs I remember from 2009. To me, Strays can be a remarkable band without Mickey, but they are, as a group that includes him, a force with the capacity to the tear through mountains, to carve a legend into that towering, craggy rock and roll canyon, to leave a legacy that will still be there when none of us are. That's how good it could be.

As I draw to the close of the current chapter, the future regarding Strays, Mutineers or even a reunion of Haven is uncertain. I hope that all involved continue to make music that matters but more than that I hope that the individuals concerned follow their hearts and enjoy whatever it is they choose to do.

It was quite moving to hear Nat say how much he felt he'd sacrificed for the band when he spoke of his plans to relocate to Cornwall with his girlfriend, and the imminent baby:

"I think I've been looking for a good reason to do that for a long time. From the time I've been here and even before I got here really, I've put the band before everything in my life, earning money, having a relationship – every single thing had to come second because that's what we trained ourselves into and also Joe's mentoring. He said if you're going to do it you've got to do it! And hat's off to him – it worked – to a degree and I think that made me… it's almost like a weight off my shoulders to think I'm going to do something for myself. And I think we'd probably all say the same – I'm the one left in the rehearsal room mixing – even at the end of the Haven thing I was mixing the record for six months and no other fucker was there! So, I like the idea of going and doing something for myself. I'm going to really cherish it. It doesn't mean I've given up or am retiring. I'm gonna be up here (in Manchester) a lot of the time. Anything that's Strays related that's gonna further what we do, I'll be up for. And you know what, I might only last six months down there and get bored. I've lived in the city for ten years now!"

I suggested to him that perhaps he could finally have the best of both worlds, though it is difficult to straddle two camps, some do manage to do this and feel the better for it.

At the end of the day though, perhaps it's a case of defining or deciding just what it is you want and then following that impulse with conviction because an ambivalence of sorts remains:

"We keep talking about possibilities with Strays," Nat explains, "I think it's literally the case where we've got a life outside the band which we have to balance so the band unfortunately has to work around that. It's a bit of a conundrum where, if we were all to take six months off work and throw ourselves headfirst into it we would stand more of a chance anyway. Like I said before, I don't even know what it is we're striving for – I really don't."

In some ways this echoes the conversation I had with Gary close to the inception of the band where he claimed there was no agenda. Freeing yourself from agendas is a good idea but I do feel it would be a great shame if Strays fizzle out and never fully embrace the journey they started. If the passion and desire are there though, they will find an outlet and an audience and I would hope, a sense of fulfilment on a deep soul level. It's clear that money in the bank, status symbols or ego aggrandisement have little or no meaning those involved.

In the current climate, the music business has almost ceased to be about music. Its fixation with vacuous talent shows parading piffle and pantomime, where commercial sponsorship is forcibly re-naming every live music venue across the globe, it feels that real musicians almost have to step outside of that circus and make music because it is what they love to do, rather than play a game that can be demeaning, destructive and plain dirty.

Nat continues to be active with Peter Hook's *The Light*, touring Australia, New Zealand, Italy, Poland and most of the major cities of America. Clearly, he's been enjoying this opportunity and it's a chance for him to play guitar, which is what he loves to do without having to worry about any of the other details. I asked him how it compared to playing with his own bands:

"I like playing in front of a crowd but it's not like playing your own music to people who've bought into what you do. In that sense I treat it like a job – do my little bit then get on. He (Peter Hook) treats me well. I'm used to be being in the back of a shit van on our way to a Travel Lodge and he's been putting us up in five star hotels so I haven't a bad word to say about the guy."

The opportunity to travel round the world in a project like this has given Nat some memorable moments: "I never imagined I'd be doing what I've been doing a year ago," he comments. "I had a bit of a defining moment in L.A. We played the Music Box in Sunset Strip and being in L.A you've got that romantic notion of being part of rock and roll history. Perry Farrell from Jane's Addiction came and sang a song with us. That was quite weird looking across the stage at a geezer like him! Jack (Hook's son) sent him an email saying "Do you fancy doing *Transmission* with us in L.A?" His reply was "What's the band wearing?" He came and did it and he did a blinding good job of it."

It is a relief for Nat to have the financial pressure taken off him a little whilst touring with The Light: "Strays is still where my heart is, the thing that gives me musical satisfaction, creative satisfaction. It doesn't earn me any money right now. It could do and I believe in it – it's got legs. But I have to be realistic and what I do with Hooky brings in good dough. As a musician I don't think you can turn your nose up at paid work like that. I wouldn't go out with an act I didn't rate. I feel I can keep my integrity in all this. I'm lucky to have been approached by Hooky who's been in some of the most credible bands historically in our world."

I was so much older then, I'm younger than that now...

When I asked Jack in March 2011 how it felt for the first time in his life not to be a band, he naturally said it felt strange. He'd had an idea for a while that perhaps Haven could reform and play together for one night only on the eve of his 30th birthday. This would be a private invite only event with no pressure, no talk of tomorrow, no post-mortem or ultimatum.

It sounded like the perfect way to celebrate what the band meant and still mean to each of them, without the dreaded scrutiny of the media or without having to think of it as anything other than a celebration for Jack.

Having said that, coming back together could only be an emotional moment for all involved. From the moment I heard Jack's party was happening at the Blue Cat, I knew that alone would instil a certain sense of nostalgia. Nat had told me over a year before how it took him a long time to even be able to play a Haven record and all of the band, except Gary, have confessed to collapsing into tears when they have:

"Yeah, it is emotional," Nat says, "if I allow myself – when I think about waking up in Tokyo in my hotel room and I don't know what the fuck is going on, totally off my face and I walk down to the lobby and I see Jack's stupid head – and he's got some amazing story to tell me and those times are so close to my heart. We went through stuff that was unspeakable – and we all went through it together."

April 28 2011

It was the eve of the first major royal wedding in years and the nation as a whole grew obsessed with every little detail of the state ceremony. The preparatory bunting burst out of most public houses and union jacks were unfurled with gusto all over town.

It was a relief to arrive at the Blue Cat Cafe that evening knowing that with Danny's political persuasions there wouldn't be any royalist celebratory trimmings in sight. This man doesn't even put up a Christmas tree and though the Sex Pistols *God Save the Queen* was not blaring out of the speakers, the area felt like a royal wedding free zone.

A celebration of a very different kind was happening though. It was Jack's 30th birthday and the band took to the Blue Cat stage for the first time since Christmas 2007.

It's hard to imagine how the band must have felt as they sailed through the set to mass applause. I know I felt a surge of confused emotion in hearing them play again and though I've never needed reminding of the power of their songs, I felt re-educated in just how natural and beautiful their music truly is. There was a lot of banter from the crowd, all of whom were personally invited by Jack. The birthday boy looked quite overwhelmed at times as the songs crashed over us all like big, dizzy waves of love laced with pain, shaken with joy.

In many ways, it seems unthinkable that a band this good and a group still young should dismantle themselves again after a performance like this. Yet, for the immediate future, this would seem to be the road being chosen.

With Nat now relocated to Cornwall and still being on the road with The Light, there is no clear path to follow.

For me, this night was a night for Jack and I feel sure it touched his heart to be surrounded by those he loves and who love him and doing what he undoubtedly loves. Haven filled the third decade of his life and that really did deserve to be marked and celebrated. I'm glad that happened on Shaw road that night.

Sweet, sweet music...

The whole point is, even if none of the members of Haven ever create or perform a single note again, this was a story worth telling. They have contributed dazzlingly to the great rock and roll songbook, a chapter that will stand the test of time. If this were to be the end of the road that would be a huge shame as they all still have so much more to offer. Inspiration can strike out of blue and in living every day there is more to experience, to learn and to share.

"I don't think people realise the amount of energy it takes to make music you believe in, bring it to life and and share it with the world, every song, every rehearsal, every gig, it's a huge investment of energy from each person," Mickey comments regarding Haven "So to have achieved what they have, I'm so proud of all those boys. They've always been such an inspiration to me, and to still be writing music with 'em now, well I hope it continues til we're old men, playing the blues, watching another young band of punks come into a jam and blow the fuckin' roof off at the start of their journey."

I hope so too.

When you go looking for an opening line, a closing line – a passage – a gateway to the magic, it will elude you. Often better to just jump in midway. I've always felt a need to understand the past, the confusing, overlapping intersection of time-zones that drop us off at a particular roundabout or junction, where there are innumerable directions we can take, even though sometimes it looks like there is only one.

Time. It whittles by us, chiselling our features, changing the landscape, sometimes so fast we can't catch our breath, sometimes so slowly we feel the dawn will never break. Yet, it does and a new cycle opens up.

I stand in the breeze on Heaton Moor road and tune into the near and distant sounds…an aeroplane cruises through the lavender tinged volcanic clouds up above, a dog barks repeatedly somewhere close by…those church-bells toll solemnly and prophetically within my hearing range and the traffic swishes onwards to wherever it's bound. Yet, there's always another sound – the one that speaks to our soul directly – even when it's only playing in our heads. I can hear music.

Ten years can disappear in the blink of an eye. The scars, smiles, sweat, dreams, tears, psychic debris dust that kicks around these same streets…same streets…some of that baggage we carry with us, some we drop – but all of it meant something at one time or another.

Every day is a new day, but your heart is the same heart that's been beating and banging and believing all the years of your life.

A thousand volumes could not contain all those beats. This book set out to capture a selection of them. To respond to the beat of the drum is as natural as breathing. This was the story of a group response. That's what it's all about.